Roll of Thunder, Hear My Cry

and Related Readings

McDougal Littell
A HOUGHTON MIFFLIN COMPANY
Evanston, Illinois   Boston   Dallas

Acknowledgments

Atheneum Books for Young Readers, an imprint of Simon & Schuster: Excerpt from *Growing Up in the Great Depression* by Richard Wormser; Copyright © 1994 by Richard Wormser. Reprinted with the permission of Atheneum Books.

Marian Reiner: "Depression" from *Hand in Hand: An American History Through Poetry* by Isabel Joshlin Glaser; Copyright © 1994 by Isabel Joshlin Glaser. Used by permission of Marian Reiner for the author.

Lucinda Vardey Agency: "The Stolen Party" from *Other Fires* by Liliana Heker, translated by Alberto Manguel; Copyright © 1982 by Liliana Heker, translation copyright © 1985 by Alberto Manguel. Reprinted by permission of Lucinda Vardey Agency.

Daisy Lee Bates: Excerpt from *The Long Shadow of Little Rock: A Memoir* by Daisy Lee Bates; Copyright © 1962 by David McKay Company. Reprinted by permission of the author.

Ellen Tarry: Excerpt from *The Third Door: An Autobiography of an American Negro Woman* by Ellen Tarry; Copyright 1955 by David McKay Company. Reprinted by permission of the author.

Continued on page 280.

Roll of Thunder, Hear My Cry Copyright © 1976 by Mildred Taylor. Reprinted by arrangement with Puffin Books, a division of Penguin Books USA, Inc.

Cover illustration by Michael Steirnagle.
Cover background photo: Bill Pogue.
Author photo: Jack Ackerman/*The Toledo Blade*.

ISBN 0-395-77530-2

567—DCI—02 01 00 99 98 97

Contents

Continued

Roll of Thunder, Hear My Cry

Mildred Taylor

Chapter 1

"Little Man, would you come on? You keep it up and you're gonna make us late."

My youngest brother paid no attention to me. Grasping more firmly his newspaper-wrapped notebook and his tin-can lunch of cornbread and oil sausages, he continued to concentrate on the dusty road. He lagged several feet behind my other brothers, Stacey and Christopher-John, and me, attempting to keep the rusty Mississippi dust from swelling with each step and drifting back upon his shiny black shoes and the cuffs of his corduroy pants by lifting each foot high before setting it gently down again. Always meticulously neat, six-year-old Little Man never allowed dirt or tears or stains to mar anything he owned. Today was no exception.

"You keep it up and make us late for school, Mama's gonna wear you out," I threatened, pulling with exasperation at the high collar of the Sunday dress Mama had made me wear for the first day of school—as if that event were something special. It seemed to me that showing up at school at all on a bright August-like October morning made for running the cool forest trails and wading barefoot in the forest pond was concession enough; Sunday clothing was asking too much. Christopher-John and Stacey were not too pleased about the clothing or school either. Only Little Man, just beginning his school career, found the prospects of both intriguing.

"Y'all go ahead and get dirty if y'all wanna," he replied without even looking up from his studied steps. "Me, I'm gonna stay clean."

"I betcha Mama's gonna 'clean' you, you keep it up," I grumbled.

"Ah, Cassie, leave him be," Stacey admonished, frowning and kicking testily at the road.

"I ain't said nothing but—"

Stacey cut me a wicked look and I grew silent. His disposition had been irritatingly sour lately. If I hadn't known the cause of it, I could have forgotten very easily that he was, at twelve, bigger than I, and that I had promised Mama to arrive at school looking clean and ladylike. "Shoot," I mumbled finally, unable to restrain myself from further comment, "it ain't my fault you gotta be in Mama's class this year."

Stacey's frown deepened and he jammed his fists into his pockets, but said nothing.

Christopher-John, walking between Stacey and me, glanced uneasily at both of us but did not interfere. A short, round boy of seven, he took little interest in troublesome things, preferring to remain on good terms with everyone. Yet he was always sensitive to others and now, shifting the handle of his lunch can from his right hand to his right wrist and his smudged notebook from his left hand to his left armpit, he stuffed his free hands into his pockets and attempted to make his face as moody as Stacey's and as cranky as mine. But after a few moments he seemed to forget that he was supposed to be grouchy and began whistling cheerfully. There was little that could make Christopher-John unhappy for very long, not even the thought of school.

I tugged again at my collar and dragged my feet in the dust, allowing it to sift back onto my socks and shoes like gritty red snow. I hated the dress. And the shoes. There was little I could do in a dress, and as for shoes, they imprisoned freedom-loving feet accustomed to the feel of the warm earth.

"Cassie, stop that," Stacey snapped as the dust billowed in swirling clouds around my feet. I looked up sharply, ready to protest. Christopher-John's whistling increased to a raucous, nervous shrill, and grudgingly I let the matter drop and trudged along in moody silence, my brothers growing as pensively quiet as I.

Before us the narrow, sun-splotched road wound like a lazy red serpent dividing the high forest bank of quiet, old trees on the left from the cotton field, forested by giant green-and-purple stalks, on the right. A barbed-wire fence ran the length of the deep field, stretching eastward for over a quarter of a mile until it met the sloping green pasture that signaled the end of our family's four hundred acres. An ancient oak tree on the slope, visible even now, was the official dividing mark between Logan land and the beginning of a dense forest. Beyond the protective fencing of the forest, vast farming fields, worked by a multitude of sharecropping families, covered two thirds of a ten-square-mile plantation. That was Harlan Granger land.

Once our land had been Granger land too, but the Grangers had sold it during Reconstruction to a Yankee for tax money. In 1887, when the land was up for sell again, Grandpa had bought two hundred acres of it, and in 1918, after the first two hundred acres had been paid off, he had bought another two hundred. It was good rich land, much of it still virgin forest, and there was no debt on half of it. But there was a mortgage on the two hundred acres bought in 1918 and there were taxes on the full four hundred, and for the past three years there had not been enough money from the cotton to pay both and live on too.

That was why Papa had gone to work on the railroad.

In 1930 the price of cotton dropped. And so, in the spring of 1931, Papa set out looking for work, going as far north as Memphis and as far south as the Delta country. He had gone west too, into Louisiana. It was there he found work laying track for the railroad. He worked the remainder of the year away from us, not returning until the deep winter when the ground was cold and barren. The following spring after the planting was finished, he did the same. Now it was 1933, and Papa was again in Louisiana laying track.

I asked him once why he had to go away, why the land was so important. He took my hand and said in his quiet way: "Look out there, Cassie girl. All that belongs to you. You ain't never had to live on nobody's place but your own and long as I live and the family survives, you'll never have to. That's important. You may not understand that now, but one day you will. Then you'll see."

I looked at Papa strangely when he said that, for I knew that all the land did not belong to me. Some of it belonged to Stacey, Christopher-John, and Little Man, not to mention the part that belonged to Big Ma, Mama, and Uncle Hammer, Papa's older brother who lived in Chicago. But Papa never divided the land in his mind; it was simply Logan land. For it he would work the long, hot summer pounding steel; Mama would teach and run the farm; Big Ma, in her sixties, would work like a woman of twenty in the fields and keep the house; and the boys and I would wear threadbare clothing washed to dishwater color; but always, the taxes and the mortgage would be paid. Papa said that one day I would understand.

I wondered.

When the fields ended and the Granger forest fanned both sides of the road with long overhanging branches, a tall, emaciated-looking boy popped suddenly from a forest trail and swung a thin arm around Stacey. It was T.J. Avery. His younger brother Claude emerged a moment later, smiling weakly as if it pained him to do so. Neither boy had on shoes, and their Sunday clothing, patched and worn, hung loosely upon their frail frames. The Avery family sharecropped on Granger land.

"Well," said T.J., jauntily swinging into step with Stacey, "here we go again startin' another school year."

"Yeah," sighed Stacey.

"Ah, man, don't look so down," T.J. said cheerfully. "Your mama's really one great teacher. I should know." He certainly should. He had failed Mama's class last year and was now returning for a second try.

"Shoot! You can say that," exclaimed Stacey. "You don't have to spend all day in a classroom with your mama."

"Look on the bright side," said T.J. "Jus' think of the advantage you've got. You'll be learnin' all sorts of stuff 'fore the rest of us. . . ." He smiled slyly. "Like what's on all them tests."

Stacey thrust T.J.'s arm from his shoulders. "If that's what you think, you don't know Mama."

"Ain't no need gettin' mad," T.J. replied undaunted. "Jus' an idea." He was quiet for a moment, then announced, "I betcha I could give y'all an earful 'bout that burnin' last night."

"Burning? What burning?" asked Stacey.

"Man, don't y'all know nothin'? The Berrys' burnin'. I thought y'all's grandmother went over there last night to see 'bout 'em."

Of course we knew that Big Ma had gone to a sick house last night. She was good at medicines and people often called her instead of a doctor when they were sick. But we didn't know anything about any burnings, and I certainly didn't know anything about any Berrys either.

"What Berrys he talking 'bout, Stacey?" I asked. "I don't know no Berrys."

"They live way over on the other side of Smellings Creek. They come up to church sometimes," said Stacey absently. Then he turned back to T.J. "Mr. Lanier come by real late and got Big Ma. Said Mr. Berry was low sick and needed her to help nurse him, but he ain't said nothing 'bout no burning."

"He's low sick all right—'cause he got burnt near to death. Him and his two nephews. And you know who done it?"

"Who?" Stacey and I and asked together.

"Well, since y'all don't seem to know nothin'," said T.J., in his usual sickening way of nursing a tidbit of information to death, "maybe I ought not tell y'all. It might hurt y'all's little ears."

"Ah, boy," I said, "don't start that mess again." I didn't like T.J. very much and his stalling around didn't help.

"Come on, T.J.," said Stacey, "out with it."

"Well . . ." T.J. murmured, then grew silent as if considering whether or not he should talk.

We reached the first of two crossroads and turned north; another mile and we would approach the second crossroads and turn east again.

Finally T.J. said, "Okay. See, them Berrys' burnin' wasn't no accident. Some white men took a match to 'em."

"Y-you mean just lit 'em up like a piece of wood?" stammered Christopher-John, his eyes growing big with disbelief.

"But why?" asked Stacey.

T.J. shrugged. "Don't know why. Jus' know they done it, that's all."

"How you know?" I questioned suspiciously.

He smiled smugly. " 'Cause your mama come down on her way to school and talked to my mama 'bout it."

"She did?"

"Yeah, and you should've seen the way she look when she come outa that house."

"How'd she look?" inquired Little Man, interested enough to glance up from the road for the first time.

T.J. looked around grimly and whispered, "Like . . . death." He waited a moment for his words to be appropriately shocking, but the effect was spoiled by Little Man, who asked lightly, "What does death look like?"

T.J. turned in annoyance. "Don't he know nothin'?"

"Well, what does it look like?" Little Man demanded to know. He didn't like T.J. either.

"Like my grandfather looked jus' 'fore they buried him," T.J. described all-knowingly.

"Oh," replied Little Man, losing interest and concentrating on the road again.

"I tell ya, Stacey, man," said T.J. morosely, shaking his head, "sometimes I jus' don't know 'bout that family of yours."

Stacey pulled back, considering whether or not T.J.'s words were offensive, but T.J. immediately erased the question by continuing amiably. "Don't get me wrong, Stacey. They some real swell kids, but that Cassie 'bout got me whipped this mornin'."

"Good!" I said.

"Now how'd she do that?" Stacey laughed.

"You wouldn't be laughin' if it'd've happened to you. She up and told your mama 'bout me goin' up to that Wallace store dancin' room and Miz Logan told Mama." He eyed me disdainfully then went on. "But don't worry, I got out of it though. When Mama asked me 'bout it, I jus' said ole Claude was always sneakin' up there to get some of that free candy Mr. Kaleb give out sometimes and I had to go and get him 'cause I knowed good and well she didn't want us up there. Boy, did he get it!" T.J laughed. "Mama 'bout wore him out."

I stared at quiet Claude. "You let him do that?" I exclaimed. But Claude only smiled in that sickly way of his and I knew that he had. He was more afraid of T.J. than of his mother.

Again Little Man glanced up and I could see his dislike for T.J. growing. Friendly Christopher-John glared at T.J., and putting his short arm around Claude's shoulder said, "Come on, Claude, let's go on ahead." Then he and Claude hurried up the road, away from T.J.

Stacey, who generally overlooked T.J.'s underhanded stunts, shook his head. "That was dirty."

"Well, what'd ya expect me to do? I couldn't let her think I was goin' up there 'cause I like to, could I? She'd've killed me!"

"And good riddance," I thought, promising myself that if he ever pulled anything like that on me, I'd knock his block off.

We were nearing the second crossroads, where deep gullies lined both sides of the road and the dense forest crept to the very edges of high, jagged, clay-walled banks. Suddenly, Stacey turned. "Quick!" he cried. "Off the road!" Without another word, all of us but Little Man scrambled up the steep right bank into the forest.

"Get up here, Man," Stacey ordered, but Little Man only gazed at the ragged red bank sparsely covered with scraggly brown briars and kept on walking. "Come on, do like I say."

"But I'll get my clothes dirty!" protested Little Man.

"You're gonna get them a whole lot dirtier you stay down there. Look!"

Little Man turned around and watched saucer-eyed as a bus bore down on him spewing clouds of red dust like a huge yellow dragon breathing fire. Little Man headed toward the bank, but it was too steep. He ran frantically along the road looking for a foothold and, finding one, hopped onto the bank, but not before the bus had sped past enveloping him in a scarlet haze while laughing white faces pressed against the bus windows.

Little Man shook a threatening fist into the thick air, then looked dismally down at himself.

"Well, ole Little Man done got his Sunday clothes dirty," T.J. laughed as we jumped down from the bank. Angry tears welled in Little Man's eyes but he quickly brushed them away before T.J. could see them.

"Ah, shut up, T.J.," Stacey snapped.

"Yeah, shut up, T.J.," I echoed.

"Come on, Man," Stacey said, "and next time do like I tell ya."

Little Man hopped down from the bank. "How's come they did that, Stacey, huh?" he asked, dusting himself off. "How's come they didn't even stop for us?"

"'Cause they like to see us run and it ain't our bus," Stacey said, balling his fists and jamming them tightly into his pockets.

"Well, where's our bus?" demanded Little Man.

"We ain't got one."

"Well, why not?"

"Ask Mamma," Stacey replied as a towheaded boy, barefooted and pale, came running down a forest path toward us. The boy quickly caught up and fell in stride with Stacey and T.J.

"Hey, Stacey," he said shyly.

"Hey, Jeremy," Stacey said.

There was an awkward silence.

"Y'all jus' startin' school today?"

"Yeah," replied Stacey.

"I wishin' ours was jus' startin'," sighed Jeremy. "Ours been goin' since the end of August." Jeremy's eyes were a whitewashed blue and they seemed to weep when he spoke.

"Yeah," said Stacey again.

Jeremy kicked the dust briskly and looked toward the north. He was a strange boy. Ever since I had begun school, he had walked with us as far as the crossroads in the morning, and met us there in the afternoon. He was often ridiculed by the other children at his school and had shown up more than once with wide red welts on his arms which Lillian Jean, his older sister, had revealed with satisfaction were the result of his associating with us. Still, Jeremy continued to meet us.

When we reached the crossroads, three more children, a girl of twelve or thirteen and two boys all looking very much like Jeremy, rushed past. The girl was Lillian Jean.

"Jeremy, come on," she said without a backward glance, and Jeremy, smiling sheepishly, waved a timid good-bye and slowly followed her.

We stood in the crossing gazing after them. Jeremy looked back once but then Lillian Jean yelled shrilly at him and he did not look back again. They were headed for the Jefferson Davis County School, a long white wooden building looming in the distance. Behind the building was a wide sports field around which were scattered rows of tiered gray-looking benches. In front of it were two yellow buses, our own tormentor and one that brought students from the other direction, and loitering students awaiting the knell of the morning-bell. In the very center of the expansive front lawn, waving red, white, and blue with the emblem of the Confederacy emblazoned in its upper left-hand corner, was the Mississippi flag. Directly below it was the American flag. As Jeremy and his sister and brothers hurried toward those transposed flags, we turned eastward toward our own school.

The Great Faith Elementary and Secondary School, one of the largest black schools in the county, was a dismal end to an hour's journey. Consisting of four weather-beaten wooden houses on stilts of brick, 320 students, seven teachers; a principal, a caretaker, and the caretaker's cow, which kept the wide crabgrass lawn sufficiently clipped in spring and summer, the school was located near three plantations, the largest and closest by far being the Granger plantation. Most of the students were from families that sharecropped on Granger land, and the others mainly from Montier and Harrison plantation families. Because the students were needed in the fields from early spring when the cotton was planted until after most of the cotton had been picked in the fall, the school adjusted its terms accordingly, beginning in October and dismissing in March. But even so, after today a number of the older students would not be seen again for a month or two, not until the last puff of cotton had been gleaned from the fields, and eventually most would drop out of school altogether. Because of this the classes in the higher grades grew smaller with each passing year.

The class buildings, with their backs practically against the forest wall, formed a semicircle facing a small one-room church at the opposite edge of the compound. It was to this church that many of the school's students and their parents belonged. As we arrived, the enormous iron bell in the church belfry was ringing vigorously, warning the milling students that only five minutes of freedom remained.

Little Man immediately pushed his way across the lawn to the well. Stacey and T.J., ignoring the rest of us now that they were on the school grounds, wandered off to be with the other seventh-grade boys, and Christopher-John and Claude rushed to reunite with their classmates of last year. Left alone, I dragged slowly to the building that held the first four grades and sat on the bottom step. Plopping my pencils and notebook into the dirt, I propped my elbows on my knees and rested my chin in the palms of my hands.

"Hey, Cassie," said Mary Lou Wellever, the principal's daughter, as she flounced by in a new yellow dress.

"Hey, yourself," I said, scowling so ferociously that she kept on walking. I stared after her a moment noting that she *would* have on a new dress. Certainly no one else did. Patches on faded pants and dresses abounded on boys and girls come so recently from the heat of the cotton fields. Girls stood awkwardly, afraid to sit, and boys pulled restlessly at starched, high-buttoned collars. Those students fortunate enough to have shoes hopped from one pinched foot to the other. Tonight the Sunday clothes would be wrapped in newspaper and hung for Sunday and the shoes would be packed away to be brought out again only when the weather turned so cold that bare feet could no longer traverse the frozen roads; but for today we all suffered.

On the far side of the lawn I spied Moe Turner speeding toward the seventh-grade-class building, and wondered at his energy. Moe was one of Stacey's friends. He lived on the Montier plantation, a three-and-a-half-hour walk from the school. Because of the distance, many children from the Montier plantation did not come to Great Faith after they had finished the four-year school near Smellings Creek. But there were some girls and boys like Moe who made the trek daily, leaving their homes while the sky was black and not returning until all was blackness again. I for one was certainly glad that I didn't live that far away. I don't think my feet would have wanted that badly for me to be educated.

The chiming of the second bell began. I stood up dusting my bottom as the first, second, third, and fourth graders crowded up the stairs into the hallway. Little Man flashed proudly past, his face and hands clean and his black shoes shining again. I glanced down at my own shoes powdered red and, raising my right foot, rubbed it against the back of my left leg, then reversed the procedure. As the last gong of the bell reverberated across the compound, I swooped up my pencils and notebook and ran inside.

A hallway extended from the front to the back door of the building. On either side of the hallway were two doorways, both leading into the same large room which was divided into two classrooms by a heavy canvas curtain. The second and third grades were on the left, the first and fourth grades on the right. I hurried to the rear of the building, turned to the right, and slid into a third-row bench occupied by Gracey Pearson and Alma Scott.

"You can't sit here," objected Gracey. "I'm saving it for Mary Lou."

I glanced back at Mary Lou Wellever depositing her lunch pail on a shelf in the back of the room and said, "Not any more you ain't."

Miss Daisy Crocker, yellow and buckeyed, glared down at me from the middle of the room with a look that said, "Soooooooo, it's you, Cassie Logan." Then she pursed her lips and drew the curtain along the rusted iron rod and tucked it into a wide loop in the back wall. With the curtain drawn back, the first graders gazed quizzically at us. Little Man sat by a window, his hands folded, patiently waiting for Miss Crocker to speak.

Mary Lou nudged me. "That's my seat, Cassie Logan."

"Mary Lou Wellever," Miss Crocker called primly, "have a seat."

"Yes, ma'am," said Mary Lou, eyeing me with a look of pure hate before turning away.

Miss Crocker walked stiffly to her desk, which was set on a tiny platform and piled high with bulky objects covered by a tarpaulin. She rapped the desk with a ruler, although the room was perfectly still, and said, "Welcome, children, to Great Faith Elementary School." Turning slightly so that she stared squarely at the left side of the room, she continued, "To all of you fourth graders, it's good to have you in my class. I'll be expecting many good and wonderful things from you." Then addressing the right side of the room, she said, "And to all our little first grade friends only today starting on the road to knowledge and education, may your tiny feet find the pathways of learning steady and forever before you."

Already bored, I stretched my right arm on the desk and rested my head in my upraised hand. Miss Crocker smiled mechanically, then rapped on her desk again. "Now, little ones," she said, still talking to the first grade, "your teacher, Miss Davis, has been held up in Jackson for a few days so I'll have the pleasure of sprinkling your little minds with the first rays of knowledge." She beamed down upon them as if she expected to be applauded for this bit of news, then with a swoop of her large eyes to include the fourth graders, she went on.

"Now since there's only one of me, we shall have to sacrifice for the next few days. We shall work, work, work, but we shall have to work like little Christian boys and girls and share, share, share. Now are we willing to do that?"

"YES'M, MIZ CROCKER," the children chorused.

But I remained silent. I never did approve of group responses. Adjusting my head in my hand, I sighed heavily, my mind on the burning of the Berrys.

"Cassie Logan?"

I looked up, startled.

"Cassie Logan!"

"Yes, ma'am?" I jumped up quickly to face Miss Crocker. "Aren't you willing to work and share?"

"Yes'm."

"Then say so!"

"Yes'm," I murmured, sliding back into my seat as Mary Lou, Gracey, and Alma giggled. Here it was only five minutes into the new school year and already I was in trouble.

By ten o'clock, Miss Crocker had rearranged our seating and written our names on her seating chart. I was still sitting beside Gracey and Alma but we had been moved from the third to the first row in front of a small potbellied stove. Although being eyeball to eyeball with Miss Crocker was nothing to look forward to, the prospect of being warm once the cold weather set in was nothing to be sneezed at either, so I resolved to make the best of my rather dubious position.

Now Miss Crocker made a startling announcement: This year we would all have books.

Everyone gasped, for most of the students had never handled a book at all besides the family Bible. I admit that even I was somewhat excited. Although Mama had several books, I had never had one of my very own.

"Now we're very fortunate to get these readers," Miss Crocker explained while we eagerly awaited the unveiling. "The county superintendent of schools himself brought these books down here for our use and we must take extra-good care of them." She moved toward her desk. "So let's all promise that we'll take the best care possible of these new books." She stared down, expecting our response. "All right, all together, let's repeat, 'We promise to take good care of our new books.'" She looked sharply at me as she spoke.

"WE PROMISE TO TAKE GOOD CARE OF OUR NEW BOOKS!"

"Fine," Miss Crocker beamed, then proudly threw back the tarpaulin.

Sitting so close to the desk, I could see that the covers of the books, a motley red, were badly worn and that the gray edges of the pages had been marred by pencils, crayons, and ink. My anticipation at having my own book ebbed to a sinking disappointment. But Miss Crocker continued to beam as she called each fourth grader to her desk and, recording a number in her roll book, handed him or her a book.

As I returned from my trip to her desk, I noticed the first graders anxiously watching the disappearing pile. Miss Crocker must have noticed them too, for as I sat down she said, "Don't worry, little ones, there are plenty of readers for you too. See there on Miss Davis's desk." Wide eyes turned to the covered teacher's platform directly in front of them and an audible sigh of relief swelled in the room.

I glanced across at Little Man, his face lit in eager excitement. I knew that he could not see the soiled covers or the marred pages from where he sat, and even though his penchant for cleanliness was often annoying, I did not like to think of his disappointment when he saw the books as they really were. But there was nothing that I could do about it, so I opened my book to its center and began browsing through the spotted pages. Girls with blond braids and boys with blue eyes stared up at me. I found a story about a boy and his dog lost in a cave and began reading while Miss Crocker's voice droned on monotonously.

Suddenly I grew conscious of a break in that monotonous tone and I looked up. Miss Crocker was sitting at Miss Davis's desk with the first-grade books stacked before her, staring fiercely down at Little Man, who was pushing a book back upon the desk.

"What's that you said, Clayton Chester Logan?" she asked.

The room became gravely silent. Everyone knew that Little Man was in big trouble for no one, but no one, ever called Little Man "Clayton Chester" unless she or he meant serious business.

Little Man knew this too. His lips parted slightly as he took his hands from the book. He quivered, but he did not take his eyes from Miss Crocker. "I—I said may I have another book please, ma'am," he squeaked. "That one's dirty."

"Dirty!" Miss Crocker echoed, appalled by such temerity. She stood up, gazing down upon Little Man like a bony giant, but Little Man raised his head and continued to look into her eyes. "Dirty! And just who do you think you are, Clayton Chester? Here the county is giving us these wonderful books during these hard times and you're going to stand there and tell me that the book's too dirty? Now you take that book or get nothing at all!"

Little Man lowered his eyes and said nothing as he stared at the book. For several moments he stood there, his face barely visible above the desk, then he turned and looked at the few remaining books and, seeming to realize that they were as badly soiled as the one Miss Crocker had given him, he looked across the room at me. I nodded and Little Man, glancing up again at Miss Crocker, slid the book from the edge of the desk, and with his back straight and his head up returned to his seat.

Miss Crocker sat down again. "Some people around here seem to be giving themselves airs. I'll tolerate no more of that," she scowled. "Sharon Lake, come get your book."

I watched Little Man as he scooted into his seat beside two other little boys. He sat for a while with a stony face looking out the window; then, evidently accepting the fact that the book in front of him was the best that he could expect, he turned and opened it. But as he stared at the book's inside cover, his face clouded, changing from sulky acceptance to puzzlement. His brows furrowed. Then his eyes grew wide, and suddenly he sucked in his breath and sprang from his chair like a wounded animal, flinging the book onto the floor and stomping madly upon it.

Miss Crocker rushed to Little Man and grabbed him up in powerful hands. She shook him vigorously, then set him on the floor again. "Now, just what's gotten into you, Clayton Chester?"

But Little Man said nothing. He just stood staring down at the open book, shivering with indignant anger.

"Pick it up," she ordered.

"No!" defied Little Man.

"No? I'll give you ten seconds to pick up that book, boy, or I'm going to get my switch."

Little Man bit his lower lip, and I knew that he was not going to pick up the book. Rapidly, I turned to the inside cover of my own book and saw immediately what had made Little Man so furious. Stamped on the inside cover was a chart which read:

PROPERTY OF THE BOARD OF EDUCATION
Spokane County, Mississippi
September, 1922

CHRONOLOGICAL ISSUANCE	DATE OF ISSUANCE	CONDITION OF BOOK	RACE OF STUDENT
1	September 1922	New	White
2	September 1923	Excellent	White
3	September 1924	Excellent	White
4	September 1925	Very Good	White
5	September 1926	Good	White
6	September 1927	Good	White
7	September 1928	Average	White
8	September 1929	Average	White
9	September 1930	Average	White
10	September 1931	Poor	White
11	September 1932	Poor	White
12	September 1933	Very Poor	nigra
13			
14			
15			

The blank lines continued down to line 20 and I knew that they had all been reserved for black students. A knot of anger swelled in my throat and held there. But as Miss Crocker directed Little Man to bend over the "whipping" chair, I put aside my anger and jumped up.

"Miz Crocker, don't, please!" I cried. Miss Crocker's dark eyes warned me not to say another word. "I know why he done it!"

"You want part of this switch, Cassie?"

"No'm," I said hastily. "I just wanna tell you how come Little Man done what he done."

"Sit down!" she ordered as I hurried toward her with the open book in my hand.

Holding the book up to her, I said, "See, Miz Crocker, see what it says. They give us these ole books when they didn't want 'em no more."

She regarded me impatiently, but did not look at the book. "Now how could he know what it says? He can't read."

"Yes'm, he can. He been reading since he was four. He can't read all them big words, but he can read them columns. See what's in the last row. Please look, Miz Crocker."

This time Miss Crocker did look, but her face did not change. Then, holding up her head, she gazed unblinkingly down at me.

"S-see what they called us," I said, afraid she had not seen.

"That's what you are," she said coldly. "Now go sit down."

I shook my head, realizing now that Miss Crocker did not even know what I was talking about. She had looked at the page and had understood nothing.

"I said sit down, Cassie!"

I started slowly toward my desk, but as the

hickory stick sliced the tense air, I turned back around. "Miz Crocker," I said, "I don't want my book neither."

The switch landed hard upon Little Man's upturned bottom. Miss Crocker looked questioningly at me as I reached up to her desk and placed the book upon it. Then she swung the switch five more times and, discovering that Little Man had no intention of crying, ordered him up.

"All right, Cassie," she sighed, turning to me, "come on and get yours."

By the end of the school day I had decided that I would tell Mama everything before Miss Crocker had a chance to do so. From nine years of trial and error, I had learned that punishment was always less severe when I poured out the whole truth to Mama on my own before she had heard anything from anyone else. I knew that Miss Crocker had not spoken to Mama during the lunch period, for she had spent the whole hour in the classroom preparing for the afternoon session.

As soon as class was dismissed I sped from the room, weaving a path through throngs of students happy to be free. But before I could reach the seventh-grade-class building, I had the misfortune to collide with Mary Lou's father. Mr. Wellever looked down on me with surprise that I would actually bump into him, then proceeded to lecture me on the virtues of watching where one was going. Meanwhile Miss Crocker briskly crossed the lawn to Mama's class building. By the time I escaped Mr. Wellever, she had already disappeared into the darkness of the hallway.

Mama's classroom was in the back. I crept silently along the quiet hall and peeped cautiously into the open doorway. Mama, pushing a strand of her long, crinkly hair back into the chignon at the base of her slender neck, was seated at her desk watching Miss Crocker thrust a book before her. "Just look at that, Mary," Miss Crocker said, thumping the book twice with her forefinger. "A perfectly good book ruined. Look at that broken binding and those foot marks all over it."

Mama did not speak as she studied the book.

"And here's the one Cassie wouldn't take," she said, placing a second book on Mama's desk with an outraged slam. "At least she didn't have a tantrum and stomp all over hers. I tell you, Mary, I just don't know what got into those children today. I always knew Cassie was rather high-strung, but Little Man! He's always such a perfect little gentleman."

Mama glanced at the book I had rejected and opened the front cover so that the offensive pages of both books faced her. "You say Cassie said it was because of this front page that she and Little Man didn't want the books?" Mama asked quietly.

"Yes, ain't that something?" Miss Crocker said, forgetting her teacher-training-school diction in her indignation. "The very idea! That's on all the books, and why they got so upset about it I'll never know."

"You punish them?" asked Mama, glancing up at Miss Crocker.

"Well, I certainly did! Whipped both of them good with my hickory stick. Wouldn't you have?" When Mama did not reply, she added defensively, "I had a perfect right to."

"Of course you did, Daisy," Mama said, turning back to the books again. "They disobeyed you." But her tone was so quiet and noncommittal that I knew Miss Crocker was not satisfied with her reaction.

"Well, I thought you would've wanted to know, Mary, in case you wanted to give them a piece of your mind also."

Mama smiled up at Miss Crocker and said rather absently, "Yes, of course, Daisy. Thank you." Then she opened her desk drawer and pulled out some paper, a pair of scissors, and a small brown bottle.

Miss Crocker, dismayed by Mama's seeming unconcern for the seriousness of the matter, thrust her shoulders back and began moving away from the desk. "You understand that if they don't have those books to study from, I'll have to fail them in both reading and composition, since I plan to base all my lessons around—" She stopped abruptly and stared in amazement at Mama. "Mary, what in the world are you doing?"

Mama did not answer. She had trimmed the paper to the size of the books and was now dipping a gray-looking glue from the brown bottle onto the inside cover of one of the books. Then she took the paper and placed it over the glue.

"Mary Logan, do you know what you're doing? That book belongs to the county. If somebody from the superintendent's office ever comes down here and sees that book, you'll be in real trouble."

Mama laughed and picked up the other book. "In the first place no one cares enough to come down here, and in the second place if anyone should come, maybe he could see all the things we need—current books for all of our subjects, not just somebody's old throwaways, desks, paper, blackboards, erasers, maps, chalk . . ." Her voice trailed off as she glued the second book

"Biting the hand that feeds you. That's what you're doing, Mary Logan, biting the hand that feeds you."

Again, Mama laughed. "If that's the case, Daisy, I don't think I need that little bit of food." With the second book finished, she stared at a small pile of seventh-grade books on her desk.

"Well, I just think you're spoiling those children, Mary. They've got to learn how things are sometime."

"Maybe so," said Mama, "but that doesn't mean they have to accept them . . . and maybe we don't either."

Miss Crocker gazed suspiciously at Mama. Although Mama had been a teacher at Great Faith for fourteen years, ever since she had graduated from the Crandon Teacher Training School at nineteen, she was still considered by many of the other teachers as a disrupting maverick. Her ideas were always a bit too radical and her statements a bit too pointed. The fact that she had not grown up in Spokane County but in the Delta made her even more suspect, and the more traditional thinkers like Miss Crocker were wary of her. "Well, if anyone ever does come from the county and sees Cassie's and Little Man's books messed up like that," she said, "I certainly won't accept the responsibility for them."

"It will be easy enough for anyone to see whose responsibility it is, Daisy, by opening any seventh-grade book. Because tomorrow I'm going to 'mess them up' too."

Miss Crocker, finding nothing else to say, turned imperiously and headed for the door. I dashed across the hall and awaited her exit, then crept back.

Mama remained at her desk, sitting very still. For a long time she did not move. When she did, she picked up one of the seventh-grade books and began to glue again. I wanted to go and help her, but something warned me that now was not the time to make my presence known, and I left.

I would wait until the evening to talk to her; there was no rush now. She understood.

Chapter 2

"Cassie, you better watch yourself, girl," Big Ma cautioned, putting one rough, large hand against my back to make sure I didn't fall.

I looked down at my grandmother from midway up one of the wooden poles Papa had set out to mark the length of the cotton field. Big Ma was Papa's mother, and like him she was tall and strongly built. Her clear, smooth skin was the color of a pecan shell. "Ah, Big Ma, I ain't gonna fall," I scoffed, then climbed onto the next strong spike and reached for a fibrous puff at the top of a tall cotton stalk.

"You sho' better not fall, girl," grumbled Big Ma. "Sometimes I wish we had more low cotton like down 'round Vicksburg. I don't like y'all children climbin' them things." She looked around, her hand on her hip. Christopher-John and Little Man farther down the field balanced skillfully on lower spikes of their own poles plucking the last of the cotton, but Stacey, too heavy now to climb the poles, was forced to remain on the ground. Big Ma eyed us all again, then with a burlap bag slung across her right shoulder and dangling at the left side of her waist she moved down the row toward Mama. "Mary, child, I think with what we picked today we oughta have ourselves another bale."

Mama was stooped over a low cotton branch. She stuffed one last puff into her bag and straightened. She was tawny-colored, thin and sinewy, with delicate features in a strong-jawed face, and though almost as tall as Big Ma, she seemed somewhat dwarfed beside her. "I expect you're right, Mama," she said. "Come Monday, we'd better haul it up to the Granger place and have it ginned. Then we can—Cassie, what's the matter?"

I didn't answer Mama. I had moved to the very top of my pole and could now see above the field to the road where two figures, one much taller than the other, were walking briskly. As the men rounded a curve in the road, they became more distinct. There was in the easy fluid gait of the shorter man a familiarity that made me gasp. I squinted, shadowing my eyes from the sun, then slipped like lightning down the pole.

"Cassie?"

"It's Papa!"

"David?" Mama questioned unbelievingly as Christopher-John and Little Man descended eagerly and dashed after Stacey and me toward the barbed-wire fence.

"Don't y'all go through that fence!" Big Ma called after us. But we pretended not to hear. We held the second and third rows of the prickly wire wide for each other to climb through: then all four of us sped down the road toward Papa.

When Papa saw us, he began running swiftly, easily, like the wind. Little Man, the first to reach him, was swept lightly upward in Papa's strong hands as Christopher-John, Stacey, and I crowded around.

"Papa, what you doing home?" asked Little Man.

Putting Little Man down, Papa said, "Just had to come home and see 'bout my babies." He hugged and kissed each of us, then stood back. "Just look at y'all," he said proudly. "Ain't y'all something? Can't hardly call y'all babies no more." He turned. "Mr. Morrison, what you think 'bout these children of mine?"

In our excitement, we had taken no notice of the

other man standing quietly at the side of the road. But now, gazing upward at the most formidable-looking being we had ever encountered, we huddled closer to Papa.

The man was a human tree in height, towering high above Papa's six feet two inches. The long trunk of his massive body bulged with muscles, and his skin, of the deepest ebony, was partially scarred upon his face and neck, as if by fire. Deep lifelines were cut into his face and his hair was splotched with gray, but his eyes were clear and penetrating. I glanced at the boys and it was obvious to me that they were wondering the same thing as I: Where had such a being come from?

"Children," said Papa, "meet Mr. L.T. Morrison."

Each of us whispered a faint hello to the giant, then the six of us started up the road toward home. Before we reached the house, Mama and Big Ma met us. When Papa saw Mama, his square, high-cheekboned face opened to a wide smile and, lifting Mama with spirited gusto, he swung her around twice before setting her down and kissing her.

"David, is something the matter?" she asked.

Papa laughed. "Something gotta be wrong, woman, for me to come see 'bout you?"

"You got my letter?"

He nodded, then hugged and kissed Big Ma before introducing them both to Mr. Morrison.

When we reached the house we climbed the long, sloping lawn to the porch and went into Mama and Papa's room, which also served as the living area. Mama offered Mr. Morrison Grandpa Logan's chair, a cushioned oak rocker skillfully crafted by Grandpa himself; but Mr. Morrison did not sit down immediately. Instead, he stood gazing at the room.

It was a warm, comfortable room of doors and

wood and pictures. From it a person could reach the front or the side porch, the kitchen, and the two other bedrooms. Its walls were made of smooth oak, and on them hung gigantic photographs of Grandpa and Big Ma, Papa and Uncle Hammer when they were boys, Papa's two eldest brothers, who were now dead, and pictures of Mama's family. The furniture, a mixture of Logan-crafted walnut and oak, included a walnut bed whose ornate headboard rose halfway up the wall toward the high ceiling, a grand chiffonier with a floor-length mirror, a large rolltop desk which had once been Grandpa's but now belonged to Mama, and the four oak chairs, two of them rockers, which Grandpa had made for Big Ma as a wedding present.

Mr. Morrison nodded when he had taken it all in, as if he approved, then sat across from Papa in front of the unlit fireplace. The boys and I pulled up straight-backed chairs near Papa as Big Ma asked, "How long you gonna be home, son?"

Papa looked across at her. "Till Sunday evening," he said quietly.

"Sunday?" Mama exclaimed. "Why, today's already Saturday."

"I know, baby," Papa said, taking her hand, "but I gotta get that night train out of Vicksburg so I can get back to work by Monday morning."

Christopher-John, Little Man, and I groaned loudly, and Papa turned to us. "Papa, can't you stay no longer than that? Last time you come home, you stayed a week," I said.

Papa gently pulled one of my pigtails. "Sorry, Cassie girl; but I stay any longer, I might lose my job."

"But, Papa—"

"Listen, all of y'all," he said, looking from me to the boys to Mama and Big Ma, "I come home special so I could bring Mr. Morrison. He's gonna stay with us awhile."

If Mama and Big Ma were surprised by Papa's words, they did not show it, but the boys and I looked with wide eyes at each other, then at the giant.

"Mr. Morrison lost his job on the railroad a while back," Papa continued, "and he ain't been able to find anything else. When I asked him if he wanted to come work here as a hired hand, he said he would. I told him we couldn't afford much—food and shelter and a few dollars in cash when I come home in the winter."

Mama turned to Mr. Morrison, studied him for a moment, and said, "Welcome to our home, Mr. Morrison."

"Miz Logan," said Mr. Morrison in a deep, quiet voice like the roll of low thunder, "I think you oughta know I got fired off my job. Got in a fight with some men . . . beat 'em up pretty bad."

Mama stared into Mr. Morrison's deep eyes. "Whose fault was it?"

Mr. Morrison stared back. "I'd say theirs."

"Did the other men get fired?"

"No, ma'am," answered Mr. Morrison. "They was white."

Mama nodded and stood. "Thank you for telling me, Mr. Morrison. You're lucky no worse happened and we're glad to have you here . . . especially now." Then she turned and went into the kitchen with Big Ma to prepare supper, leaving the boys and me to wonder about her last words.

"Stacey, what you think?" I asked as we milked the cows in the evening. "How come Papa come home and brung Mr. Morrison?"

Stacey shrugged. "Like he said, I guess."

I thought on that a moment. "Papa ain't never brung nobody here before."

Stacey did not reply.

"You think . . . Stacey, you think it's cause of them burnings T.J. was talking 'bout?"

"Burnings?" piped Little Man, who had interrupted his feeding of the chickens to visit with Lady, our golden mare. "What's burnings gotta do with anything?"

"That happened way over by Smellings Creek," said Stacey slowly, ignoring Little Man. "Papa got no need to think . . ." His voice trailed off and he stopped milking.

"Think what?" I asked.

"Nothin'," he muttered, turning back to the cow. "Don't worry 'bout it."

I glared at him. "I ain't worrying. I just wanna know, that's all, and I betcha anything Mr. Morrison come here to do more'n work. Sure wish I knew for sure."

Stacey made no reply, but Christopher-John, his pudgy hands filled with dried corn for the chickens and his lower lip quivering, said, "I—I know what I wish. I wish P-Papa didn't never have to go 'way no more. I wish he could just stay . . . and stay. . . ."

At church the next morning, Mrs. Silas Lanier leaned across me and whispered to Big Ma, "John Henry Berry died last night." When the announcement was made to the congregation, the deacons prayed for the soul of John Henry Berry and the recovery of his brother, Beacon, and his uncle, Mr. Samuel Berry. But after church, when some of the members stopped by the house to visit, angry hopeless words were spoken.

"The way I hears it," said Mr. Lanier, "they been after John Henry ever since he come back from the war and settled on his daddy's place up by Smellings Creek. Had a nice little place up there too, and was doing pretty well. Left a wife and six children."

Big Ma shook her head. "Just in the wrong place at the wrong time."

The boys and I sat at our study table pretending not to listen, but listening still.

"Henrietta Toggins," said Mrs. Lanier, "you know, Clara Davis's sister that live up there in Strawberry? Well, she's kin to the Berrys and she was with John Henry and Beacon when the trouble got started. They was gonna drop her off at home—you know John Henry had him one of them old Model-T pickups—but they needed some gas so they stopped by that fillin' station up there in Strawberry. They was waitin' there for they gas when some white men come up messin' with them—been drinkin', you know. And Henrietta heard 'em say; 'That's the nigger Sallie Ann said was flirtin' with her.' And when she heard that, she said to John Henry, 'Let's get on outa here.' He wanted to wait for the gas, but she made him and Beacon get in that car, and them men jus' watched them drive off and didn't mess with 'em right then.

"John Henry, he took her on home then headed back for his own place, but evidently them men caught up with him and Beacon again and starts rammin' the back of they car—least that's what Beacon and John Henry told they aunt and uncle when they seed 'em. John Henry knowed he was runnin' outa gas and he was 'fraid he couldn't make it to his own place, so he stopped at his uncle's. But them men dragged him and Beacon both outa that house, and when old man Berry tried to stop it, they lit him afire with them boys."

"It's sho' a shame, all right," said T.J.'s father, a frail, sickly man with a hacking cough. "These folks gettin' so bad in here. Heard tell they lynched a boy a few days ago at Crosston."

"And ain't a thing gonna be done 'bout it," said Mr. Lanier. "That's what's so terrible! When Henrietta went to the sheriff and told him what she'd seed, he called her a liar and sent her on home. Now I hear tells that some of them men that done it been 'round braggin' 'bout it. Sayin' they'd do it again if some other uppity nigger get out of line."

Mrs. Avery tisked, "Lord have mercy!"

Papa sat very quietly while the Laniers and the Averys talked, studying them with serious eyes. Finally, he took the pipe from his mouth and made a statement that seemed to the boys and me to be totally disconnected with the conversation. "In this family, we don't shop at the Wallace store."

The room became silent. The boys and I stared at the adults wondering why. The Laniers and the Averys looked uneasily about them and when the silence was broken, the subject had changed to the sermon of the day.

After the Laniers and the Averys had left, Papa called us to him. "Your mama tells me that a lot of the older children been going up to that Wallace store after school to dance and buy their bootleg liquor and smoke cigarettes. Now she said she's already told y'all this, but I'm gonna tell y'all again, so listen good. We don't want y'all going to that place. Children going there are gonna get themselves in a whole lot of trouble one day. There's drinking up there and I don't like it—and I don't like them Wallaces either. If I ever find out y'all been up there, for any reason, I'm gonna wear y'all out. Y'all hear me?"

"Yessir, Papa," piped Christopher-John readily. "I ain't never going up there."

The rest of us agreed; Papa always meant what he said—and he swung a mean switch.

Chapter 3

By the end of October the rain had come, falling heavily upon the six-inch layer of dust which had had its own way for more than two months. At first the rain had merely splotched the dust, which seemed to be rejoicing in its own resiliency and laughing at the heavy drops thudding against it; but eventually the dust was forced to surrender to the mastery of the rain and it churned into a fine red mud that oozed between our toes and slopped against our ankles as we marched miserably to and from school.

To shield us from the rain, Mama issued us dried calfskins which we flung over our heads and shoulders like stiff cloaks. We were not very fond of the skins, for once they were wet they emitted a musty odor which seeped into our clothing and clung to our skins. We preferred to do without them; unfortunately, Mama cared very little about what we preferred.

Since we usually left for school after Mama, we solved this problem by dutifully cloaking ourselves with the skins before leaving home. As soon as we were beyond Big Ma's eagle eyes, we threw off the cloaks and depended upon the overhanging limbs of the forest trees to keep us dry. Once at school, we donned the cloaks again and marched into our respective classrooms properly attired.

If we had been faced only with the prospect of the rain soaking through our clothing each morning and evening, we could have more easily endured the journey between home and school. But as it was, we also had to worry about the Jefferson Davis school bus zooming from behind and splashing us with the murky waters of the road. Knowing that the bus driver liked to entertain his passengers by sending us slipping along the road to the almost inaccessible forest banks washed to a smooth baldness by the constant rains, we continuously looked over our shoulders when we were between the two crossroads so that we could reach the bank before the bus was upon us. But sometimes the rain pounded so heavily that it was all we could do to stay upright, and we did not look back as often nor listen as carefully as we should; we consequently found ourselves comical objects to cruel eyes that gave no thought to our misery.

No one was more angered by this humiliation than Little Man. Although he had asked Mama after the first day of school why Jefferson Davis had two buses and Great Faith had none, he had never been totally satisfied by her answer. She had explained to him, as she had explained to Christopher-John the year before and to me two years before that, that the county did not provide buses for its black students. In fact, she said, the county provided very little and much of the money which supported the black schools came from the black churches. Great Faith Church just could not afford a bus, so therefore we had to walk.

This information cut deeply into Little Man's brain, and each day when he found his clean clothes splashed red by the school bus, he became more and more embittered until finally one day he stomped angrily into the kitchen and exploded, "They done it again, Big Ma! Just look at my clothes!"

Big Ma clucked her tongue as she surveyed us. "Well, go on and get out of 'em, honey, and wash 'em out. All of y'all, get out of them clothes and dry yo'selves," she said, turning back to the huge iron-bellied stove to stir her stew.

"But, Big Ma, it ain't fair!" wailed Little Man. "It just ain't fair."

Stacey and Christopher-John left to change into their work clothes, but Little Man sat on the side bench looking totally dejected as he gazed at his pale-blue pants crusted with mud from the knees down. Although each night Big Ma prepared a pot of hot soapy water for him to wash out his clothing, each day he arrived home looking as if his pants had not been washed in more than a month.

Big Ma was not one for coddling any of us, but now she turned from the stove and, wiping her hands on her long white apron, sat down on the bench and put her arm around Little Man. "Now, look here, baby, it ain't the end of the world. Lord, child, don't you know one day the sun'll shine again and you won't get muddy no more?"

"But, Big Ma," Little Man protested, "ifn that ole bus driver would slow down, I wouldn't get muddy!" Then he frowned deeply and added, "Or ifn we had a bus like theirs."

"Well, he don't and you don't," Big Ma said, getting up. "So ain't no use frettin' 'bout it. One day you'll have a plenty of clothes and maybe even a car of yo' own to ride 'round in, so don't you pay no mind to them ignorant white folks. You jus' keep on studyin' and get yo'self a good education and you'll be all right. Now, go on and wash out yo' clothes and hang 'em by the fire so's I can iron 'em 'fore I go to bed."

Turning, she spied me. "Cassie, what you want, girl? Go change into yo' pants and hurry on back here so's you can help me get this supper on the table time yo' mama get home."

That night when I was snug in the deep feathery bed beside Big Ma, the tat-tat of the rain against the tin roof changed to a deafening roar that sounded as if thousands of giant rocks were being hurled against the earth. By morning the heavy rain had become a drizzle, but the earth was badly sodden from the night's downpour. High rivers of muddy water flowed in the deep gullies, and wide lakes shimmered on the roads.

As we set out for school the whiteness of the sun attempted to penetrate the storm clouds, but by the time we had turned north toward the second crossing it had given up, slinking meekly behind the blackening clouds. Soon the thunder rolled across the sky, and the rain fell like hail upon our bent heads.

"Ah, shoot! I sure am gettin' tired of this mess," complained T.J.

But no one else said a word. We were listening for the bus. Although we had left home earlier than usual to cover the northern road before the bus came, we were not overly confident that we would miss it, for we had tried this strategy before. Sometimes it worked; most times it didn't. It was as if the bus were a living thing, plaguing and defeating us at every turn. We could not outwit it.

We plodded along feeling the cold mud against our feet, walking faster and faster to reach the crossroads. Then Christopher-John stopped. "Hey, y'all, I think I hear it," he warned.

We looked around, but saw nothing.

"Ain't nothin' yet," I said.

We walked on.

"Wait a minute," said Christopher-John, stopping a second time. "There it is again."

We turned but still there was nothing.

"Why don't you clean out your ears?" T.J. exclaimed.

"Wait," said Stacey, "I think I hear it too."

We hastened up the road to where the gully was narrower and we could easily swing up the bank into the forest.

Soon the purr of a motor came closer and Mr. Granger's sleek silver Packard eased into view. It was a grand car with chrome shining even in the rain, and the only one like it in the county, so it was said.

We groaned. "Jus' ole Harlan," said T.J. flippantly as the expensive car rounded a curve and disappeared, then he and Claude started down the bank.

Stacey stopped them. "Long as we're already up here, why don't we wait awhile," he suggested. "The bus oughta be here soon and it'll be harder to get up on the bank further down the road."

"Ah, man, that bus ain't comin' for a while yet," said T.J. "We left early this mornin', remember?"

Stacey looked to the south, thinking. Little Man, Christopher-John and I waited for his decision.

"Come on, man," T.J. persuaded. "Why stay up here waitin' for that devilish bus when we could be at school outa this mess?"

"Well . . ."

T.J. and Claude jumped from the bank. Then Stacey, frowning as if he were doing this against his better judgment, jumped down too. Little Man, Christopher-John, and I followed.

Five minutes later we were skidding like frightened puppies toward the bank again as the bus accelerated and barreled down the narrow rain-soaked road but there was no place to which we could run, for Stacey had been right. Here the gullies were too wide, filled almost to overflowing, and there were no briars or bushes by which we could swing up onto the bank.

Finally, when the bus was less than fifty feet behind us, it veered dangerously close to the right edge of the road where we were running, forcing us to attempt the jump to the bank; but all of us fell short and landed in the slime of the gully.

Little Man, chest-deep in water, scooped up a handful of mud and in an uncontrollable rage scrambled up to the road and ran after the retreating bus. As moronic rolls of laughter and cries of "Nigger! Nigger! Mud eater!" wafted from the open windows, Little Man threw his mudball, missing the wheels by several feet. Then, totally dismayed by what had happened, he buried his face in his hands and cried.

T.J. climbed from the gully grinning at Little Man, but Stacey, his face burning red beneath his dark skin, glared so fiercely at T.J. that he fell back. "Just one word outa you, T.J.," he said tightly. "Just one word."

Christopher-John and I looked at each other. We had never seen Stacey look like this, and neither had T.J.

"Hey, man, I ain't said nothin'! I'm jus' as burnt as you are."

Stacey glowered at T.J. a moment longer, then walked swiftly to Little Man and put his long arm around his shoulders, saying softly, "Come on, Man. It ain't gonna happen no more, least not for a long while. I promise you that."

Again, Christopher-John and I looked questioningly at each other, wondering how Stacey could make such a rash promise. Then, shrugging, we hurried after him.

When Jeremy Simms spied us from his high perch on the forest path, he ran hastily down and joined us.

"Hey," he said, his face lighting into a friendly grin. But no one spoke to him.

The smile faded and, noticing our mud-covered clothing, he asked, "Hey, St-Stacey, wh-what happened?"

Stacey turned, stared into his blue eyes and said coldly, "Why don't you leave us alone? How come you always hanging 'round us anyway?"

Jeremy grew even more pale. "C-cause I just likes y'all," he stammered. Then he whispered, "W-was it the bus again?"

No one answered him and he said no more. When we reached the crossroads, he looked hopefully at us as if we might relent and say good-bye. But we did not relent and as I glanced back at him standing alone in the middle of the crossing, he looked as if the world itself was slung around his neck. It was only then that I realized that Jeremy never rode the bus, no matter how bad the weather.

As we crossed the school lawn, Stacey beckoned Christopher-John, Little Man, and me aside. "Look," he whispered, "meet me at the toolshed right at noon."

"Why?" we asked.

He eyed us conspiratorily. "I'll show y'all how we're gonna stop that bus from splashing us."

"How?" asked Little Man, eager for revenge.

"Don't have time to explain now. Just meet me. And be on time. It's gonna take us all lunch hour."

"Y-you mean we ain't gonna eat no lunch!" Christopher-John cried in dismay.

"You can miss lunch for one day," said Stacey, moving away. But Christopher-John looked sourly after him as if he greatly questioned the wisdom of a plan so drastic that it could exclude lunch.

"You gonna tell T.J. and Claude?" I asked.

Stacey shook his head. "T.J.'s my best friend, but he's got no stomach for this kinda thing. He talks too much, and we couldn't include Claude without T.J."

"Good," said Little Man.

At noon, we met as planned and ducked into the unlocked toolshed where all the church and school garden tools were kept. Stacey studied the tools available while the rest of us watched. Then, grabbing the only shovels, he handed one to me, holding on to the other himself, and directed Little Man and Christopher John to each take two buckets.

Stealthily emerging from the toolshed into the drizzle, we eased along the forest edge behind the class buildings to avoid being seen. Once on the road, Stacey began to run. "Come on, hurry," he ordered. "We ain't got much time."

"Where we going?" asked Christopher-John, still not quite adjusted to the prospect of missing lunch.

"Up to where that bus forced us off the road. Be careful now," he said to Christopher-John, already puffing to keep up.

When we reached the place where we had fallen into the gully, Stacey halted. "All right," he said, "start digging." Without another word, he put his bare foot upon the top edge of the shovel and sank it deep into the soft road. "Come on, come on," he ordered, glancing up at Christopher-John, Little Man and me, who were wondering whether he had finally gone mad.

"Cassie, you start digging over there on that side of the road right across from me. That's right, don't get too near the edge. It's gotta look like it's been washed out. Christopher-John, you and Little Man start scooping out mud from the middle of the road. Quick now," he said, still digging as we began to carry out his commands. "We only got 'bout thirty minutes so's we can get back to school on time."

We asked no more questions. While Stacey and I shoveled ragged holes almost a yard wide and a foot deep toward each other, dumping the excess mud into the water-filled gullies, Little Man and Christopher-John scooped bucketfuls of the red earth from the road's center. And for once in his life, Little Man was happily oblivious to the mud spattering upon him.

When Stacey's and my holes merged into one big hole with Little Man's and Christopher-John's, Stacey and I threw down our shovels and grabbed the extra buckets. Then the four of us ran back and forth to the gullies, hastily filling the buckets with the murky water and dumping it into the hole.

Now understanding Stacey's plan, we worked wordlessly until the water lay at the same level as the road. Then Stacey waded into the gully water and pulled himself up onto the forest bank. Finding three rocks, he stacked them to identify the spot.

"It might look different this afternoon," he explained, jumping down again.

Christopher-John looked up at the sky. "Looks like it's gonna rain real hard some more."

"Let's hope so," said Stacey. "The more rain, the better. That'll make it seem more likely that the road could've been washed away like that. It'll also keep cars and wagons away." He looked around, surveying the road. "And let's hope don't nothin' come along 'fore that bus. Let's go.

Quickly we gathered our buckets and shovels and hurried back to school. After returning the tools to the toolshed, we stopped at the well to wash the mud from our arms and feet, then rushed into our classes, hoping that the mud caked on our clothes would go unnoticed. As I slipped into my seat Miss Crocker looked at me oddly and shook her head, but when she did the same thing as Mary Lou and Alma sat down, I decided that my mud was no more noticeable than anyone else's.

Soon after I had settled down to the boredom of Miss Crocker, the rain began to pound down again, hammering with great intensity upon the tin roof. After school it was still raining as the boys and I, avoiding T. J. and Claude, rushed along the slippery road recklessly bypassing more cautious students.

"You think we'll get there in time to see, Stacey?" I asked.

"We should. They stay in school fifteen minutes longer than we do and it always takes them a few minutes to load up."

When we reached the crossing, we glanced toward Jefferson Davis. The buses were there but the students had not been dismissed. We hastened on.

Expecting to see the yard-wide ditch we had dug at noon, we were not prepared for the twelve-foot lake which glimmered up at us.

"Holy smokes! What happened?" I exclaimed.

"The rain," said Stacey. "Quick, up on the bank." Eagerly, we settled onto the muddy forest floor and waited.

"Hey, Stacey," I said, "won't that big a puddle make that ole driver cautious?"

Stacey frowned, then said uncertainly, "I don't know. Hope not. There's big puddles down the road that ain't deep, just water heavy."

"If I was to be walking out there when the bus comes, that ole bus driver would be sure to speed up so's he could splash me," I suggested.

"Or maybe me," Little Man volunteered, ready to do anything for his revenge.

Stacey thought a moment, but decided against it.

"Naw. It's better none of us be on the road when it happens. It might give 'em ideas."

"Stacey, what if they find out we done it?" asked Christopher-John nervously.

"Don't worry, they won't," assured Stacey.

"Hey, I think it's coming," whispered Little Man.

We flattened ourselves completely and peered through the low bushes.

The bus rattled up the road, though not as quickly as we had hoped. It rolled cautiously through a wide puddle some twenty feet ahead; then, seeming to grow bolder as it approached our man-made lake, it speeded up, spraying the water in high sheets of backward waterfalls into the forest. We could hear the students squealing with delight. But instead of the graceful glide through the puddle that its occupants were expecting, the bus emitted a tremendous crack and careened drunkenly into our trap. For a moment it swayed and we held our breath, afraid that it would topple over. Then it sputtered a last murmuring protest and died, its left front wheel in our ditch, its right wheel in the gully, like a lopsided billy goat on its knees.

We covered our mouths and shook with silent laughter.

As the dismayed driver opened the rear emergency exit, the rain poured down upon him in sharp-needled darts. He stood in the doorway looking down with disbelief at his sunken charge; then, holding on to the bus, he poked one foot into the water until it was on solid ground before gingerly stepping down. He looked under the bus. He looked at the steaming hood. He looked at the water. Then he scratched his head and cursed.

"How bad is it, Mr. Grimes?" a large, freckle-faced boy asked, pushing up one of the cracked windows and sticking out his head. "Can we push it out and fix it?"

"Push it out? Fix it?" the bus driver echoed angrily. "I got me a broken axle here and a water-logged engine no doubt and no tellin' what-all else and you talkin' bout fixin' it! Y'all come on, get outa there! Y'all gonna have to walk home."

"Mister Grimes," a girl ventured, stepping hesitantly from the rear of the bus, "you gonna be able to pick us up in the mornin'?"

The bus driver stared at her in total disbelief. "Girl, all y'all gonna be walkin' for at least two weeks by the time we get this thing hauled outa here and up to Strawberry to get fixed. Now y'all get on home." He kicked a back tire, and added, "And get y'all's daddies to come on up here and give me a hand with this thing."

The students turned dismally from the bus. They didn't know how wide the hole actually was. Some of them took a wild guess and tried to jump it; but most of them miscalculated and fell in, to our everlasting delight. Others attempted to hop over the gullies to the forest to bypass the hole; however, we knew from much experience that they would not make it.

By the time most of the students managed to get to the other side of the ditch, their clothes were dripping with the weight of the muddy water. No longer laughing, they moved spiritlessly toward their homes while a disgruntled Mr. Grimes leaned moodily against the raised rear end of the bus.

Oh, how sweet was well-maneuvered revenge!

With that thought in mind, we quietly eased away and picked our way through the dense forest toward home.

At supper Mama told Big Ma of the Jefferson Davis bus being stuck in the ditch. "It's funny, you know, such a wide ditch in one day. I didn't even notice the beginning of it this morning—did you, children?"

"No'm," we chorused.

"You didn't fall in, did you?"

"We jumped onto the bank when we thought the bus would be coming," said Stacey truthfully.

"Well, good for you," approved Mama. "If that bus hadn't been there when I came along, I'd probably have fallen in myself."

The boys and I looked at each other. We hadn't thought about that.

"How'd you get across, Mama?" Stacey asked.

"Somebody decided to put a board across the washout.

"They gonna haul that bus outa there tonight?" Big Ma inquired.

"No, ma'am," said Mama. "I heard Mr. Granger telling Ted Grimes—the bus driver—that they won't be able to get it out until after the rain stops and it dries up a bit. It's just too muddy now."

We put our hands to our mouths to hide happy grins. I even made a secret wish that it would rain until Christmas.

Mama smiled. "You know I'm glad no one was hurt—could've been too with such a deep ditch—but I'm also rather glad it happened."

"Mary!" Big Ma exclaimed.

"Well, I am," Mama said defiantly, smiling smugly to herself and looking very much like a young girl. "I really am."

Big Ma began to grin. "You know somethin'? I am too."

Then all of us began to laugh and were deliciously happy.

Later that evening the boys and I sat at the study

table in Mama and Papa's room attempting to concentrate on our lessons; but none of us could succeed for more than a few minutes without letting out a triumphant giggle. More than once Mama scolded us, telling us to get down to business. Each time she did, we set our faces into looks of great seriousness, resolved that we would be adult about the matter and not gloat in our hour of victory. Yet just one glance at each other and we were lost, slumping on the table in helpless, contagious laughter.

"All right," Mama said finally. "I don't know what's going on here, but I suppose I'd better do something about it or you'll never get any work done."

It occurred to us that Mama might be preparing to whip us and we shot each other warning glances. But even that thought couldn't dampen our laughter, now uncontrollable, welling up from the pits of our stomachs and forcing streams of laughter tears down our faces. Stacey, holding his sides, turned to the wall in an attempt to bring himself under control. Little Man put his head under the table. But Christopher-John and I just doubled up and fell upon the floor.

Mama took my arm and pulled me up. "Over here, Cassie," she said, directing me to a chair next to the fireplace and behind Big Ma, who was ironing our clothes for the next day.

I peeped around Big Ma's long skirts and saw Mama guiding Stacey to her own desk. Then back she went for Little Man and, picking him up bodily, set him in the chair beside her rocker. Christopher-John she left alone at the study table. Then she gathered all our study materials and brought them to us along with a look that said she would tolerate no more of this foolishness.

With Big Ma before me, I could see nothing else and I grew serious enough to complete my arithmetic assignment. When that was finished, I lingered before opening my reader, watching Big Ma as she hung up my ironed dress, then placed her heavy iron on a small pile of embers burning in a corner of the fireplace and picked up a second iron already warming there. She tested the iron with a tap of her finger and put it back again.

While Big Ma waited for the iron to get hot, I could see Mama bending over outspread newspapers scraping the dried mud off the old field shoes of Papa's which she wore daily, stuffed with wads of newspaper, over her own shoes to protect them from the mud and rain. Little Man beside her was deep into his first-grade reader, his eyebrows furrowed in concentration. Ever since Mama had brought the reader home with the offensive inside cover no longer visible, Little Man had accepted the book as a necessary tool for passing the first grade. But he took no pride in it. Looking up, he noticed that Big Ma was now preparing to iron his clothes, and he smiled happily. Then his eyes met mine and silent laughter creased his face. I muffled a giggle and Mama looked up.

"Cassie, you start up again and I'm sending you to the kitchen to study," she warned.

"Yes'm," I said, settling back in my chair and beginning to read. I certainly did not want to go to the kitchen. Now that the fire no longer burned in the stove, it was cold in there.

The room grew quiet again, except for the earthy humming of Big Ma's rich alto voice, the crackle of the hickory fire, and the patter of rain on the roof. Engrossed in a mystery, I was startled when the comfortable sounds were shattered by three rapid knocks on the side door.

Rising quickly, Mama went to the door and called, "Who is it?"

"It's me, ma'am," came a man's gravelly voice. "Joe Avery."

Mama opened the door and Mr. Avery stepped dripping into the room.

"Why, Brother Avery," Mama said, "what are you doing out on a night like this? Come on in. Take off your coat and sit by the fire. Stacey, get Mr. Avery a chair."

"No'm," said Mr. Avery, looking rather nervously over his shoulder into the night. "I ain't got but a minute." He stepped far enough into the room so that he could close the door, then nodded to the rest of us. "Evenin', Miz Caroline, how you t'night?"

"Oh, I'll do, I reckon," said Big Ma, still ironing. "How's Miz Fannie?"

"She's fine," he said without dwelling on his wife. "Miz Logan . . . uh, I come to tell you somethin' . . . somethin' important—Mr. Morrison here?"

Mama stiffened. "David. You heard something about David?"

"Oh, no'm," replied Mr. Avery hastily. "Ain't heard nothin' 'bout yo' husband, ma'am."

Mama regarded him quizzically.

"It's . . . it's them again. They's ridin' t'night."

Mama, her face pale and frightened, glanced back at Big Ma; Big Ma held her iron in midair.

"Uh . . . children," Mama said, "I think it's your bedtime."

"But, Mama—" we chorused in protest, wanting to stay and hear who was riding.

"Hush," Mama said sternly. "I said it was time to go to bed. Now go!"

Groaning loudly enough to voice our displeasure,

but not loudly enough to arouse Mama's anger, we stacked our books upon the study table and started toward the boys' room.

"Cassie, I said go to bed. That's not your room."

"But, Mama, it's cold in there," I pouted. Usually, we were allowed to build small fires in the other rooms an hour before bedtime to warm them up.

"You'll be warm once you're under the covers. Stacey, take the flashlight with you and light the lantern in your room. Cassie, take the lamp from the desk with you."

I went back and got the kerosene lamp, then entered my bedroom, leaving the door slightly ajar.

"Close that door, Cassie!"

Immediately, the door was closed.

I put the lamp on the dresser, then silently slid the latch off the outside door and slipped onto the wet front porch. I crossed to the boys' room. Tapping lightly, I whispered, "Hey, let me in."

The door creaked open and I darted in. The room was bathed in darkness.

"What they say?" I asked.

"Shhhhh!" came the answer.

I crept to the door leading into Mama's room and huddled beside the boys.

The rain softened upon the roof and we could hear Mama asking, "But why? Why are they riding? What's happened?"

"I don't rightly know," said Mr. Avery. "But y'all knows how they is. Anytime they thinks we steppin' outa our place, they feels like they gotta stop us. You know what some of 'em done to the Berrys." He paused, then went on bitterly, "It don't take but a little of nothin' to set them devilish night men off."

"But somethin' musta happened," Big Ma said. "How you know 'bout it?"

"All's I can tell ya, Miz Caroline, is what Fannie heard when she was leavin' the Grangers' this evenin'. She'd just finished cleanin' up the supper dishes when Mr. Granger come home with Mr. Grimes—ya know, that white school's bus driver—and two other mens. . . ."

A clap of deafening thunder drowned Mr. Avery's words, then the rain quickened and the conversation was lost.

I grabbed Stacey's arm. "Stacey, they're coming after *us!*"

"What!" squeaked Christopher-John.

"Hush," Stacey said harshly. "And Cassie, let go. That hurts."

"Stacey, somebody musta seen and told on us," I persisted.

"No . . ." Stacey replied unconvincingly. "It couldn't be."

"Couldn't be?" cried Christopher-John in a panic "Whaddaya mean it couldn't be?"

"Stacey," said Little Man excitedly, "whaddaya think they gonna do to us? Burn us up?"

"Nothin'!" Stacey exclaimed, standing up suddenly. "Now why don't y'all go to bed like y'all s'pose to?"

We were stunned by his attitude. He sounded like Mama and I told him so.

He collapsed in silence by the door, breathing hard, and although I could not see him, I knew that his face was drawn and that his eyes had taken on a haggard look. I touched his arm lightly. "Ain't no call to go blaming yourself," I said. "We all done it."

"But I got us into it," he said listlessly.

"But we all wanted to do it," I comforted.

"Not me!" denied Christopher-John. "All I wanted to do was eat my lunch!"

"Shhhhh," hissed Little Man. "I can hear 'em again."

"I'd better go tell Mr. Morrison," Mr. Avery was saying. "He out back?"

"I'll tell him," said Mama.

We could hear the side door open and we scrambled up.

"Cassie, get back to your room quick," Stacey whispered. "They'll probably come check on us now."

"But what'll we do?"

"Nothin' now, Cassie. Them men probably won't even come near here."

"Ya really believe that?" asked Christopher-John hopefully.

"But shouldn't we tell Mama?" I asked.

"No! We can't ever tell nobody!" declared Stacey adamantly. "Now go on, hurry!"

Footsteps neared the door. I dashed onto the porch and hastened back to my own room, where I jumped under the bedcovers with my clothes still on. Shivering, I pulled the heavy patchwork quilts up to my chin.

A few moments later Big Ma came in, leaving the door to Mama's room open. Knowing that she would be suspicious of such an early surrender to sleep, I sighed softly and, making sleepy little sounds, turned onto my stomach, careful not to expose my shirt sleeves. Obviously satisfied by my performance, Big Ma tucked the covers more closely around me and smoothed my hair gently. Then she stooped and started fishing for something under our bed.

I opened my eyes. Now what the devil was she looking for down there? While she was searching, I heard Mama approaching and I closed my eyes again.

"Mama?"

"Stacey, what're you doing up?"

"Let me help."

"Help with what?"

"With . . . with whatever's the matter."

Mama was silent a moment, then said softly, "Thank you, Stacey, but Big Ma and I can handle it."

"But Papa told me to help you!"

"And you do, more than you know. But right now you could help me most by going back to bed. It's a school day tomorrow, remember?"

"But, Mama—"

"If I need you, I'll call you. I promise."

I heard Stacey walk slowly away, then Mama whispering in the doorway, "Cassie asleep?"

"Yeah, honey," Big Ma said. "Go on and sit back down. I'll be out in a minute."

Then Big Ma stood up and turned down the wick of the kerosene lamp. As she left the room, my eyes popped open again and I saw her outlined in the doorway, a rifle in her hands. Then she closed the door and I was left to the darkness.

For long minutes I waited, wide awake, wondering what my next move should be. Finally deciding that I should again consult with the boys, I swung my legs over the edge of the bed, but immediately had to swing them back again as Big Ma reentered the room. She passed the bed and pulled a straight-backed chair up to the window. Parting the curtains so that the blackness of the night mixed with the blackness of the room, she sat down without a sound.

I heard the door to the boys' room open and close and I knew that Mama had gone in. I waited for the sound of the door opening again, but it did not come. Soon the chill of the cotton sheets beneath me began to fade and as Big Ma's presence lulled me into a security I did not really feel, I fell asleep.

When I awoke, it was still nightly dark. "Big Ma?" I called. "Big Ma, you there?" But there was no reply from the chair by the window. Thinking that Big Ma had fallen asleep, I climbed from the bed and felt my way to her chair.

She wasn't there.

Outside, an owl hooted into the night, quiet now except for the drip-drap of water falling from the roof. I stood transfixed by the chair, afraid to move.

Then I heard a noise on the porch. I could not control my trembling. Again the noise, this time close to the door, and it occurred to me that it was probably the boys coming to confer with me. No doubt Mama had left them alone too.

Laughing silently at myself, I hurried onto the porch. "Stacey," I whispered. "Christopher-John?" There was a sudden movement near the end of the porch and I headed toward it, feeling along the wall of the house. "Little Man? Hey, y'all, stop fooling 'round and answer me."

I crept precariously near the edge of the high porch, my eyes attempting to penetrate the blackness of the night. From below, a scratchy bristlyness sprang upon me, and I lost my balance and tumbled with a thud into the muddy flower bed. I lay paralyzed with fear. Then a long wet tongue licked my face.

"Jason? Jason, that you?"

Our hound dog whined his reply.

I hugged him, then instantly let him go. "Was that you all the time? Look what you gone and done," I fussed, thinking of the mess I was in with mud all over me.

Jason whined again and I got up.

I started to climb back up onto the porch but froze as a caravan of headlights appeared suddenly in the east, coming fast along the rain-soaked road like cat eyes in the night. Jason whined loudly, growing skittish as the lights approached, and when they slowed and braked before the house he slunk beneath the porch. I wanted to follow, but I couldn't. My legs would not move.

The lead car swung into the muddy driveway and a shadowy figure outlined by the headlights of the car behind him stepped out. The man walked slowly up the drive.

I stopped breathing.

The driver of the next car got out, waiting. The first man stopped and stared at the house for several long moments as if uncertain whether it was the correct destination. Then he shook his head, and without a word returned to his car. With a wave of his hand he sent the other driver back inside, and in less than a minute the lead car had backed into the road, its headlights facing the other cars. Each of the cars used the driveway to turn around, then the caravan sped away as swiftly as it had come, its seven pairs of rear lights glowing like distant red embers until they were swallowed from view by the Granger forest.

Jason began barking now that the danger had passed, but he did not come out. As I reached for the porch to steady myself, there was a sense of quiet movement in the darkness. The moon slid from its dark covers, cloaking the earth in a shadowy white light, and I could see Mr. Morrison clearly, moving silently, like a jungle cat, from the side of the house to the road, a shotgun in his hand. Feeling sick, I crawled onto the porch and crept trembling toward the door.

Once inside the house, I leaned against the latch while waves of sick terror swept over me. Realizing that I must get into bed before Mama or Big Ma came from the other room, I pulled off my muddy clothes, turning them inside out to wipe the mud from my body, and put on my night clothes. Then I climbed into the softness of the bed. I lay very still for a while, not allowing myself to think. But soon, against my will, the vision of ghostly headlights soaked into my mind and an uncontrollable trembling racked my body. And it remained until the dawn, when I fell into a restless sleep.

Chapter 4

"Cassie, what's the matter with you, girl?" Big Ma asked as she thrust three sticks of dried pine into the stove to rekindle the dying morning fire. "You sure are takin' a sorrowful long time to churn that butter."

"Nothin'," I muttered.

"Nothin'?" Big Ma turned and looked directly at me. "You been mopin' 'round here for the past week like you got the whoopin' cough, flu, and measles all put together."

I sighed deeply and continued to churn.

Big Ma reached out and felt my forehead, then my cheeks. Frowning, she pulled her hand away as Mama entered the kitchen. "Mary, feel this child's face," she said. "She seem warm to you?"

Mama cupped my face in her thin hands. "You feel sick, Cassie?"

"No'm."

"How do you feel?"

"All right," I said, still churning.

Mama studied me with the same disturbed look Big Ma wore and a tiny frown line appeared on her brow. "Cassie," she said softly, fixing her dark eyes upon me, "is there something you want to tell me?"

I was on the verge of blurting out the awful truth about the bus and the men in the night, but then I remembered the pact Stacey had made us all swear to when I had told him, Christopher-John, and Little Man about the caravan and I said instead, "No, ma'am," and began to churn again. Abruptly, Mama took hold of the churning stick, her eyes searching mine. As she studied me, she seemed about to ask me something, then the question faded and she pulled away, lifting the lid of the churn. "It looks ready now," she said with a sigh. "Dip out the butter like I showed you and wash it down. I'll take care of the milk."

I scooped the butter from the churning lid onto a plate and went through the curtain to the small pantry off the kitchen to get the molding dish. It had been placed on a high shelf under several other dishes and I had to stand on a stool to get it. As I eased it out, Mama and Big Ma spoke softly in worried tones on the other side of the curtain.

"Somethin' the matter with that child, Mary."

"She's not sick, Mama."

"There's all sorts of sickness. She ain't ate right for goin' on over a week. She ain't sleepin' right neither. Restless and murmurin' in her sleep all night long. And she won't hardly even go out and play, rather be in here helpin' us. Now you know that ain't like that child."

There was a moment's pause, then Mama whispered so I could hardly hear her. "You think . . . Mama, you think she could've seen—"

"Oh, Lord, no, child," Big Ma exclaimed hastily. "I checked in there right after they passed and she was sound asleep. She couldn't've seen them ole devils. The boys neither."

Mama sighed. "The boys, they're not themselves either. All of them, too quiet. Here it is Saturday morning and they're quiet as church mice. I don't like it, and I can't shake the feeling it's got something to do with—Cassie!"

Without warning, I had lost my balance and with an absurd topple from the knee-high stool crashed upon the floor with the molding dish. "Cassie, you hurt?" Mama asked, stooping beside me.

"No'm," I mumbled, feeling very clumsy and close to tears. I knew that if I let the tears fall, Mama's suspicion that something was wrong would be confirmed for I never cried about such a silly thing as a fall; in fact, I seldom ever cried. So instead of crying, I jumped up quickly and began to pick up the broken pieces of the dish.

"I'm sorry, Mama," I said.

"That's all right," she said, helping me. When we had swept the chips away with the long field-straw broom, she told me, "Leave the butter, Cassie, and go on in with the boys."

"But, Mama—"

"I'll do the butter. Now go on, do like I say."

I stared up at Mama, wondering if she would ever know what we had done, then joined the boys who were sitting listlessly around the fire absently listening to T.J.

"See, fellows, there's a system to getting out of work," T.J. was expounding as I sat down. "Jus' don't be 'round when it's got to be done. Only thing is, you can't let your folks know that's what you're doin'. See, you should do like me. Like this mornin' when Mama wanted to bring back them scissors she borrowed from Miz Logan, I ups and volunteers so she don't have to make this long trip down here, she bein' so busy and all. And naturally when I got here, y'all wanted me to stay awhile and talk to y'all, so what could I do? I couldn't be impolite, could I? And by the time I finally convince y'all I gotta go, all the work'll be done at home." T.J. chuckled with satisfaction. "Yeah, you just have to use the old brain, that's all."

He was quiet a moment, expecting some comment on his discourse, but no one said a word.

T.J.'s eyes roamed the length of the room, then he admonished, "See, if you was smart like me, Stacey, you'd use the old brain to get the questions on that big test comin' up. Just think, they probably jus' sittin' right here in this very room waitin' to be discovered."

Stacey cast T.J. an annoyed look, but did not speak.

"Y'all sure are a sorry lot this mornin'," T.J. observed. "A fellow's just wastin' his know-how talkin' to y'all."

"Ain't nobody asked you to give it," said Stacey.

"Well, you don't have to get snippety about it," replied T.J. haughtily. Again, silence prevailed; but that would not do for T.J. "Say, how 'bout we sneak down to that ole Wallace store and learn how to do them new dances?"

"Mama told us not to go down there," Stacey said.

"You some mama's boy or somethin' you gotta do everything your mama tells—"

"You go on if you wanna," said Stacey quietly, not rising to T.J.'s bait, "but we staying here."

Again, silence.

Then T.J. said: "Say, y'all hear the latest 'bout them night men?" Suddenly, all eyes turned from the fire and riveted themselves upon him. Our faces were eager question marks; we were totally in T.J.'s power.

"What 'bout them?" Stacey asked, almost evenly.

T.J., of course, intended to nurse the moment for as long as he could. "You see when a fellow's as smart as me, he gets to know things that other folks don't. Now, this kind of information ain't for the ears of little kids so I really shouldn't even tell y'all—"

"Then don't!" said Stacey with smooth finality, turning back toward the fire as if he cared not at all about the night men. Taking his cue, I nudged Christopher-John and Christopher-John nudged Little Man, and the three of us forced ourselves to stare into the fire in feigned disinterest.

Without a captive audience, T.J. had to reinterest us by getting to the point. "Well, 'bout a week ago, they rode down to Mr. Sam Tatum's place—you know, down the Jackson Road toward Strawberry—and you know what they done?"

Stacey, Little Man, and I kept our eyes upon the fire, but Christopher-John piped eagerly, "What?"

I poked Christopher-John and he turned guiltily around, but T.J., triumphant with an assured audience of one, settled back in his chair ready to prolong the suspense. "You know Mama'd kill me if she knowed I was tellin' this. I heard her and Miz Claire Thompson talkin' 'bout it. They was real scared. Don't know why though. Them ole night men sure wouldn't scare me none. Like I told Claude—"

"Hey, y'all," Stacey said, standing and motioning us up. "Mama said she wanted us to take some milk and butter down to Miz Jackson before noon. We'd better get started."

I nodded, and Christopher-John, Little Man, and I got up.

"Tarred and feathered him!" T.J. announced hastily. "Poured the blackest tar they could find all over him, then plastered him with chicken feathers." T.J. laughed. "Can you imagine that?"

"But why?" asked Little Man, forgetting our ploy.

This time T.J. did not slow down. "I dunno if y'all's little ears should hear this, but it seems he called Mr. Jim Lee Barnett a liar—he's the man who runs the Mercantile down in Strawberry. Mr. Tatum's s'pose to done told him that he ain't ordered up all them things Mr. Barnett done charged him for. Mr. Barnett said he had all them things Mr. Tatum ordered writ down and when Mr. Tatum asked to see that list of his, Mr. Barnett says, 'You callin' me a liar, boy?' And Mr. Tatum says, 'Yessuh, I guess I is!' That done it!"

"Then it wasn't 'cause of the bus?" Christopher-John blurted out.

"Bus? What's a bus got to do with it?"

"Nothin'," said Stacey quickly. "Nothin' at all."

"Well, if anybody said them night men was down in here 'cause of some stupid bus, they crazy," said T.J. authoritatively. "'Cause my information come direct from Miz Claire Thompson who seen Mr. Tatum herself."

"You sure?" Stacey asked.

"Sure? Sure, I'm sure. When do I ever say anythin' when I ain't sure?"

Stacey smiled with relief. "Come on, let's get the milk."

All of us went into the kitchen, then to the bedrooms to get our coats. When we got outside, T.J remembered that he had left his cap by the fire and ran back to retrieve it. As soon as we were alone, Little Man asked, "Stacey, you really think them night men put tar and feathers all over Mr. Tatum?"

"I s'pose so," said Stacey.

Little Man frowned. but it was Christopher-John who spoke, whispering shrilly as if a stray morning ghost might overhear. "If they ever find out 'bout the bus, you think they gonna put tar and feathers all over us?"

Little Man's frown deepened and he observed gravely, "If they did, we'd never get clean again."

"Cassie," said Christopher-John, his eyes wide, "w-was you real s-scared when you seen 'em?"

Little Man shivered with excitement. "I wish I could've seen 'em."

"Well, I don't," declared Christopher-John. "In fact, I wish I'd never heard of no night men or buses or secrets or holes in the road!" And with that outburst, he stuffed his pudgy hands into his thin jacket, pressed his lips firmly together, and refused to say another word.

After a few moments, Stacey said, "What's keeping T.J.?" The rest of us shrugged, then followed Stacey back up the porch into Mama's room. As we entered, T.J. jumped. He was standing at the desk with Mama's W.E.B. Du Bois's *The Negro* in his hands.

"That don't look like your cap," said Stacey.

"Aw, man, I ain't done nothin'. Jus' lookin' at Miz Logan's history book, that's all. I'm mighty interested in that place called Egypt she been tellin' us 'bout and them black kings that was rulin' back then." Still talking, he casually put down the book and picked up his cap.

All four of us looked accusingly at T.J. and he halted. "Say, what is this? What's the meanin' of sneakin' up on me like that anyway? Y'all think I was lookin' for them test questions or somethin'? Shoot, a fellow'd think you didn't trust him." Then, thrusting his arm around Stacey's shoulders, he chided, "Friends gotta trust each other, Stacey, 'cause ain't nothin' like a true friend." And with those words of wisdom he left the room, leaving us to wonder how he had managed to slink out of this one.

The Monday after his arrival Mr. Morrison had moved into the deserted tenant shack that stood in the south pasture. It was a sorry mess, that house. Its door hung sadly from a broken hinge; its porch floorboards were rotted; and its one-room interior was densely occupied by rats, spiders, and other field creatures. But Mr. Morrison was a quiet man, almost shy, and although Mama had offered him lodging in our house, he preferred the old shack. Mama sensed that Mr. Morrison was a private person and she did not object to the move, but she did send the boys and me to the house to help clean it.

Little Man, Christopher-John, and I took to Mr. Morrison immediately and had no objections to the cleaning. Anybody who was a friend of Papa's was all right in our book; besides, when he was near, night men and burnings and-midnight tarrings faded into a hazy distance. But Stacey remained aloof and had little to do with him.

After the cleaning I asked Mama if Christopher-John, Little Man, and I could go visit Mr. Morrison, but she said no.

"But, Mama, I wanna know more 'bout him," I explained. "I just wanna know how come he's so big."

"You know about as much as you need to know," she decided. "And long as Mr. Morrison stays here, that's his house. If he wants you down there, he'll ask you."

"Don't know how come y'all wanna go down there noway," Stacey said moodily when Mama was out of hearing.

"'Cause we like him, that's why," I answered, tired of his distant attitude toward Mr. Morrison. Then, as discreetly as I could, I said, "What's the matter with you, boy, not liking Mr. Morrison?"

Stacey shrugged. "I like him all right."

"Don't act that way."

Stacey looked away from me. "Don't need him here. All that work he doing, I could've done it myself."

"Ah, you couldn't've done no such thing. Besides"—I looked around to be certain that Big Ma and Mama were not near—"besides, Papa didn't just bring him here to do no work. You know how come he really here."

Stacey turned toward me haughtily. "I could've taken care of that too."

I rolled my eyes at him, but held my peace. I didn't feel like a fight, and as long as Mr. Morrison was within hollering distance of the back porch, it made little difference to me what Stacey *thought* he could do.

"I sure wouldn't want that big ole man stayin' at my place," said T.J. on the way to school. "I betcha he get mad one time, he'd take ole Little Man and swing him over that tree yonder like he wasn't nothin' but a twig." He laughed then as Little Man set his lips and stared angrily up. "Course, I could probably 'bout do that myself."

"Couldn't neither!" denied Little Man.

"Hush, Man," said Stacey. "T.J., leave Man alone."

"Aw, I ain't botherin' him. Little Man's my buddy, ain't ya, Man?" Little Man scowled, but didn't reply. T.J. turned back to Stacey. "You ready for that history test?"

"Hope so," said Stacey. "But I keep forgetting them dates."

"Betcha I could help ya, if you be nice."

"How? You worse than I am 'bout dates."

T.J. grinned, then slyly pulled a folded sheet of paper from his pocket and handed it to Stacey. Stacey unfolded it, looked at it curiously, then frowned. "You planning on cheating?"

"Well, naw, I ain't plannin' on it," said T.J. seriously. "Jus' if I gotta."

"Well, you ain't gonna," said Stacey, tearing the paper in two.

"Hey, what's the matter with you, man!" cried T.J. grabbing for the paper. But Stacey turned his back to him and tore the paper into bits; then deposited them in the gully. "Man, that sho' ain't right! I wouldn't do you that way!"

"Maybe not," replied Stacey. "But at least this way you won't get into no trouble."

T.J. mumbled, "If failin' ain't trouble, I don't know what is."

Little Man, Christopher-John, Claude, and I were sitting on the bottom step of the seventh-grade class building after school waiting for Stacey and T.J. when the front door banged open and T.J. shot out and tore across the yard. "What's the matter with him?" asked Christopher-John. "Ain't he gonna wait for Stacey?"

The rest of the seventh grade, led by Little Willie Wiggins and Moe Turner, spilled from the building. "There he go!" cried Little Willie as T.J. disappeared on the forest road. Moe Turner yelled, "Let's see where he goin'!" Then he and three other boys dashed away in pursuit of T.J. But the others stood restlessly near the steps as if school had not yet ended.

"Hey, what's going on?" I asked Little Willie. "What's everybody waiting 'round for?"

"And where's Stacey?" demanded Little Man.

Little Willie smiled. "Stacey inside with Miz Logan. He got whipped today."

"Whipped!" I cried. "Why, can't nobody whip Stacey. Who done it?"

"Your mama," laughed Little Willie.

"Mama!" Christopher-John, Little Man, and I exclaimed.

Little Willie nodded. "Yep. In front of everybody."

I swallowed hard, feeling very sorry for my older brother. It was bad enough to be whipped in front of thirty others by a teacher, but to get it by one's own mother—now that was downright embarrassing.

"Why'd Mama do that?" asked Christopher-John.

"She caught him with cheat notes during the history examination."

"Mama knows Stacey wouldn't cheat!" I declared.

Little Willie shrugged. "Well, whether she knowed it or not, she sho' 'nough whipped him. . . . Course, now, she give him a chance to get out of it when he said he wasn't cheatin' and she asked him how he got them cheat notes. But Stacey wouldn't tell on ole T.J., and you know good and well ole T.J. wasn't 'bout to say them notes was his."

"Cheat notes! But how'd T.J. get cheat notes? Stacey got rid of them things this morning!"

"Come noontime though," replied Little Willie, "T.J. was in them woods busy writing himself another set. Me and Moe seen him."

"Well, what the devil was Stacey doing with 'em?"

"Well, we was in the middle of the examination and ole T. J. slips out these cheat notes—me and Clarence here was sittin' right behind him and T.J. and seen the whole thing. Stacey was sittin' right side of T.J. and when he seen them notes, he motioned T.J. to put 'em away. At first T.J wouldn't do it, but then he seen Miz Logan startin' toward 'em and he slipped Stacey the notes. Well, Stacey didn't see Miz Logan comin' when he took them notes, and by the time he saw her it was too late to get rid of 'em. Wasn't nothin' Miz Logan could do but whip him. Failed him too."

"And ole T.J. just sat there and ain't said a word," interjected Clarence, laughing.

"But knowin' Stacey, I betcha ole T.J. ain't gonna

get away with it," chuckled Little Willie. "And T.J. know it too. That's why he lit outa here like he done, and I betcha—Hey, Stacey!"

Everyone turned as Stacey bounded down the steps. His square face was unsmiling, but there was no anger in his voice when he asked quietly, "Anybody seen T.J.?" All the students answered at once, indicating that T.J. had headed west toward home, then surrounded Stacey as he started across the lawn. Christopher-John, Little Man, Claude, and I followed.

When we reached the crossroads, Moe Turner was waiting. "T.J. went down to the Wallace store," he announced.

Stacey stopped and so did everyone else. Stacey stared past Jefferson Davis, then back down the road toward Great Faith. Looking over his shoulder, he found me and ordered, "Cassie, you and Christopher-John and Man go on home."

"You come too," I said, afraid of where he was going.

"Got something to take care of first," he said, walking away.

"Mama gonna take care of you, too!" I hollered after him. "You know she said we wasn't to go down there, and she find out, she gonna wear you out again! Papa too! " But Stacey did not come back. For a moment, Little Man, Christopher-John, Claude, and I stood watching Stacey and the others heading swiftly northward. Then Little Man said, "I wanna see what he gonna do."

"I don't," declared Christopher-John.

"Come on," I said, starting after Stacey with Little Man and Claude beside me.

"I don't want no whipping!" objected Christopher-John, standing alone in the crossroads. But when he saw that we were not coming back, he puffed to join us, grumbling all the while.

The Wallace store stood almost a half mile beyond Jefferson Davis, on a triangular lot that faced the Soldiers Bridge crossroads. Once the Granger plantation store, it had been run by the Wallaces for as long as I could remember, and most of the people within the forty-mile stretch between Smellings Creek and Strawberry shopped there. The other three corners of the crossroads were forest land, black and dense. The store consisted of a small building with a gas pump in front and a storage house in back. Beyond the store, against the forest edge, were two gray clapboard houses and a small garden. But there were no fields; the Wallaces did not farm.

Stacey and the other students were standing in the doorway of the store when Little Man, Christopher-John, Claude, and I ran up. We squeezed through so we could see inside. A man we all knew was Kaleb Wallace stood behind the counter. A few other men sat around a stove playing checkers, and Jeremy's older brothers, R.W. and Melvin, who had dropped out of school long ago, leaned sleepy-eyed against the counter staring at us.

"Y'all go on to the back," said Kaleb Wallace, "lessn y'all wanna buy something. Mr. Dewberry got the music goin' already."

As we turned away from the entrance, Melvin Simms said, "Just look at all the little niggers come to dance," and the laughter of the men filled the room.

Christopher-John tugged at my arm. "I don't like this place, Cassie. Let's go on home."

"We can't leave without Stacey," I said.

Music beckoned from the storage room where

Dewberry Wallace was placing round brown bottles on a small table as we crowded in. Aside from the table, there was no furniture in the room. Boxes lined the walls and the center floor had been cleared for dancing—several older couples from Great Faith were already engaged in movements I had never seen before.

"What they doing?" asked Little Man.

I shrugged. "I guess that's what they call dancing."

"There he go!" someone shouted as the back door of the storeroom slammed shut. Stacey turned quickly and sped to the back of the building. T.J. was fleeing straight toward Soldiers Road. Stacey tore across the Wallace yard and, leaping high like a forest fox, fell upon T.J., knocking him down. The two boys rolled toward the road, each trying to keep the other's back pinned to the ground, but then Stacey, who was stronger, gained the advantage and T.J., finding that he could not budge him, cried, "Hey, wait a minute, man, let me explain—"

Stacey did not let him finish. Jumping up, he pulled T.J up too and hit him squarely in the face. T.J. staggered back holding his eyes as if he were badly hurt, and Stacey momentarily let down his guard. At that moment, T.J. rammed into Stacey, forcing the fight to the ground again.

Little Man, Christopher-John, and I, with the others, circled the fighters, chanting loudly as they rolled back and forth punching at each other. All of us were so engrossed in the battle that no one saw a mule wagon halt on the road and a giant man step out. It wasn't until I realized that the shouting had stopped behind us and that the girls and boys beside me were falling back that I looked up.

Mr. Morrison towered above us.

He did not look at me or Christopher-John or

Little Man, although I knew he had seen us, but walked straight to the fighters and lifted a still-swinging Stacey off T.J. After a long, tense moment, he said to Stacey, "You and your sister and brothers get on in the wagon."

We walked through the now-silent crowd. Kaleb and Dewberry Wallace, standing on the front porch of the store with the Simmses, stared at Mr. Morrison as we passed, but Mr. Morrison looked through them as if they were not there. Stacey sat in front of the wagon with Mr. Morrison; the rest of us climbed into the back. "Now we gonna get it," shuddered Christopher-John. "I told y'all we shoulda gone on home."

Before Mr. Morrison took the reins, he handed Stacey a handkerchief in which to wrap his bruised right hand, but he did not say a word and it wasn't until we had passed the crossroads leading to Great Faith that the silence was broken.

"Mr. Morrison . . . you gonna tell Mama?" Stacey asked huskily.

Mr. Morrison was very quiet as Jack the mule clopped noisily along the dry road. "Seems I heard your mama tell y'all not to go up to that Wallace store," he said at last.

"Y-yessir," said Stacey, glancing nervously at Mr. Morrison. Then he blurted out, "But I had good reason!"

"Ain't never no reason good enough to go disobey your mama."

The boys and I looked woefully at each other and my bottom stung from the awful thought of Mama's leather strap against it. "But Mr. Morrison," I cried anxiously, "T.J. was hiding there 'cause he thought Stacey wouldn't never come down there to get him. But Stacey had to go down there cause T.J. was cheating and—"

"Hush, Cassie," Stacey ordered, turning sharply around.

I faltered for only a moment before deciding that my bottom was more important than Stacey's code of honor "—and Stacey had to take the blame for it and Mama whipped him right in front of God and everybody!" Once the truth had been disclosed, I waited with dry throat and nauseous stomach for Mr. Morrison to say something. When he did, all of us strained tensely forward.

"I ain't gonna tell her," he said quietly.

Christopher-John sighed with relief. "Ain't going down there no more neither," he promised. Little Man and I agreed. But Stacey stared long and hard at Mr. Morrison.

"How come, Mr. Morrison?" he asked. "How come you ain't gonna tell Mama?"

Mr. Morrison slowed Jack as we turned into the road leading home. " 'Cause I'm leaving it up to you to tell her."

"What!" we exclaimed together.

"Sometimes a person's gotta fight," he said slowly. "But that store ain't the place to be doing it. From what I hear, folks like them Wallaces got no respect at all for colored folks and they just think it's funny when we fight each other. Your mama knowed them Wallaces ain't good folks, that's why she don't want y'all down there, and y'all owe it to her and y'allselves to tell her. But I'm gonna leave it up to y'all to decide."

Stacey nodded thoughtfully and wound the handkerchief tighter around his wounded hand. His face was not scarred, so if he could just figure out a way to explain the bruises on his hand to Mama without lying he was in the clear, for Mr. Morrison had not said that he *had* to tell her. But for some reason I could not understand he said, "All right, Mr. Morrison, I'll tell her."

"Boy, you crazy!" I cried as Christopher-John and Little Man speedily came to the same conclusion. If he did not care about his own skin, he could at least consider ours.

But he seemed not to hear us as his eyes met Mr. Morrison's and the two of them smiled in subtle understanding, the distance between them fading.

As we neared the house, Mr. Granger's Packard rolled from the dusty driveway. Mr. Morrison directed Jack to the side of the road until the big car had passed, then swung the wagon back into the road's center and up the drive. Big Ma was standing by the yard gate that led onto the drive, gazing across the road at the forest.

"Big Ma, what was Mr. Granger doing here?" Stacey asked, jumping from the wagon and going to her. Little Man, Christopher-John, and I hopped down and followed him.

"Nothin'," Big Ma replied absently, her eyes still on the forest. "Just worryin' me 'bout this land again."

"Oh," said Stacey, his tone indicating that he considered the visit of no importance. Mr. Granger had always wanted the land. He turned and went to help Mr. Morrison. Little Man and Christopher-John went with him, but I remained by the gate with Big Ma.

"Big Ma," I said, "what Mr. Granger need more land for?"

"Don't need it," Big Ma said flatly. "Got more land now than he know what to do with."

"Well, what he want with ours then?"

"Just like to have it, that's all."

"Well, seems to me he's just being greedy. You ain't gonna sell it to him, are you?"

Big Ma did not answer me. Instead, she pushed open the gate and walked down the drive and across the road into the forest. I ran after her. We walked in silence down the narrow cow path which wound through the old forest to the pond. As we neared the pond, the forest gapped open into a wide, brown glade, man-made by the felling of many trees, some of them still on the ground. They had been cut during the summer after Mr. Andersen came from Strawberry with an offer to buy the trees. The offer was backed with a threat, and Big Ma was afraid. So Andersen's lumbermen came, chopping and sawing, destroying the fine old trees. Papa was away on the railroad then but Mama sent Stacey for him. He returned and stopped the cutting, but not before many of the trees had already fallen.

Big Ma surveyed the clearing without a word, then, stepping around the rotting trees, she made her way to the pond and sat down on one of them. I sat close beside her and waited for her to speak. After a while she shook her head and said: "I'm sho' glad your grandpa never had to see none of this. He dearly loved these here old trees. Him and me, we used to come down here early mornin's or just 'fore the sun was 'bout to set and just sit and talk. He used to call this place his thinkin' spot and he called that old pond there Caroline, after me."

She smiled vaguely, but not at me.

"You know, I . . . I wasn't hardly eighteen when Paul Edward married me and brung me here. He was older than me by 'bout eight years and he was smart. Ow-ow, my Lord, that was one smart man! He had himself a mind like a steel trap. Anything he seen done, he could do it. He had done learned carpentry back up there near Macon, Georgia, where he was born. Born into slavery he was, two years 'fore freedom come, and him and his mama stayed on at that plantation after the fightin' was finished. But then when he got to be fourteen and his mama died, he left that place and worked his way 'cross here up to Vicksburg."

"That's where he met you, ain't it, Big Ma?" I asked, already knowing the answer.

Big Ma nodded, smiling. "Sho' was. He was carpenterin' up there and my papa took me in with him to Vicksburg—we was tenant farmin' 'bout thirty miles from there—to see 'bout gettin' a store-bought rocker for my mama, and there was ole Paul Edward workin' in that furniture shop just as big. Had himself a good job, but that ole job wasn't what he wanted. He wanted himself some land. Kept on and kept on talkin' 'bout land, and then this place come up for sell."

"And he bought himself two hundred acres from that Yankee, didn't he?"

Big Ma chuckled. "That man went right on over to see Mr. Hollenbeck and said, 'Mr. Hollenbeck, I understand you got land to sell and I'd be interested in buyin' me 'bout two hundred acres if yo' price is right.' Ole Mr. Hollenbeck questioned him good 'bout where he was gonna get the money to pay him, but Paul Edward just said, 'Don't seem to me it's your worry 'bout how I'm gonna get the money just long as you get paid your price.' Didn't nothin' scare that man!" She beamed proudly. "And Mr. Hollenbeck went on and let him have it. Course now, he was just 'bout as eager to sell this land as Paul Edward was to buy. He'd had it for goin' on nigh twenty years—bought it during Reconstruction from the Grangers—"

"'Cause they didn't have no money to pay their taxes—"

"Not only didn't have tax money, didn't have no money at all! That war left them plumb broke. Their ole Confederate money wasn't worth nothin' and both Northern and Southern soldiers had done ransacked their place. Them Grangers didn't have nothin' but they land left and they had to sell two thousand acres of it to get money to pay them taxes and rebuild the rest of it, and that Yankee bought the whole two thousand—"

"Then he turned 'round and tried to sell it back to 'em, huh, Big Ma?"

"Sho' did . . . but not till eighty-seven, when your grandpa bought himself that two hundred acres. As I hears it, that Yankee offered to sell all two thousand acres back to Harlan Granger's daddy for less'n the land was worth, but that old Filmore Granger was just 'bout as tight with a penny as anybody ever lived and he wouldn't buy it back. So Mr. Hollenbeck just let other folks know he was sellin', and it didn't take long 'fore he sold all of it 'cause it was some mighty fine land. Besides your grandpa, a bunch of other small farmers bought up eight hundred acres and Mr. Jamison bought the rest."

"But that wasn't *our* Mr. Jamison," I supplied knowingly. "That was his daddy."

"Charles Jamison was his name," Big Ma said. "A fine old gentleman, too. He was a good neighbor and he always treated us fair . . . just like his son. The Jamisons was what folks call 'Old South' from up in Vicksburg, and as I understands it, before the war they had as much money as anybody and even after the war they managed better than some other folks 'cause they had made themselves some Northern money. Anyways, old Mr. Jamison got it into his mind that he wanted to farm and he moved his family from Vicksburg down in here. Mr. Wade Jamison wasn't but 'bout eight years old then."

"But he didn't like to farm," I said.

"Oh, he liked it all right. Just wasn't never much hand at it though, and after he went up North to law school and all he just felt he oughta practice his law."

"Is that how come he sold Grandpa them other two hundred acres?"

"Sho' is . . . and it was mighty good of him to do it, too. My Paul Edward had been eyein' that two hundred acres ever since 1910 when he done paid off the bank for them first two hundred, but ole Mr. Jamison didn't wanna sell. 'Bout that same time, Harlan Granger 'come head of the Granger plantation—you know, him and Wade Jamison 'bout the same year's children—and he wanted to buy back every inch of land that used to belong to the Grangers. That man crazy 'bout anythin' that was before that war and he wantin' his land to be every bit like it was then. Already had more'n four thousand acres, but he just itchin' to have back them other two thousand his granddaddy sold. Got back eight hundred of 'em, too, from them other farmers that bought from Mr. Hollenbeck—"

"But Grandpa and old Mr. Jamison wasn't interested in selling, period, was they, Big Ma? They didn't care how much money Mr. Granger offered 'em!" I declared with an emphatic nod.

"That's the truth of it all right," agreed Big Ma. "But when Mr. Jamison died in 1918 and Wade 'come head of the family, he sold them two hundred acres to Paul Edward and the rest of his land to Harlan Granger, and moved his family into Strawberry. He could've just as easy sold the full thousand acres to the Grangers and gotten more money, but he didn't . . . and till this day Harlan Granger still hold it 'gainst him 'cause he didn't. . . ."

The soft swish of falling leaves made Big Ma look up from the pond and at the trees again. Her lips curved into a tender smile as she looked around thoughtfully. "You know," she said, "I can still see my Paul Edward's face the day Mr. Jamison sold him them two hundred acres. He put his arms 'round me and looked out at his new piece of land, then he said 'zactly the same thing he said when he grabbed himself that first two hundred acres. Said, 'Pretty Caroline, how you like to work this fine piece of earth with me?' Sho' did . . . said the 'zact same thing."

She grew quiet then and rubbed the wrinkles down one hand as if to smooth them away. I gazed at the pond, glassy gray and calm, until she was ready to go on. I had learned that at times like these it was better to just sit and wait than to go asking disrupting questions which might vex her.

"So long ago now," she said eventually, in a voice that was almost a whisper. "We worked real hard gettin' them crops sown, gettin' 'em reaped. We had us a time. . . . But there was good times too. We was young and strong when we started out and we liked to work. Neither one of us, I'm proud to say, never was lazy and we didn't raise us no lazy children neither. Had ourselves six fine children. Lost our girls when they was babies, though. . . . I s'pose that's one of the reasons I love your sweet mama so much. . . . But them boys grew strong and all of 'em loved this place as much as Paul Edward and me. They go away, they always come back to it. Couldn't leave it."

She shook her head and sighed. "Then Mitchell, he got killed in the war and Kevin got drowned. . . ."

Her voice faded completely, but when she spoke again it had hardened and there was a determined glint in her eyes. "Now all the boys I got is my baby boys, your papa and your Uncle Hammer, and this they place as much as it is mine. They blood's in this land, and here that Harlan Granger always talkin' 'bout buyin' it. He pestered Paul Edward to death 'bout buyin' it, now he pesterin' me. Humph!" she grumped angrily. "He don't know nothin' 'bout me or this land, he think I'm gonna sell!"

She became silent again.

A cold wind rose, biting through my jacket, and I shivered. Big Ma looked down at me for the first time. "You cold?"

"N-no, ma'am," I stuttered, not ready to leave the forest.

"Don't you be lyin' to me girl!" she snapped, putting out her hand. "It's time we was goin' back to the house anyways. Your mama'll be home soon."

I took her hand, and together we left the Caroline.

Despite our every effort to persuade Stacey otherwise, when Mama came home he confessed that he had been fighting T.J. at the Wallace store and that Mr. Morrison had stopped it. He stood awkwardly before her, disclosing only those things which he could honorably mention. He said nothing of T.J.'s cheating or that Christopher-John, Little Man, and I had been with him, and when Mama asked him a question he could not answer honestly, he simply looked at his feet and refused to speak. The rest of us sat fidgeting nervously throughout the interview and when Mama looked our way, we swiftly found somewhere else to rest our eyes.

Finally, seeing that she had gotten all the information she was going to get from Stacey, Mama turned to us.

"I suppose you three went to the store too, huh?" But before any of us could squeak an answer, she exclaimed, "That does it!" and began to pace the floor, her arms folded, her face cross.

Although she scolded us severely, she did not whip us. We were sent to bed early but we didn't consider that a punishment, and we doubted that Mama did either. How we had managed to escape a whipping we couldn't fathom until Saturday, when Mama woke us before dawn and piled us into the wagon. Taking us southwest toward Smellings Creek, she said, "Where we're going the man is very sick and he doesn't look like other people. But I don't want you to be afraid or uncomfortable when you see him. Just be yourselves."

We rode for almost two hours before turning onto a backwoods trail. We were jarred and bounced over the rough road until we entered a clearing where a small weather-grayed house stood and fields stretched barren beyond it. As Mama pulled up on the reins and ordered us down, the front door cracked warily open, but no one appeared. Then Mama said, "Good morning, Mrs. Berry. It's Mary Logan, David's wife."

The door swung wide then and an elderly woman, frail and toothless, stepped out. Her left arm hung crazily at her side as if it had been broken long ago but had not mended properly, and she walked with a limp; yet she smiled widely, throwing her good arm around Mama and hugging her. "Land sakes, child, ain't you somethin'!" she exclaimed. "Comin' to see 'bout these old bones. I jus' sez to Sam, I sez, 'Who you reckon comin' to see old folks like us?' These yo' babies, ain't they? Lord a'mighty, ain't they fine! Sho' is!" She hugged each of us and ushered us into the house.

The interior was dark, lit only by the narrow slat

of gray daylight allowed in by the open door. Stacey and I carried cans of milk and butter, and Christopher-John and Little Man each had a jar of beef and a jar of crowder peas which Mama and Big Ma had canned. Mrs. Berry took the food, her thanks intermingled with questions about Big Ma, Papa, and others. When she had put the food away, she pulled stools from the darkness and motioned us to sit down, then she went to the blackest corner and said, "Daddy, who you s'pose done come to see 'bout us?"

There was no recognizable answer, only an inhuman guttural wheezing. But Mrs. Berry seemed to accept it and went on. "Miz Logan and her babies. Ain't that somethin'?" She took a sheet from a nearby table. "Gots to cover him," she explained. "He can't hardly stand to have nothin' touch him." When she was visible again, she picked up a candle stump and felt around a table for matches. "He can't speak no more. The fire burned him too bad. But he understands all right." Finding the matches, she lit the candle and turned once more to the corner.

A still form lay there staring at us with glittering eyes. The face had no nose, and the head no hair; the skin was scarred, burned and the lips were wizened black, like charcoal. As the wheezing sound echoed from the opening that was a mouth, Mama said, "Say good morning to Mrs. Berry's husband, children." The boys and I stammered a greeting, then sat silently trying not to stare at Mr. Berry during the hour that we remained in the small house. But Mama talked softly to both Mr. and Mrs. Berry, telling them news of the community as if Mr. Berry were as normal as anyone else.

After we were on the main road again, having ridden in thoughtful silence over the wooded trail, Mama said quietly, "The Wallaces did that, children.

They poured kerosene over Mr. Berry and his nephews and lit them afire. One of the nephews died, the other one is just like Mr. Berry." She allowed this information to penetrate the silence, then went on. "Everyone knows they did it, and the Wallaces even laugh about it, but nothing was ever done. They're bad people, the Wallaces. That's why I don't want you to ever go to their store again—for any reason. You understand?"

We nodded, unable to speak as we thought of the disfigured man lying in the darkness.

On the way home we stopped at the homes of some of Mama's students, where families poured out of tenant shacks to greet us. At each farm Mama spoke of the bad influence of the Wallaces, of the smoking and drinking permitted at their store, and asked that the family's children not be allowed to go there.

The people nodded and said she was right.

She also spoke of finding another store to patronize, one where the proprietors were more concerned about the welfare of the community. But she did not speak directly of what the Wallaces had done to the Berrys for, as she explained later, that was something that wavered between the known and the unknown and to mention it outright to anyone outside of those with whom you were closest was not wise. There were too many ears that listened for others besides themselves, and too many tongues that wagged to those they shouldn't.

The people only nodded, and Mama left.

When we reached the Turner farm, Moe's widowed father rubbed his stubbled chin and squinted across the room at Mama. "Miz Logan," he said, "you know I feels the same way you do 'bout them low-down Wallaces, but it ain't easy to jus' stop shoppin' there. They overcharges me and I has to pay them high interest, but I gots credit there 'cause Mr. Montier signs for me. Now you know most folks 'round here sharecroppin' on Montier, Granger, or Harrison land and most of them jus' 'bout got to shop at that Wallace store or up at the mercantile in Strawberry, which is jus' 'bout as bad. Can't go no place else."

Mama nodded solemnly, showing she understood, then she said, "For the past year now, our family's been shopping down at Vicksburg. There are a number of stores down there and we've found several that treat us well."

"Vicksburg?" Mr. Turner echoed, shaking his head. "Lord, Miz Logan, you ain't expectin' me to go all the way to Vicksburg? That's an overnight journey in a wagon down there and back."

Mama thought on that a moment. "What if someone would be willing to make the trip for you? Go all the way to Vicksburg and bring back what you need?"

"Won't do no good," retorted Mr. Turner. "I got no cash money. Mr. Montier signs for me up at that Wallace store so's I can get my tools, my mule, my seed, my fertilizer, my food, and what few clothes I needs to keep my children from runnin' plumb naked. When cotton-pickin' time comes, he sells my cotton, takes half of it, pays my debt up at that store and my interest for they credit, then charges me ten to fifteen percent more as 'risk' money for signin' for me in the first place. This year I earned me near two hundred dollars after Mr. Montier took his half of the crop money, but I ain't seen a penny of it. In fact, if I manages to come out even without owin' that man nothin', I figures I've had a good year. Now, who way down in Vicksburg gonna give a man like me credit?"

Mama was very quiet and did not answer.

"I sho' sorry, Miz Logan. I'm gonna keep my younguns from up at that store, but I gots to live. Y'all got it better'n most the folks 'round here 'cause y'all gots your own place and y'all ain't gotta cowtail to a lot of this stuff. But you gotta understand it ain't easy for sharecroppin' folks to do what you askin'."

"Mr. Turner," Mama said in a whisper, "what if someone backed your signature? Would you shop up in Vicksburg then?"

Mr. Turner looked at Mama strangely. "Now, who'd sign for me?"

"If someone would, would you do it?"

Mr. Turner gazed into the fire, burning to a low ash, then got up and put another log on it, taking his time as he watched the fire shoot upward and suck in the log. Without turning around he said, "When I was a wee little boy, I got burnt real bad. It healed over but I ain't never forgot the pain of it. . . . It's an awful way to die." Then, turning, he faced Mama. "Miz Logan, you find someone to sign my credit, and I'll consider it deeply."

After we left the Turners', Stacey asked, "Mama, who you gonna get to sign?" But Mama, her brow furrowed, did not reply. I started to repeat the question, but Stacey shook his head and I settled back wondering, then fell asleep.

Chapter 5

The blue-black shine that had so nicely encircled T.J.'s left eye for over a week had almost completely faded by the morning T.J. hopped into the back of the wagon beside Stacey and snuggled in a corner not occupied by the butter, milk, and eggs Big Ma was taking to sell at the market in Strawberry. I sat up front beside Big Ma, still sandy-eyed and not believing that I was actually going.

The second Saturday of every month was market day in Strawberry, and for as far back as I could remember the boys and I had been begging Big Ma to take us to it. Stacey had actually gone once, but Christopher-John, Little Man, and I had always been flatly denied the experience. We had, in fact, been denied so often that our pestering now occurred more out of habit than from any real belief that we would be allowed to go. But this morning, while the world lay black, Big Ma called: "Cassie, get up, child, if you gonna go to town with me, and be quiet 'bout it. You wake up Christopher-John or Little Man and I'll leave you here. I don't want them cryin' all over the place 'cause they can't go."

As Jack swept the wagon into the gray road, Big Ma pulled tightly on the reins and grumbled, "Hold on! You, Jack, hold on! I ain't got no time to be putting up with both you and T.J.'s foolishness."

"T.J!" Stacey and I exclaimed together. "He going?"

Big Ma didn't answer immediately; she was occupied in a test of wills with Jack. When hers had prevailed and Jack had settled into a moderate trot, she replied moodily, "Mr. Avery come by after y'all was asleep last night wanting T.J. to go to Strawberry to do some shopping for a few things he couldn't get at the Wallace store. Lord, that's all I need with all the trouble about is for that child to talk me to death for twenty-two miles." Big Ma didn't need to say any more and she didn't. T.J. was far from her favorite person and it was quite obvious that Stacey and I owed our good fortune entirely to T.J.'s obnoxious personality.

T.J., however, was surprisingly subdued when he settled into the wagon; I suppose that at three-thirty in the morning even T.J.'s mouth was tired. But by dawn, when the December sun was creeping warily upward shooting pale streams of buff-colored light through the forest, he was fully awake and chattering like a cockatoo. His endless talk made me wish that he had not managed to wheedle his way so speedily back into Stacey's good graces, but Big Ma, her face furrowed in distant thoughts, did not hush him. He talked the rest of the way into Strawberry, announcing as we arrived, "Well, children, open your eyes and take in Strawberry, Mississippi!"

"Is this it?" I cried, a gutting disappointment enveloping me as we entered the town. Strawberry was nothing like the tough, sprawling bigness I had envisioned. It was instead a sad, red place. As far as I could see, the only things modern about it were a paved road which cut through its center and fled northward, away from it, and a spindly row of electrical lines. Lining the road were strips of red dirt splotched with patches of brown grass and drying mud puddles, and beyond the dirt and the mud puddles, gloomy store buildings set behind raised wooden sidewalks and sagging verandas.

"Shoot!" I grumbled. "It sure ain't nothing to shout about."

"Hush up; Cassie," Big Ma said. "You, too, T.J. Y'all in town now and I expects y'all to act like it. In another hour this place'll be teeming up with folks from all over the county and I don't want no trouble."

As the stores gave way to houses still sleeping, we turned onto a dirt road which led past more shops and beyond to a wide field dotted with wooden stalls. Near the field entrance several farm wagons and pickups were already parked, but Big Ma drove to the other side of the field where only two wagons were stationed. Climbing from the wagon, she said, "Don't seem like too many folks ahead of us. In the summer, I'd've had to come on Friday and spent the night to get a spot like this." She headed toward the back of the wagon. "Stacey, you and T.J. stay up here a minute and push them milk cans over here so's I can reach 'em."

"Big Ma," I said, following her, "all them folks up there selling milk and eggs too?"

"Not all, I reckon. Some of 'em gots meats and vegetables, quilts and sewing and such. But I guess a good piece of 'em sellin' the same as us."

I studied the wagons parked at the field entrance, then exclaimed, "Well, what the devil we doing way back here then! Can't nobody see us."

"You watch your mouth, girl," warned Big Ma. Then, arranging the milk cans and baskets of eggs near the wagon's edge, she softened her voice and promised, "We'll do all right. I got me some regular customers and they'll check to see if I'm here 'fore they buy."

"Not back here they won't," I grumbled. Maybe Big Ma knew what she was doing, but it made absolutely no sense to me to be so far from the entrance. Most of the other farmers seemed to have the right idea, and I couldn't help but try to make her see the business sense in moving the wagon forward. "Why don't we move our wagon up there with them other wagons, Big Ma? There's plenty of room, and we could sell more."

"Them's white folks' wagons, Cassie," Big Ma said gruffly, as if that explained everything. "Now, hush up and help me get this food out."

"Shoot," I mumbled, taking one of the buckets from Stacey, "by the time a body walk way back here, they'll have bunions on their soles and corns on their toes."

By noon the crowd which had covered the field during the early morning had thinned noticeably, and wagons and trucks began to pack up and head for town. After we had eaten our cold lunch of oil sausages and cornbread washed down with clabber milk, we did the same.

On the main street of Strawberry once more, Big Ma parked the wagon in front of a building where four shingles hung from a rusted post. One of the shingles read: "Wade W. Jamison, Attorney-at-Law."

"Mr. Jamison live here?" I cried, scrambling down. "I wanna see him."

"He don't live here," said Big Ma, opening her large purse. She pulled out a long manila envelope, checked inside, then gingerly put it back again. "This here's his office and I got some business with him. You get on back in the wagon." Big Ma climbed down, but I didn't get back in. "Can't I just go up and say 'Hey'?" I persisted.

"I'm gonna 'Hey' you," Big Ma said, "you keep pesterin' me." She glanced over at Stacey and T.J. "Y'all wait here for me and soon's I get back, we'll go do that shoppin' so's we can get on home 'fore it gets dark."

When she had gone inside, T.J. said, "What you wanna see that ole white man for anyway, Cassie? What you and him got to talk 'bout?"

"I just wanted to see him, that's all," I said, going to the raised sidewalk and taking a seat. I liked Mr. Jamison and I didn't mind admitting it. He came to see us several times a year, mainly on business, and although the boys and I were somewhat shy of him, we were always glad to see him. He was the only white man I had ever heard address Mama and Big Ma as "Missus," and I liked him for it. Besides that, in his way he was like Papa: Ask him a question and he would give it to you straight with none of this pussyfooting-around business. I liked that.

After several minutes of watching farmers in faded overalls and their women in flour-sack-cut dresses promenading under the verandas, T.J. said, "Why don't we go on down to the mercantile and look around?"

Stacey hesitated. "I don't know. I think Big Ma wanted to go with us."

"Ah, shoot, man, we'll be doin' her a favor. We go on down to the mercantile now and order up our stuff, we'll save her some time so when she come from seein' that lawyer, we can jus' go on home. Besides, I got somethin' to show ya."

Stacey pondered the suggestion for a long moment. "Well, I guess it'll be all right," he said finally.

"Big Ma said stay here!" I objected, hoping that Mr. Jamison would come out with Big Ma.

"Stay here then," Stacey called over his shoulder as he crossed the street with T.J.

I dashed after them. I wasn't about to stay on that sidewalk by myself.

The Barnett Mercantile had everything. Its shelves,

counters, and floor space boasted items from ladies' ribbons to burlap bags of seeds; from babies' bottles to brand-new potbellied stoves. T.J., who had been to the store several times before, wove his way among the farmers and led us to a counter at the far corner of the room. The counter had a glass top, and beneath the glass were handguns artfully displayed on a bolt of red velvet.

"Jus' look at it," T.J. said dreamily. "Ain't she somethin'?"

"What?" I said.

"That pearl-handled one. Stacey, man, you ever seen a gun like that before in your whole life? I'd sell my life for that gun. One of these days I'm gonna have it, too."

"I reckon I ain't," said Stacey politely. "It's a nice-looking gun all right."

I stared down at the gun. A price tag of $35.95 stared back at me. "Thirty-five dollars and ninety-five cents!" I almost screamed. "Just for an ole gun? What the devil you gonna use it for? Can't hunt with it."

T.J. looked at me with disgust. "Ain't 'pose to hunt with it. It's for protection."

"Protection of what?" I asked, thinking of Papa's sturdy shotgun that hung over his and Mama's bed, and the sleek Winchester rifle which Big Ma kept locked in the trunk beneath our own bed. "That thing couldn't hardly kill a rattlesnake."

"There's other things a body needs protectin' from more than a rattlesnake," he said haughtily. "I get me that gun and ain't nobody gonna mess with me. I wouldn't need nobody."

Stacey backed away from the counter. He seemed nervous being in the store. "We better get those things you need and get on outa here 'fore Big Ma comes looking for us."

"Ah, man, there's plenty of time," said T.J., looking longingly at the gun. "Sure wish I could jus' hold it, jus' once."

"Come on, T.J.," ordered Stacey, "or me and Cassie's gonna go on back outside."

"Oh, all right." T.J. turned reluctantly away and went to a counter where a man was measuring nails onto a scale. We stood patiently waiting behind the people in front of us and when our turn came, T.J. handed his list to the man. "Mr. Barnett, sir," he said, "I got me this here list of things my mama want."

The storekeeper studied the list and without looking up he asked, "You one of Mr. Granger's people?"

"Yessir," answered T.J.

Mr. Barnett walked to another counter and began filling the order, but before he finished a white woman called, "Mr. Barnett, you waiting on anybody just now?"

Mr. Barnett turned around. "Just them," he said, indicating us with a wave of his hand. "What can I do for you, Miz Emmaline?" The woman handed him a list twice as long as T.J.'s and the storekeeper, without a word of apology to us, proceeded to fill it.

"What's he doing?" I objected.

"Hush, Cassie," said Stacey, looking very embarrassed and uncomfortable. T.J.'s face was totally bland, as if nothing at all had happened.

When the woman's order was finally filled, Mr. Barnett again picked up T.J.'s list, but before he had gotten the next item his wife called, "Jim Lee, these folks needing help over here and I got my hands full." And as if we were not even there, he walked away.

"Where's he going?" I cried.

"He'll be back," said T.J., wandering away.

After waiting several minutes for Mr. Barnett's return, Stacey said, "Come on, Cassie, let's go." He started toward the door and I followed. But as we passed one of the counters, I spied Mr. Barnett wrapping an order of pork chops for a white girl. Adults were one thing; I could almost understand that. They ruled things and there was nothing that could be done about them. But some kid who was no bigger than me was something else again. Certainly Mr. Barnett had simply forgotten about T.J.'s order. I decided to remind him and, without saying anything to Stacey, I turned around and marched over to Mr. Barnett.

"Uh . . . 'scuse me, Mr. Barnett," I said as politely as I could, waiting a moment for him to look up from his wrapping. "I think you forgot, but you was waiting on us 'fore you was waiting on this girl here, and we been waiting a good while now for you to get back."

The girl gazed at me strangely, but Mr. Barnett did not look up. I assumed that he had not heard me. I was near the end of the counter so I merely went to the other side of it and tugged on his shirt sleeve to get his attention.

He recoiled as if I had struck him.

"Y-you was helping us," I said, backing to the front of the counter again.

"Well, you just get your little black self back over there and wait some more," he said in a low, tight voice.

I was hot. I had been as nice as I could be to him and here he was talking like this. "We been waiting on you for near an hour," I hissed, "while you 'round here waiting on everybody else. And it ain't fair. You got no right—"

"Whose little nigger is this!" bellowed Mr. Barnett.

Everyone in the store turned and stared at me. "I ain't nobody's little nigger!" I screamed, angry and humiliated. "And you ought not be waiting on everybody 'fore you wait on us."

"Hush up, child, hush up," someone whispered behind me. I looked around. A woman who had occupied the wagon next to ours at the market looked down upon me. Mr. Barnett, his face red and eyes bulging, immediately pounced on her.

"This gal yourn, Hazel?"

"No, suh," answered the woman meekly, stepping hastily away to show she had nothing to do with me. As I watched her turn her back on me, Stacey emerged and took my hand.

"Come on, Cassie, let's get out of here."

"Stacey!" I exclaimed, relieved to see him by my side. "Tell him! You know he ain't fair making us wait—"

"She your sister, boy?" Mr. Barnett spat across the counter.

Stacey bit his lower lip and gazed into Mr. Barnett's eyes, "Yessir."

"Then you get her out of here," he said with hateful force. "And make sure she don't come back till yo' mammy teach her what she is."

"I already know what I am!" I retaliated. "But I betcha you don't know what you are! And I could sure tell you, too, you ole—"

Stacey jerked me forward, crushing my hand in the effort, and whispered angrily, "Shut up, Cassie!" His dark eyes flashed malevolently as he pushed me in front of him through the crowd.

As soon as we were outside, I whipped my hand from his. "What's the matter with you? You know he was wrong!"

Stacey swallowed to flush his anger, then said gruffly, "I know it and you know it, but he don't know it, and that's where the trouble is. Now come on 'fore you get us into a real mess. I'm going up to Mr. Jamison's to see what's keeping Big Ma."

"What 'bout T.J.?" I called as he stepped into the street. Stacey laughed wryly. "Don't worry 'bout T.J. He knows exactly how to act." He crossed the street sullenly then, his hands jammed in his pockets.

I watched him go, but did not follow. Instead, I ambled along the sidewalk trying to understand why Mr. Barnett had acted the way he had. More than once I stopped and gazed over my shoulder at the mercantile. I had a good mind to go back in and find out what had made Mr. Barnett so mad. I actually turned once and headed toward the store, then remembering what Mr. Barnett had said about my returning, I swung back around, kicking at the sidewalk, my head bowed.

It was then that I bumped into Lillian Jean Simms. "Why don't you look where you're going?" she asked huffily. Jeremy and her two younger brothers were with her. "Hey, Cassie," said Jeremy.

"Hey, Jeremy," I said solemnly, keeping my eyes on Lillian Jean.

"Well, apologize," she ordered.

"What?"

"You bumped into me. Now you apologize."

I did not feel like messing with Lillian Jean. I had other things on my mind. "Okay," I said, starting past, "I'm sorry."

Lillian Jean sidestepped in front of me. "That ain't enough. Get down in the road."

I looked up at her. "You crazy?"

"You can't watch where you going, get in the road. Maybe that way you won't be bumping into decent white folks with your little nasty self."

This second insult of the day was almost more than I could bear. Only the thought of Big Ma up in Mr. Jamison's office saved Lillian Jean's lip. "I ain't nasty," I said, properly holding my temper in check, "and if you're so afraid of getting bumped, walk down there yourself."

I started past her again, and again she got in my way. "Ah, let her pass, Lillian Jean," said Jeremy. "She ain't done nothin' to you."

"She done something to me just standing in front of me." With that, she reached for my arm and attempted to push me off the sidewalk. I braced myself and swept my arm backward, out of Lillian Jean's reach. But someone caught it from behind, painfully twisting it, and shoved me off the sidewalk into the road. I landed bottom first on the ground.

Mr. Simms glared down at me. "When my gal Lillian Jean says for you to get yo'self off the sidewalk, you get, you hear?"

Behind him were his sons R.W. and Melvin. People from the store began to ring the Simmses. "Ain't that the same little nigger was cuttin' up back there at Jim Lee's?" someone asked.

"Yeah, she the one," answered Mr. Simms. "You hear me talkin' to you, gal? You 'pologize to Miz Lillian Jean this minute."

I stared up at Mr. Simms, frightened. Jeremy appeared frightened too. "I—I apologized already."

Jeremy seemed relieved that I had spoken. "She d-did, Pa. R-right now, 'fore y'all come, she did—"

Mr. Simms turned an angry gaze upon his son and Jeremy faltered, looked at me, and hung his head.

Then Mr. Simms jumped into the street. I moved away from him, trying to get up. He was a mean-looking man, red in the face and bearded. I was afraid he was going to hit me before I could get to my feet, but he didn't. I scrambled up and ran blindly for the wagon. Someone grabbed me and I fought wildly, attempting to pull loose. "Stop, Cassie!" Big Ma said. "Stop, it's me. We're going home now."

"Not 'fore she 'pologizes to my gal, y'all ain't," said Mr. Simms.

Big Ma gazed down at me, fear in her eyes, then back at the growing crowd. "She jus' a child—"

"Tell her, Aunty—"

Big Ma looked at me again, her voice cracking as she spoke. "Go on, child . . . apologize."

"But, Big Ma—"

Her voice hardened. "Do like I say."

I swallowed hard.

"Go on!"

"I'm sorry," I mumbled.

"I'm sorry, *Miz* Lillian Jean," demanded Mr. Simms.

"Big Ma!" I balked.

"Say it, child."

A painful tear slid down my cheek and my lips trembled. "I'm sorry . . . M-Miz . . . Lillian Jean."

When the words had been spoken, I turned and fled crying into the back of the wagon. No day in all my life had ever been as cruel as this one.

Chapter 6

The ride home was long and silent. None of us felt like talking, not even T.J. Big Ma had informed him shortly after leaving Strawberry that she did not want to hear another word out of him before we reached home. He sulked for a while with a few audible grumbles which no one paid any attention to, but finally he fell asleep and did not awaken until we had driven up the Granger road and stopped in front of the Avery house.

By the time Jack pulled into our own yard, the night was a thick blackness and smelled of a coming rain. Big Ma climbed wearily down from the wagon and went into the house without a word. I stayed with Stacey to help him put the wagon inside the barn and unhitch and feed Jack. While I held the flashlight on the barn doors, Stacey slowly slid aside the plank of wood that held the doors fastened. "Cassie," he said, in a quiet, thoughtful voice, "don't go blaming Big Ma for what she done."

"Why not?" I asked angrily. "She made me apologize to that ole ugly Lillian Jean 'bout something wasn't even my fault. She took them ole Simmses' side without even hearing mine."

"Well, maybe she couldn't help it, Cassie. Maybe she had to do it."

"Had to do it!" I practically screamed. "She didn't have to do nothin'! She's grown just like that Mr. Simms and she should've stood up for me. I wouldn't've done her that way."

Stacey put the plank on the ground and leaned against the barn. "There's things you don't understand, Cassie—"

"And I s'pose you do, huh? Ever since you went down into Louisiana to get Papa last summer you think you know so doggone much! Well, I betcha I know one thing. If that had been Papa, he wouldn't've made me apologize! He would've listened to me!"

Stacey sighed and swung open the barn doors. "Well, Papa . . . that's different. But Big Ma ain't Papa and you can't expect . . ." His voice trailed off as he peered into the barn. Suddenly he cried, "Cassie, give me that flashlight!" Then, before I could object, he tore the flashlight from my hand and shone it into the barn.

"What's Mr. Granger's car doing in our barn?" I exclaimed as the silver Packard was unveiled by the light. Without answering me, Stacey swiftly turned and ran toward the house. I followed closely behind. Throwing open the door to Mama's room, we stood dumbfounded in the doorway. Instead of Mr. Granger, a tall, handsome man, nattily dressed in a gray pin-striped suit and vest, stood by the fire with his arm around Big Ma. For a moment we swayed with excitement, then as if by signal we both cried, "Uncle Hammer!" and dashed into his arms.

Uncle Hammer was two years older than Papa and, unmarried, he came every winter to spend the Christmas season with us. Like Papa, he had dark, red-brown skin, a square-jawed face, and high cheekbones; yet there was a great difference between them somehow. His eyes, which showed a great warmth as he hugged and kissed us now, often had a cold, distant glaze, and there was an aloofness in him which the boys and I could never quite bridge.

When he let us go, Stacey and I both grew consciously shy, and we backed away. I sat down beside Christopher-John and Little Man, who were silently gazing up at Uncle Hammer, but Stacey stammered, "Wh-what's Mr. Granger's car doing in our barn?"

"That's your Uncle Hammer's car," Mama said. "Did you unhitch Jack?"

"Uncle Hammer's!" Stacey exclaimed, exchanging shocked glances with me. "No kidding?"

Big Ma stammered, "Hammer, you—you went and got a car like Harlan Granger's?"

Uncle Hammer smiled a strange, wry smile. "Well, not exactly like it, Mama. Mine's a few months newer. Last year when I come down here, I was right impressed with that big ole Packard of Mr. Harlan Filmore Granger's and I thought I'd like to own one myself. It seems that me and Harlan Granger just got the same taste." He winked slyly at Stacey. "Don't it, Stacey?"

Stacey grinned.

"You like, maybe we'll all go riding in it one day. If it's all right with your mama."

"Oh, boy!" cried Little Man.

"You mean it, Uncle Hammer?" I asked. "Mama, can we?"

"We'll see," Mama said. "But in any case, not tonight. Stacey, go take care of Jack and draw up a bucket of water for the kitchen. We've done the other chores."

Since no one told me to help Stacey, I forgot all about Jack and settled back to listen to Uncle Hammer. Christopher-John and Little Man, who Big Ma had feared would be moping because they had not been allowed to go to town, seemed not at all concerned that Stacey and I had gone. They were awestruck by Uncle Hammer, and compared to his arrival a day in Strawberry was a minor matter.

For a while Uncle Hammer talked only to Mama and Big Ma, laughing from deep down inside himself like Papa, but then to my surprise he turned from them and addressed me. "I understand you had your first trip to Strawberry today, Cassie," he said. "What did you think?"

Big Ma stiffened, but I was pleased to have this opportunity to air my side of the Strawberry affair. "I didn't like it," I said. "Them ole Simmses—"

"Mary, I feel a bit hungry," Big Ma interrupted abruptly. "Supper still warm?"

"Yes, ma'am," said Mama standing. "I'll set it on the table for you."

As Mama stood up, I started again. "Them ole Simmses—"

"Let Cassie get it, Mary," said Big Ma nervously. "You must be tired."

I looked strangely at Big Ma, then up at Mama.

"Oh, I don't mind," said Mama, heading for the kitchen. "Go ahead, Cassie, and tell your uncle about Strawberry."

"That ole Lillian Jean Simms made me so mad I could just spit. I admit that I bumped into her, but that was 'cause I was thinking 'bout that ole Mr. Barnett waiting on everybody else in his ole store 'fore he waited on us—"

"Jim Lee Barnett?" asked Uncle Hammer, turning toward Big Ma. "That ole devil still living?"

Big Ma nodded mutely, and I went on. "But I told him he shouldn't've been 'round there waiting on everybody else 'fore he got to us—"

"Cassie!" Big Ma exclaimed, hearing this bit of news for the first time.

Uncle Hammer laughed. "You told him that!"

"Yessir," I said softly, wondering why he was laughing.

"Oh, that's great! Then what happened?"

"Stacey made me leave and Mr. Barnett told me I couldn't come back no more and then I bumped into that confounded Lillian Jean and she tried to make me get off the sidewalk and then her daddy come along and he—"

Big Ma's eyes grew large and she whispered hoarsely, "Cassie, I don't think—"

"—and he twisted my arm and knocked me off the sidewalk!" I exclaimed, unwilling to muffle what Mr. Simms had done. I glanced triumphantly at Big Ma, but she wasn't looking at me. Her eyes, frightened and nervous, were on Uncle Hammer. I turned and looked at him too.

His dark eyes had narrowed to thin, angry slits. He said: "He knocked you off the sidewalk, Cassie? A grown man knocked you off the sidewalk?"

"Y-yessir."

"This Lillian Jean Simms, her daddy wouldn't be Charlie Simms, would it?"

"Y-yessir."

Uncle Hammer grasped my shoulders. "What else he do to you?"

"N-nothin'," I said, frightened by his eyes. " 'Cepting he wanted me to apologize to Lillian Jean 'cause I wouldn't get in the road when she told me to."

"And you did?"

"Big Ma said I had to."

Uncle Hammer released me and sat very still. No one said a word. Then he stood slowly, his eyes icing into that cold distant way they could, and he started toward the door, limping slightly on his left leg. Christopher-John, Little Man, and I stared after him wonderingly, but Big Ma jumped up from her chair, knocking it over in her haste, and dashed after him. She grabbed his arm. "Let it be, son!" she cried.

"That child ain't hurt!"

"Not hurt! You look into her eyes and tell me she ain't hurt!"

Mama came back from the kitchen with Stacey behind her. "What is it?" she asked, looking from Big Ma to Uncle Hammer.

"Charlie Simms knocked Cassie off the sidewalk in Strawberry and the child just told Hammer," said Big Ma in one breath, still holding on to Uncle Hammer's arm.

"Oh, Lord," Mama groaned. "Stacey, get Mr. Morrison. Quick, now!" As Stacey sped from the room, Mama's eyes darted to the shotgun over the bed, and she edged between it and Uncle Hammer. Uncle Hammer was watching her and he said quietly, "Don't worry. I ain't gotta use David's gun. . . . I got my own."

Suddenly Mama lunged to the side door, blocking it with her slender body. "Hammer, now you listen to me—"

But Uncle Hammer gently but firmly pushed her to one side and, brushing Big Ma from his arm, opened the door and bounded down the steps into the light rain.

Little Man, Christopher-John, and I dashed to the door as Big Ma and Mama ran after him. "Get back inside," Mama called over her shoulder, but she was too busy trying to grab Uncle Hammer to see to it that we obeyed, and we did not move. "Hammer, Cassie's all right," she cried. "Don't go making unnecessary trouble!"

"Unnecessary trouble! You think my brother died and I got my leg half blown off in their German war to have some red-neck knock Cassie around anytime it suits him? If I'd've knocked his girl down, you know what'd've happened to me? Yeah, you know all right. Right now I'd be hanging from that oak over yonder. Let go of me, Mary."

Mama and Big Ma could not keep him from reaching the car. But just as the Packard roared to life, a huge figure loomed from the darkness and jumped into the other side, and the car zoomed angrily down the drive into the blackness of the Mississippi night.

"Where'd he go?" I asked as Mama slowly climbed the steps. Her face under the glow of the lamp was tired, drained "He went up to the Simmses', didn't he? Didn't he, Mama?"

"He's not going anywhere," Mama said, stepping aside and waiting until both Big Ma and Stacey were inside; then she locked the door.

"Mr. Morrison'll bring him back," said Christopher-John confidently, although he looked somewhat bewildered by all that had happened.

"If he don't," said Little Man ominously, "I betcha Uncle Hammer'll teach that ole Mr. Simms a thing or two. 'Round here hitting on Cassie."

"I hope he knocks his block off," I said.

Mama's gaze blazed down upon us. "I think little mouths that have so much to say must be very tired."

"No, ma'am, Mama, we ain't—"

"Go to bed."

"Mama, it ain't but—" Mama's face hardened, and I knew that it would not be in my best interest to argue further; I turned and did as I was told. Christopher-John and Little Man did the same. When I got to my door, I asked, "Ain't Stacey coming?"

Mama glanced down at Stacey sitting by the fire. "I don't recall his mouth working so hard, do you?"

"No'm," I muttered and went into my room. After a few minutes Mama came in. Without a word of reprimand, she picked up my clothes from where I had tossed them at the foot of the bed, and absently draping them over the back of a chair, she said, "Stacey tells me you blame Big Ma for what happened today. Is that right?"

I thought over her question and answered, "Not for all of it. Just for making me apologize to that ole dumb Lillian Jean Simms. She oughtn't't've done that, Mama. Papa wouldn't't've—"

"I don't want to hear what Papa wouldn't have done!" Mama snapped. "Or what Mr. Morrison wouldn't have done or Uncle Hammer! You were with Big Ma and she did what she had to do and believe me, young lady, she didn't like doing it one bit more than you did."

"Well," I muttered, "maybe so, but—"

"There's no maybe to it."

"Yes'm," I said softly, deciding that it was better to study the patchwork pattern on the quilt until the anger left Mama's eyes and I could talk to her again. After a moment she sat beside me on the bed and raised my chin with the tip of her forefinger. "Big Ma didn't want you to be hurt," she said. "That was the only thing on her mind . . . making sure Mr. Simms didn't hurt you."

"Yes'm," I murmured, then flared, "But, Mama, that Lillian Jean ain't got the brains of a flea! How come I gotta go 'round calling her 'Miz' like she grown or something?"

Mama's voice grew hard. "Because that's the way of things, Cassie."

"The way of what things?" I asked warily.

"Baby, you had to grow up a little today. I wish . . . well, no matter what I wish. It happened and you have to accept the fact that in the world outside this house, things are not always as we would have them to be."

"But, Mama, it ain't fair. I didn't do nothin' to that confounded Lillian Jean. How come Mr. Simms went and pushed me like he did?"

Mama's eyes looked deeply into mine, locked into them, and she said in a tight, clear voice, "Because he thinks Lillian Jean is better than you are, Cassie, and when you—"

"That ole scrawny, chicken-legged, snaggle-toothed, cross—"

"Cassie." Mama did not raise her voice, but the quiet force of my name silenced me. "Now," she said, folding my hand in hers, "I didn't say that Lillian Jean *is* better than you. I said Mr. Simms only *thinks* she is. In fact, he thinks she's better than Stacey or Little Man or Christopher-John—"

"Just 'cause she's his daughter?" I asked, beginning to think Mr. Simms was a bit touched in the head.

"No, baby, because she's white."

Mama's hold tightened on mine, but I exclaimed, "Ah, shoot! White ain't nothin'!"

Mama's grip did not lessen. "It is something, Cassie. White is something just like black is something. Everybody born on this earth is something and nobody, no matter what color, is better than anybody else."

"Then how come Mr. Simms don't know that?"

"Because he's one of those people who has to believe that white people are better than black people to make himself feel big." I stared questioningly at Mama, not really understanding. Mama squeezed my hand and explained further. "You see, Cassie, many years ago when our people were first brought from Africa in chains to work as slaves in this country—"

"Like Big Ma's papa and mama?"

Mama nodded. "Yes, baby, like Papa Luke and Mama Rachel, except they were born right here in Mississippi. But their grandparents were born in Africa, and when they came there were some white people who thought that it was wrong for any people to be slaves; so the people who needed slaves to work in their fields and the people who were making money bringing slaves from Africa preached that black people weren't really people like white people were, so slavery was all right.

"They also said that slavery was good for us because it taught us to be good Christians—like the white people." She sighed deeply, her voice fading into a distant whisper. "But they didn't teach us Christianity to save our souls, but to teach us obedience. They were afraid of slave revolts and they wanted us to learn the Bible's teachings about slaves being loyal to their masters. But even teaching us Christianity didn't make us stop wanting to be free, and many slaves ran away—"

"Papa Luke ran away," I reminded her, thinking of the story of how Great-Grandpa had run away three times. He had been caught and punished for his disobedience, but his owners had not tried to break him, for he had had a knowledge of herbs and cures. He had tended both the slaves and the animals of the plantation, and it was from him that Big Ma had learned medicines.

Mama nodded again. "That's right, honey. He was hiding in a cave when freedom came, so I understand." She was silent a moment, then went on. "Well, after a while, slavery became so profitable to people who had slaves and even to those who didn't that most folks decided to believe that black people really weren't people like everybody else. And when the Civil War was fought and Mama Rachel and

Papa Luke and all the other slaves were freed, people continued to think that way. Even the Northerners who fought the war didn't really see us equal to white people. So now, even though seventy years have passed since slavery, most white people still think of us as they did then— that we're not as good as they are—and people like Mr. Simms hold on to that belief harder than some other folks because they have little else to hold on to. For him to believe that he is better than we are makes him think that he's important, simply because he's white."

Mama relaxed her grip. I knew that she was waiting for me to speak. There was a sinking feeling in my stomach and I felt as if the world had turned itself upside down with me in it. Then I thought of Lillian Jean and a surging anger gurgled upward and I retaliated, "Well, they ain't!" But I leaned closer to Mama, anxiously hoping that she would agree with me.

"Of course they aren't," Mama said. "White people may demand our respect, but what we give them is not respect but fear. What we give to our own people is far more important because it's given freely. Now you may have to call Lillian Jean 'Miss' because the white people say so, but you'll also call our own young ladies at church 'Miss' because you really do respect them.

"Baby, we have no choice of what color we're born or who our parents are or whether we're rich or poor. What we do have is some choice over what we make of our lives once we're here." Mama cupped my face in her hands. "And I pray to God you'll make the best of yours." She hugged me warmly then and motioned me under the covers.

As she turned the lamp down low, I asked, "Mama, Uncle Hammer. If Mr. Morrison can't stop him, what'll happen?"

"Mr. Morrison will bring him back."

"But just what if he can't and Uncle Hammer gets to Mr. Simms?"

A shadowy fear fleeted across her face, but disappeared with the dimming light. "I think . . . I think you've done enough growing up for one day, Cassie," she said without answering my question. "Uncle Hammer'll be all right. Now go to sleep."

Mama had been right about Uncle Hammer. When I awoke the next morning and followed the smell of frying ham and baking biscuits into the kitchen, there he sat at the table drinking coffee with Mr. Morrison. He was unshaven and looked a bit bleary-eyed, but he was all right; I wondered if Mr. Simms looked so good. I didn't get a chance to ask, because as soon as I had said good morning Mama called me into her room, where a tub of hot water was waiting by the fireplace.

"Hurry up," she said. "Uncle Hammer's going to take us to church."

"In his car?"

Mama's brow furrowed. "Well, I just don't know. He did say something about hitching up Jack . . ."

My smile faded, but then I caught the teasing glint in her eyes, and she began to laugh. "Ah, Mama!" I laughed, and splashed into the water.

After my bath I went into my room to dress. When I rejoined Mama she was combing her hair, which fanned her head like an enormous black halo. As I watched, she shaped the long thickness into a large chignon at the nape of her neck and stuck six sturdy hairpins into it. Then, giving the chignon a pat, she reached for her pale-blue cotton dress sprinkled with tiny yellow-and-white flowers and polished white buttons running from top to bottom along its front.

She glanced down at me. "You didn't comb your hair."

"No'm. I want you to fix me my grown-up hairdo."

Mama began buttoning the top of her dress with long, flying fingers as I slowly fastened the lower buttons. I loved to help Mama dress. She always smelled of sunshine and soap. When the last button had slipped into place, she buckled a dark-blue patent-leather belt around her tiny waist and stood ready except for her shoes. She looked very pretty.

"Where's your brush?"

"Right here," I said, picking up the brush from where I had laid it on the chair.

Mama sat down in Papa's rocker and I sat on the deerskin rug in front of her. Mama divided my hair from ear to ear into two sections and braided the front section to one side and the back section right in the center. Then she wound each braid into a flat chignon against my head. My hair was too thick and long for me to do it well myself, but Mama could do it perfectly. I figured I looked my very best that way.

When Mama finished, I ran to the mirror, then turned, facing her with a grin. She grinned back and shook her head at my vanity.

"One day, Mama, you gonna fix my hair like yours?"

"That'll be a few years yet," she answered, readjusting the cardboard lining she had placed in her shoes to protect her feet from the dirt and gravel which could easily seep through the large holes in the soles. She set the shoes on the floor and stepped into them. Now, with the soles facing downward and Mama's feet in them, no one could tell what the shiny exteriors hid; yet I felt uncomfortable for Mama and wished that we had enough money for her to have her shoes fixed or, better still, buy new ones.

After breakfast Stacey, Christopher-John, Little Man, and I sat impatiently by the dying morning fire waiting for Mama, Big Ma, and Uncle Hammer. Uncle Hammer was dressing in the boys' room and Mama was in with Big Ma. I checked to make sure none of them was about to appear, then leaned toward Stacey and whispered, "You think Uncle Hammer whipped Mr. Simms?"

"No," said Stacey quietly.

"No!" cried Little Man.

"Y-you don't mean Mr. Simms whipped Uncle Hammer?" stammered an unbelieving Christopher-John.

"Nothin' happened," said Stacey in explanation as he tugged irritably at his collar.

"Nothin'?" I repeated, disappointed.

"Nothin'."

"How you know?" asked Little Man suspiciously.

"Mama said so. I asked her straight out this morning."

"Oh," replied Little Man, resigned.

"But something must've happened," I said. "I mean Uncle Hammer and Mr. Morrison look like they haven't even been to bed. How come they look like that if nothin' happened?"

"Mama said Mr. Morrison talked all night to Uncle Hammer. Talked him tired and wouldn't let him go up to the Simmses'."

"Ah, shoot!" I exclaimed, my dream of revenge against the Simmses vanishing as Stacey talked. I propped my elbows on my knees, then settled my head in my upraised hands and stared into the glowing embers. A burning knot formed in my throat and I felt as if my body was not large enough to hold the frustration I felt, nor deep enough to drown the rising anger.

"It ain't fair," Christopher-John sympathized, patting me lightly with his pudgy hand.

"Sho' ain't," agreed Little Man.

"Cassie," Stacey said softly. At first I didn't look at him, thinking he would go ahead and say what he had to say. But when he didn't, I turned toward him. He leaned forward secretively and automatically Christopher-John and Little Man did the same. "Y'all better be glad nothin' happened," he said in a whisper. " 'Cause I heard Big Ma tell Mama last night that if Mr. Morrison didn't stop Uncle Hammer, Uncle Hammer might get killed."

"Killed?" we echoed as the fire sputtered and died. "Who'd do that?" I cried. "Not one of them puny Simmses?"

Stacey started to speak, but then Mama and Big Ma entered, and he cautioned us into silence.

When Uncle Hammer joined us, freshly shaven and in another suit, the boys and I put on our coats and headed for the door; Uncle Hammer stopped us. "Stacey, that the only coat you got, son?" he asked.

Stacey looked down at his faded cotton jacket. Everyone else did too. The jacket was too small for him, that was obvious, and compared to Little Man's and Christopher-John's and mine, it was admittedly in sadder shape. Yet we were all surprised that Uncle Hammer would ask about it, for he knew as well as anyone that Mama had to buy our clothes in shifts, which meant that we each had to wait our turn for new clothes. Stacey looked up at Mama, then back at Uncle Hammer. "Y-yessir," he answered.

Uncle Hammer stared at him, then waving his hand ordered, "Take it off." Before Stacey could question why, Uncle Hammer disappeared into the boys' room.

Again Stacey looked at Mama. "You'd better do like he says," she said.

Uncle Hammer returned with a long box, store wrapped in shiny red Christmas paper and a fancy green ribbon. He handed the package to Stacey. "It was supposed to be your Christmas present, but I think I'd better give it to you now. It's cold out there."

Gingerly, Stacey took the box and opened it.

"A coat!" cried Little Man joyously, clapping his hands.

"Wool," Mama said reverently. "Go ahead, Stacey. Try it on."

Stacey eagerly slipped on the coat; it was much too big for him, but Mama said that she could take up the sleeves and that he would grow into it in another year. Stacey beamed down at the coat, then up at Uncle Hammer. A year ago he would have shot into Uncle Hammer's arms and hugged his thanks, but now at the manly age of twelve he held out his hand, and Uncle Hammer shook it.

"Come on, we'd better go," said Mama.

The morning was gray as we stepped outside, but the rain had stopped. We followed the path of bedded rocks that led to the barn, careful not to slip into the mud, and got into the Packard, shining clean and bright from the washing Uncle Hammer and Mr. Morrison had given it after breakfast. Inside the Packard, the world was a wine-colored luxury. The boys and I, in the back, ran our hands over the rich felt seats, tenderly fingered the fancy door handles and window knobs, and peered down amazed at the plush carpet peeping out on either side of the rubber mats. Mr. Morrison, who was not a churchgoing man, waved good-bye from the barn and we sped away.

As we drove onto the school grounds and parked, the people milling in front of the church turned, staring at the Packard. Then Uncle Hammer stepped from the car and someone cried, "Well, I'll be doggone! It's our Hammer! Hammer Logan!" And in a body, the crowd engulfed us.

T.J. ran up with Moe Turner and Little Willie Wiggins to admire the car. "It's Uncle Hammer's," said Stacey proudly. But before the boys could sufficiently admire the car, Mama and Big Ma shooed us toward the church for the service. It was then that T.J. noticed Stacey's new coat.

"Uncle Hammer gave it to him," I said. "Ain't it something?"

T.J. ran his long fingers over the lapels, and shrugged. "It's all right, I guess, if you like that sort of thing."

"All right!" I cried, indignant at his casual reaction to the coat. "Boy, that's the finest coat you ever did lay eyes on and you know it!"

T.J. sighed. "Like I said, it's all right . . . if you like lookin' like a fat preacher." Then he and Little Willie and Moe laughed, and went on ahead.

Stacey looked down at the coat with its long sleeves and wide shoulders. His smile faded. "He don't know what he's talking 'bout," I said. "He's just jealous, that's all."

"I know it," snapped Stacey sourly.

As we slid into the pew in front of T.J., T.J. whispered, "Here comes the preacher," then leaned forward and said snidely, "How do you do, Reverend Logan?"

Stacey turned on T.J., but I poked him hard. "Mama's looking," I whispered, and he turned back around.

After church, as T.J. and the others looked

longingly at the car, Mama said, "Stacey, maybe T.J. wants to ride."

Before Stacey could reply, I spoke up hurriedly. "No, ma'am, Mama, he got something else he gotta do." Then under my breath so that I would not be guilty of a lie, I added, "He gotta walk home like he always do."

"That'll teach him," whispered Little Man.

"Yeah," agreed Christopher-John, but Stacey sulked by the window and said nothing.

The sun was out now and Uncle Hammer suggested that we take a real ride before going home. He drove us the full twenty-two miles up to Strawberry by way of the Jackson Road, one of two roads leading to the town. But Mama and Big Ma objected so much to going through Strawberry that he turned the big car around and headed back toward home, taking the old Soldiers Road. Supposedly, Rebel soldiers had once marched up the road and across Soldiers Bridge to keep the town from falling into the hands of the Yankee Army, but I had my doubts about that. After all, who in his right mind would want to capture Strawberry . . . or defend it either for that matter?

The road was hilly and curving, and as we sped over it scattered road stones hit sharply against the car's underbelly and the dust swelled up in rolls of billowing clouds behind us. Little Man, Christopher-John, and I shrieked with delight each time the car climbed a hill and dropped suddenly downward, fluttering our stomachs. Eventually, the road intersected with the Jefferson Davis School Road. Uncle Hammer stopped the car at the intersection and, leaning his right arm heavily over the steering wheel, motioned languidly at the Wallace store. "Got me a good mind to burn that place out," he said.

"Hammer, hush that kind of talk!" ordered Big Ma, her eyes growing wide.

"Me and John Henry and David grew up together. And John Henry and me even fought in their war together. What good was it? A black man's life ain't worth the life of a cowfly down here."

"I know that, son, but that kinda talk get you hung and you know it."

Mama touched Uncle Hammer's arm. "There might be another way, Hammer . . . like I told you. Now don't go do something foolish. Wait for David—talk to him."

Uncle Hammer looked glassy-eyed at the store, then sighed and eased the Packard across the road toward Soldiers Bridge. We were taking the long way home.

Soldiers Bridge was built before the Civil War. It was spindly and wooden, and each time I had to cross it I held my breath until I was safely on the other side. Only one vehicle could cross at a time, and whoever was on the bridge first was supposed to have the right of way, although it didn't always work that way. More than once when I had been in the wagon with Mama or Big Ma, we had had to back off the bridge when a white family started across after we were already on it.

As the bridge came into view the other side of the river was clearly visible, and it was obvious to everyone that an old Model-T truck, overflowing with redheaded children, had reached the bridge first and was about to cross, but suddenly Uncle Hammer gassed the Packard and sped onto the creaking structure. The driver of the truck stopped, and for no more than a second hesitated on the bridge, then without a single honk of protest backed off so that we could pass.

"Hammer!" Big Ma cried. "They think you're Mr. Granger."

"Well, now, won't they be surprised when we reach the other side," said Uncle Hammer.

As we came off the bridge, we could see the Wallaces, all three of them—Dewberry, Thurston, and Kaleb—touch their hats respectfully, then immediately freeze as they saw who we were. Uncle Hammer, straight-faced and totally calm, touched the brim of his own hat in polite response and without a backward glance sped away, leaving the Wallaces gaping silently after us.

Stacey, Christopher-John, Little Man, and I laughed, but Mama's cold glance made us stop. "You shouldn't have done that, Hammer," she said quietly.

"The opportunity, dear sister, was too much to resist."

"But one day we'll have to pay for it. Believe me," she said, "one day we'll pay."

Chapter 7

"Stacey, go bring me your coat," Mama said a few days later as we gathered around the fire after supper. "I've got time to take up the sleeves now."

"Uh-oh!" exclaimed Christopher-John, then immediately opened his reader as Mama looked down at him.

Little Man cupped his hand and whispered to me, "Boy, now he's gonna get it!"

"Uh . . . th-that's all right, Mama," stuttered Stacey. "The c-coat's all right like it is."

Mama opened her sewing box. "It's not all right. Now go get it for me."

Stacey stood up and started slowly toward his room. Little Man, Christopher-John, and I watched him closely, wondering what he was going to do. He actually went into the room, but was gone only a moment before he reappeared and nervously clutched the back of his chair. "I ain't got the coat, Mama," he said.

"Not got the coat!" cried Big Ma. Uncle Hammer looked up sharply from his paper, but remained silent.

"Stacey," Mama said irritably, "bring me that coat, boy."

"But, Mama, I really ain't got it! I gave it to T.J."

"T.J.!" Mama exclaimed.

"Yes, ma'am, Mama," Stacey answered, then went on hurriedly as Mama's eyes glittered with rising anger. "The coat was too big for me and . . . and T.J. said it made me look like . . . like a preacher . . . and he said since it fit him just right, he'd . . . he'd take it off my hands till I grow into it, then thataway all the guys would stop laughing at me and calling me preacher." He paused, waiting for someone to speak; but the only sound was a heavy breathing and the crackle of burning hickory. Then, seeming more afraid of the silence than putting his neck further into the noose, he added, "But I didn't give it to him for good, Mama—just lent it to him till I get big enough for it and then . . ."

Stacey's voice faded into an inaudible whisper as Mama slowly put the sewing box on the table behind her. I thought she was headed for the wide leather strap hanging in the kitchen, but she did not rise. In quiet anger she glared at Stacey and admonished, "In this house we do not give away what loved ones give to us. Now go bring me that coat."

Backing away from her anger, Stacey turned to leave, but Uncle Hammer stopped him. "No," he said, "leave the coat where it is."

Mama turned bewildered toward Uncle Hammer. "Hammer, what're you saying? That's the best coat Stacey's ever had and probably ever will have as long as he lives in this house. David and I can't afford a coat like that."

Uncle Hammer leaned back in his chair, his eyes cold on Stacey. "Seems to me if Stacey's not smart enough to hold on to a good coat, he don't deserve it. As far as I'm concerned, T.J. can just keep that coat permanently. At least he knows a good thing when he sees it."

"Hammer," Big Ma said, "let the boy go get the coat. That T.J. probably done told him all sorts—"

"Well, ain't Stacey got a brain? What the devil should he care what T.J. thinks or T.J. says? Who is this T.J. anyway? Does he put clothes on Stacey's back or food in front of him?" Uncle Hammer stood and walked over to Stacey as Little Man, Christopher-John, and I followed him fearfully with our eyes. "I suppose if T.J. told you it was summertime out there and you should run buck naked down the road because everybody else was doing it, you'd do that too, huh?"

"N-no sir," Stacey replied, looking at the floor.

"Now you hear me good on this—look at me when I talk to you, boy!" Immediately Stacey raised his head and looked at Uncle Hammer. "If you ain't got the brains of a flea to see that this T.J. fellow made a fool of you, then you'll never get anywhere in this world. It's tough out there, boy, and as long as there are people, there's gonna be somebody trying to take what you got and trying to drag you down. It's up to you whether you let them or not. Now it seems to me you wanted that coat when I gave it to you, ain't that right?"

Stacey managed a shaky "Yessir."

"And anybody with any sense would know it's a good thing, ain't that right?"

This time Stacey could only nod.

"Then if you want something and it's a good thing and you got it in the right way, you better hang on to it and don't let nobody talk you out of it. You care what a lot of useless people say 'bout you you'll never get anywhere, 'cause there's a lotta folks don't want you to make it. You understand what I'm telling you?"

"Y-yessir, Uncle Hammer," Stacey stammered. Uncle Hammer turned then and went back to his paper without having laid a hand on Stacey, but Stacey shook visibly from the encounter.

Christopher-John, Little Man, and I exchanged apprehensive glances. I don't know what they were thinking, but I for one was deciding right then and there not to do anything to rub Uncle Hammer the wrong way; I had no intention of ever facing a tongue-lashing like that. Papa's bottom-warming whippings were quite enough for me, thank you.

The last days of school before Christmas seemed interminable. Each night I fell asleep with the hope that the morning would bring Papa, and each morning when he wasn't there I trudged to school consoling myself that he would be home when I returned. But the days passed, prickly cold and windy, and he did not come.

Added to the misery of the waiting and the cold was Lillian Jean, who managed to flounce past me with a superior smirk twice that week. I had already decided that she had had two flounces too many, but since I hadn't yet decided how to handle the matter, I postponed doing anything until after I had had a chance to talk with Papa about the whole Strawberry business. I knew perfectly well that he would not tear out of the house after Mr. Simms as Uncle Hammer had done, for he always took time to think through any move he made, but he would certainly advise me on how to handle Lillian Jean.

Then too there was T.J., who, although not really my problem, was so obnoxiously flaunting Stacey's wool coat during these cold days that I had just about decided to deflate him at the same time I took care of Lillian Jean. Ever since the night Mr. Avery had brought him to the house to return the coat and he had been told by Uncle Hammer and a faltering Stacey that the coat was his, T.J. had been more unbearable than usual. He now praised the coat from the wide tips of its lapels to the very edges of its deep hem. No one had ever had a finer coat; no one had ever looked better in such a coat; no one could ever hope to have such a coat again.

Stacey was restrained from plugging T.J.'s mouth by Uncle Hammer's principle that a man did not blame others for his own stupidity; he learned from his mistake and became stronger for it. I, however, was not so restrained and as far as I was concerned, if T.J. kept up with this coat business, he could just hit the dirt at the same time as "Miss" Lillian Jean.

The day before Christmas I awoke to the soft murmuring of quiet voices gathered in the midnight blackness of morning. Big Ma was not beside me, and without a moment's doubt I knew why she was gone. Jumping from the bed, my feet barely hitting the deerskin rug, I rushed into Mama's room.

"Oh Papa!" I cried. "I knew it was you!"

"Ah, there's my Cassie girl!" Papa laughed, standing to catch me as I leapt into his arms.

By the dawn, the house smelled of Sunday: chicken frying, bacon sizzling, and smoke sausages baking. By evening, it reeked of Christmas. In the kitchen sweet-potato pies, egg-custard pies, and rich butter pound cakes cooled; a gigantic coon which Mr. Morrison, Uncle Hammer, and Stacey had secured in a night's hunt baked in a sea of onions, garlic, and fat orange-yellow yams; and a choice sugar-cured ham brought from the smokehouse awaited its turn in the oven. In the heart of the house, where we had gathered after supper, freshly cut branches of long-needled pines lay over the fireplace mantle adorned by winding vines of winter holly and bright red Christmas berries. And in the fireplace itself, in a black pan set on a high wire rack, peanuts roasted over the hickory fire as the waning light of day swiftly deepened into a fine velvet night speckled with white forerunners of a coming snow, and the warm sound of husky voices and rising laughter mingled in tales of sorrow and happiness of days past but not forgotten.

". . . Them watermelons of old man Ellis' seemed like they just naturally tasted better than anybody else's," said Papa, "and ole Hammer and me, we used to sneak up there whenever it'd get so hot you couldn't hardly move and take a couple of them melons on down to the pond and let them get real chilled. Then talking 'bout eating! We did some kind of good eating."

"Papa, you was stealing?" asked an astonished Little Man. Although he usually strongly disapproved of being held, he was now reclining comfortably in Papa's lap.

"Well . . ." Papa said, "not exactly. What we'd do was exchange one of the melons from our patch for his. Course it was still wrong for us to do it, but at the time it seemed all right—"

"Problem was, though," laughed Uncle Hammer, "old man Ellis grew them ole fat green round watermelons and ours was long and striped—"

"And Mr. Ellis was always right particular 'bout his melons," interjected Papa. "He took the longest time to figure out what we was up to, but, Lord, Lord, when he did—"

"—You should've seen us run," Uncle Hammer said, standing. He shot one hand against and past the other. "Ma—an! We was gone! And that ole man was right behind us with a hickory stick hitting us up side the head—"

"Ow—weee! That ole man could run!" cried Papa. I didn't know nobody's legs could move that fast."

Big Ma chuckled. "And as I recalls, your Papa 'bout wore y'all out when Mr. Ellis told him what y'all'd been up to. Course, you know all them Ellises was natural-born runners. Y'all remember Mr. Ellis' brother, Tom Lee? Well, one time he . . ."

Through the evening Papa and Uncle Hammer and Big Ma and Mr. Morrison and Mama lent us their memories, acting out their tales with stageworthy skills, imitating the characters in voice, manner, and action so well that the listeners held their sides with laughter. It was a good warm time. But as the night deepened and the peanuts in the pan grew shallow, the voices grew hushed, and Mr. Morrison said:

". . . They come down like ghosts that Christmas of seventy-six. Them was hard times like now and my family was living in a shantytown right outside Shreveport. Reconstruction was just 'bout over then, and them Northern soldiers was tired of being in the South and they didn't hardly care 'bout no black folks in shantytown. And them Southern whites, they was tired of the Northern soldiers and free Negroes, and they was trying to turn things back 'round to how they used to be. And the colored folks . . . well, we was just tired. Warn't hardly no work, and during them years I s'pose it was jus' 'bout as hard being free as it was being a slave. . .

"That night they come—I can remember just as good—it was cold, so cold we had to huddle all 'gainst each other just trying to keep warm, and two boys— 'bout eighteen or nineteen, I reckon—come knocking on my daddy's door. They was scairt, clean out of their heads with fright. They'd just come back from Shreveport. Some white woman done accused them of molestin' her and they didn't know nowhere to run so they come up to my daddy's 'cause he had a good head and he was big, bigger than me. He was strong too. So strong he could break a man's leg easy as if he was snapping a twig—I seen him do it that night. And the white folks was scairt of him. But my daddy didn't hardly have time to finish hearing them boys' story when them devilish night men swept down—"

"Night men!" I echoed in a shrill, dry whisper. Stacey sitting beside me on the floor stiffened; Christopher-John nudged me knowingly; Little Man leaned forward on Papa's lap.

"David . . ." Mama started, but Papa enfolded her slender hand in his and said quietly, "These are things they need to hear, baby. It's their history."

Mama sat back, her hand still in Papa's, her eyes wary. But Mr. Morrison seemed not to notice. ". . . swept down like locusts," he continued in a faraway voice. "Burst in on us with their Rebel sabers, hacking and killing, burning us out. Didn't care who they kilt. We warn't nothing to them. No better than dogs. Kilt babies and old women. Didn't matter."

He gazed into the fire.

"My sisters got kilt in they fire, but my Mama got me out. . . ." His voice faded and he touched the scars on his neck. "She tried to get back into the house to save the girls, but she couldn't. Them night men was all over her and she threw me—just threw me like I was a ball—hard as she could, trying to get me away from them. Then she fought. Fought like a wild thing right 'side my daddy. They was both of them from breeded stock and they was strong like bulls—"

"Breeded stock?" I said. "What's that?"

"Cassie, don't interrupt Mr. Morrison," said Mama, but Mr. Morrison turned from the fire and explained. "Well, Cassie, during slavery there was some farms that mated folks like animals to produce more slaves. Breeding slaves brought a lot of money for them slave owners, 'specially after the government said they couldn't bring no more slaves from Africa, and they produced all kinds of slaves to sell on the block. And folks with enough money, white men and even free black men, could buy 'zactly what they wanted. My folks was bred for strength like they folks and they grandfolks 'fore 'em. Didn't matter none what they thought 'bout the idea. Didn't nobody care.

"But my mama and daddy they loved each other and they loved us children, and that Christmas they fought them demons out of hell like avenging angels of the Lord." He turned back toward the fire and grew very quiet; then he raised his head and looked at us. "They died that night. Them night men kilt 'em. Some folks tell me I can't remember what happened that Christmas—I warn't hardly six years old—but I remembers all right. I makes myself remember."

He grew silent again and no one spoke. Big Ma poked absently at the red-eyed logs with the poker, but no one else stirred. Finally Mr. Morrison stood, wished us a good night, and left.

Uncle Hammer stood also. "Guess I'll turn in too. It's near one o'clock."

"Wait awhile, Hammer," said Big Ma. "Now you and David both home, I gotta talk to y'all—'bout the land. . . ."

Visions of night men and fire mixed in a caldron of fear awakened me long before dawn. Automatically, I rolled toward the comforting presence of Big Ma, but she was not beside me.

A soft light still crept under the door from Mama and Papa's room and I immediately hurried toward it. As I opened the door and stepped into the shadowy room, lit now only by the flickering yellow of the low fire, Big Ma was saying, ". . . y'all start messin' with these folks down in here, no telling what'll happen."

"Is it better to just sit back and complain about how they do us?" Mama snapped, her voice rising. "Everybody from Smellings Creek to Strawberry knows it was them but what do we do about it? We line their pockets with our few pennies and send our children up to their store to learn things they've got no business learning. The older children are drinking regularly there now, even though they don't have any money to pay, and the Wallaces are simply adding the liquor charges to the family bill . . . just more money for them as they ruin our young people. As I see it the least we can do is stop shopping there. It may not be real justice, but it'll hurt them and we'll have done something. Mr. Turner and the Averys and the Laniers and over two dozen other families, and perhaps even more, say they'll think about not shopping there if they can get credit somewhere else. We owe it to the Berrys—"

"Frankly," interrupted Uncle Hammer, "I'd rather burn them out myself."

"Hammer, you go to burning and we'll have nothing," Mama retorted.

"Ain't gonna have nothing noway," replied Uncle Hammer. "You think by shopping up at Vicksburg you gonna drive them Wallaces out, then you got no idea of how things work down here. You forgetting Harlan Granger backs that store?"

"Mary, child, Hammer's right," Big Ma said. "I'm doing what I told y'all 'bout this land 'cause I don't want some legal thing to come up after I'm gone that let that Harlan Granger get this place. But we go backing folks' credit with our land, we'd lose it sure; and we do that, I couldn't face Paul Edward—"

"I didn't say we should back it," Mama said, "but we're just about the only family with any collateral at all."

Papa looked up from the fire. "That may be, honey, but we put up this land to back this thing and it'll be just like giving it away. Times like they are, it ain't likely that any of these people can pay the bills they make—as much as they might mean to—and if they can't pay, where would we be? We've got no cash money to pay other folks' debts." He shook his head. "No . . . we'll have to find another way. . . . Go to Vicksburg maybe and see what we can arrange—" His eyes fell upon me in the shadows and he leaned forward. "Cassie? What is it, sugar?"

"Nothin', Papa," I mumbled. "I just woke up, that's all."

Mama started to rise but Papa motioned her down and got up himself. Escorting me back to bed, he said gently, "Got no cause for bad dreams, Cassie girl. Not tonight anyway."

"Papa," I said, snuggling under the warm quilts as he tucked them around me, "we gonna lose our land?"

Papa reached out and softly touched my face in the darkness. "If you remember nothing else in your whole life, Cassie girl, remember this: We ain't never gonna lose this land. You believe that?"

"Yessir, Papa."

"Then go to sleep. Christmas is coming."

"Books!" cried Little Man on Christmas morning.

For Stacey there was *The Count of Monte Cristo;* for me, *The Three Musketeers;* and for Christopher-John and Little Man, two different volumes of *Aesop's Fables.* On the inside cover of each book in Mama's fine hand was written the name of the owner. Mine read: "This book is the property of Miss Cassie Deborah Logan. Christmas, 1933."

"Man sold me them books told me these two was

written by a black man," Papa said, opening my book and pointing to a picture of a man in a long, fancy coat and a wigful of curly hair that fell to his shoulders. "Name of Alexander Dumas, a French fellow. His daddy was a mulatto and his grandmama was a slave down on one of them islands—Mar-ti-nique, it says here. Man said to me, they right hard reading for children, but I told him he didn't know my babies. They can't read 'em now, I said, they'll grow into 'em.'"

In addition to the books there was a sockful of once-a-year store-bought licorice, oranges, and bananas for each of us and from Uncle Hammer a dress and a sweater for me, and a sweater and a pair of pants each for Christopher-John and Little Man. But nothing compared to the books. Little Man, who treasured clothes above all else, carefully laid his new pants and sweater aside and dashed for a clean sheet of brown paper to make a cover for his book, and throughout the day as he lay upon the deerskin rug looking at the bright, shining pictures of faraway places, turning each page as if it were gold, he would suddenly squint down at his hands, glance at the page he had just turned, then dash into the kitchen to wash again—just to make sure.

After the church services, the Averys returned home with us for Christmas dinner. All eight of the Avery children, including the four pre-schoolers, crowded into the kitchen with the boys and me, smelling the delicious aromas and awaiting the call to eat. But only the eldest girls, who were helping Mama, Big Ma, and Mrs. Avery prepare the finishing touches to the meal, were allowed to remain. The rest of us were continuously being shooed out by Big Ma. Finally, the announcement we were all waiting for was made and we were allowed to begin the Christmas feast.

The meal lasted for over two hours through firsts, seconds, and thirds, talk and laughter, and finally dessert. When we were finished the boys and I, with Claude and T.J., went outside, but the half-inch layer of snow made everything sloppy, so we soon went back in and joined the adults by the fire. Shortly afterward, there was a timid knock on the front door. Stacey opened the door and found Jeremy Simms standing there looking frozen and very frightened as he peered into the bright room. Everyone turned to stare at him. Stacey glanced around at Papa, then back at Jeremy. "You—you wanna come in?" he asked awkwardly.

Jeremy nodded and stepped hesitantly inside. As Stacey motioned him toward the fire, Uncle Hammer's eyes narrowed, and he said to Papa, "He looks like a Simms."

"I believe he is," agreed Papa.

"Then what the devil—"

"Let me handle it," Papa said.

Jeremy, who had heard, flushed a deep red and quickly handed Mama a small burlap bag. "I—I brung them for y'all." Mama took the bag. As she opened it, I peeped over her shoulder; the bag was full of nuts.

"Nuts?" I questioned. "Nuts! Why we got more nuts now than we know what—"

"Cassie!" Mama scowled. "What have I told you about that mouth of yours?" Then she turned to Jeremy. "This is very thoughtful of you, Jeremy, and we appreciate them. Thank you."

Jeremy nodded slightly as if he did not know how to accept her thanks, and stiffly handed a slender, paper-wrapped object to Stacey. "Made this for ya," he said.

Stacey looked at Papa to see if he should take it. For a long moment Papa studied Jeremy, then he nodded. "It—it ain't much," stammered Jeremy as Stacey tore off the wrapping. "M-made it myself." Stacey slid his fingers down the smooth, sanded back of a wooden flute. "Go 'head and try it," said a pleased Jeremy. "It blows real nice."

Again Stacey looked at Papa, but this time Papa gave him no indication what he should do. "Thanks, Jeremy, it's real nice," he said finally. Then, flute in hand, he stood uncomfortably by the door waiting for Jeremy to leave.

When Jeremy did not move, Papa asked; "You Charlie Simms's boy?"

Jeremy nodded. "Y-yessir."

"Your daddy know you here?"

Jeremy bit his lower lip, and looked at his feet. "N-no sir, I reckon not."

"Then I expect you'd better be getting on home, son, 'fore he come looking for you."

"Yessir," said Jeremy, backing away.

As he reached the door, I cried after him, "Merry Christmas, Jeremy!" Jeremy looked back and smiled shyly. "Merry Christmas to y'all too."

T.J. made no comment on Jeremy's visit until both Papa and Uncle Hammer had left the room. He was afraid of Papa and downright terrified of Uncle Hammer, so he never had much to say when either was around, but now that they had gone outside with Mr. Avery, he said, "You ain't gonna keep that thing, are you?"

Stacey looked malevolently at T.J. and I knew that he was thinking of the coat. "Yeah, I'm gonna keep it. Why?"

T.J. shrugged. "Nothin'. 'Ceptin' I sure wouldn't

want no whistle some ole white boy been blowin' on."

I watched Stacey closely to see if he was going to allow himself to be goaded by T.J.; he was not. "Ah, stuff it, T.J.," he ordered.

"Ah, man, don't get me wrong," said T.J. quickly. "You wanna keep the ole thing, it's up to you. But for me, somebody give me something, I want it to be something fine—like that pretty little pearl-handled pistol. . . ."

When the Averys had left, Stacey asked, "Papa, how come Jeremy give me this flute? I mean, I didn't give him nothin'."

"Maybe you did give him something," said Papa, lighting his pipe.

"No sir, Papa. I ain't never give him nothin'!"

"Not even your friendship?"

"Well . . . not really. I mean . . . he's a crazy kid and he likes to walk to school with us, but—"

"You like him?"

Stacey frowned, thinking. "I told him I didn't want him walking with us, but he keeps on anyway and the white kids laugh at him 'cause he do. But he don't seem to let it bother him none. . . . I s'pose I like him all right. Is that wrong?"

"No," Papa said carefully. "That ain't wrong."

"Actually, he's much easier to get along with than T.J.," Stacey went on. "And I s'pose if I let him, he could be a better friend than T.J."

Papa took the pipe from his mouth, rubbed his moustache and spoke quietly. "Far as I'm concerned, friendship between black and white don't mean that much 'cause it usually ain't on a equal basis. Right now you and Jeremy might get along fine, but in a few years he'll think of himself as a man but you'll probably still be a boy to him. And if he feels that way, he'll turn on you in a minute."

"But Papa, I don't think Jeremy'd be that way."

Papa's eyes narrowed and his resemblance to Uncle Hammer increased. "We Logans don't have much to do with white folks. You know why? 'Cause white folks mean trouble. You see blacks hanging 'round with whites, they're headed for trouble. Maybe one day whites and blacks can be real friends, but right now the country ain't built that way. Now you could be right 'bout Jeremy making a much finer friend than T.J. ever will be. The trouble is, down here in Mississippi, it costs too much to find out. . . . So I think you'd better not try."

Stacey looked full into Papa's face and read his meaning.

On my way to bed, I stopped by the boys' room to retrieve an orange Christopher-John had swiped from my stocking and spied Stacey fingering the flute. As I stood in the doorway, he lingered over it, then, carefully rewrapping it, placed it in his box of treasured things. I never saw the flute again.

The day after Christmas Papa summoned Stacey, Christopher-John, Little Man, and me into the barn. We had hoped against hope that Mama would not tell him about our trip to the Wallace store or, if she did, that he would forget what he had promised. We should have known better. Mama always told Papa everything, and Papa never forgot anything.

After we had received our punishment, we emerged sore and teary-eyed and watched Papa, Uncle Hammer, and Mr. Morrison climb into the Packard and speed away. Mama said they were going to Vicksburg.

"Why Vicksburg, Mama?" asked Stacey.

"They've got some business to attend to," she said shortly. "Come on now, get busy. We've got chores to do."

In the late afternoon, shortly after the men had returned, Mr. Jamison arrived. He brought with him a fruit cake sent by Mrs. Jamison and a bag of lemon drops for each of the boys and me. Mama allowed us to say our thanks, then sent us outside. We played for a while in the patches of snow that remained, but when that grew tiresome, I popped into the house to see what was happening; Mama ordered me to pop back out again.

"What they doing?" asked Little Man.

"Looking at a whole bunch of papers," I said. "And Uncle Hammer was signing something."

"What kind of papers?" asked Stacey.

I shrugged. "I dunno. But Mr. Jamison was saying something 'bout selling the land."

"Selling the land?" questioned Stacey. "You sure?"

I nodded. "He said: 'Y'all sign them papers and Miz Caroline got no more legal right to this land. Can't sell it, can't sign on it. It'll be in y'all's name and it'll take both of y'all to do anything with it.' "

"Both of who?"

I shrugged again. "Papa and Uncle Hammer, I guess."

After a while it grew chilly and we went inside. Mr. Jamison, sitting next to Big Ma, was putting some papers into his briefcase. "I hope you feel better now that that's done, Miz Caroline," he said, his voice a soft mixture of Southern aristocracy and Northern schooling.

"Hammer and David, they been takin' care of things a long time now," Big Ma said. "Them and Mary works hard to pay the taxes and mortgage on this here place and I been wantin' to make sure while I'm still breathin' that they gets title to this place under the law without no trouble. I ain't wantin' a whole lot of problems after I'm gone 'bout who gots rights to this land." She paused a moment, then added, "That happens sometimes, you know."

Mr. Jamison nodded. He was a long, thin man in his mid-fifties with a perfect lawyer face, so placid that it was difficult to guess what thoughts lay behind it.

The boys and I sat down silently at the study table, and the silence allowed us to stay. I figured that Mr. Jamison would be leaving now. His business was evidently finished and despite the fact that the family thought well of him, he was not considered a friend in the usual sense, and there seemed no reason for him to stay longer. But now Mr. Jamison put his briefcase back on the floor, indicating that he was not leaving, and looked first at Big Ma and Mama, then across at Papa and Uncle Hammer.

"There's talk that some of the people around here are looking to shop in Vicksburg," he said.

Big Ma looked around at Papa and Uncle Hammer, but neither of them acknowledged her glance; their eyes were pinned on Mr. Jamison.

"There's talk too why folks are looking to shop there." He paused, met Papa's eyes, then Uncle Hammer's, and went on. "As you know, my family has roots in Vicksburg—we've a number of friends there still. I got a call from one of them this morning. Said you were looking to find credit for about thirty families."

Papa and Uncle Hammer neither affirmed nor denied this. "You know as well as I do that credit doesn't come easy these days," continued Mr. Jamison. "You expect to get any, you'll need something to back it."

"I reckon we know that," said Uncle Hammer.

Mr. Jamison glanced at Uncle Hammer and

nodded. "I reckoned you did. But as far as I can see, the only thing any of you got to back that credit with is this land . . . and I'd hate to see you put it up."

"Why's that?" asked Uncle Hammer, wary of his interest.

"Because you'd lose it."

The fire popped and the room grew silent. Then Papa said, "What you getting at?"

"I'll back the credit."

Again, silence. Mr. Jamison allowed Papa and Uncle Hammer several moments to search for a motive behind his masklike face. "I'm a Southerner, born and bred, but that doesn't mean I approve of all that goes on here, and there are a lot of other white people who feel the same."

"If you and so many others feel that way," said Uncle Hammer with a wry sneer, "then how come them Wallaces ain't in jail?"

"Hammer—" Big Ma started.

"Because," answered Mr. Jamison candidly, "there aren't enough of those same white people who would admit how they feel, or even if they did, would hang a white man for killing a black one. It's as simple as that."

Uncle Hammer smiled slightly and shook his head, but his eyes showed a grudging respect for Mr. Jamison.

"Backing the loan will be strictly a business matter. In the fall when the crops are in, those people who've bought the goods in Vicksburg will have to pay for them. If they don't, then I'll have to. Of course, as a businessman, I'm hoping that I won't have to put out a penny—my own cash box isn't exactly overflowing—so there'll have to be a credit limit. Still, it would lend me a great deal of satisfaction to know that I was a part of all this." He looked around. "What do you think?"

"You know it ain't hardly likely," Papa said, "that after accounts are figured, there'll be any money to pay any debts at all, except those up at that Wallace store."

Mr. Jamison nodded knowingly. "But the offer still stands."

Papa inhaled deeply. "Well, then, I'd say it's up to those people who'd be buying on your signature. They want to do it, then we got no say in it. We always pay cash."

"You know if you sign that credit," said Uncle Hammer, "you won't be the most popular man down in here. You thought about that?"

"Yes," said Mr. Jamison thoughtfully, "my wife and I discussed it fully. We realize what could happen. . . . But I'm just wondering if you do. Besides the fact that a number of white folks around here resent this land you've got and your independent attitude, there's Harlan Granger. Now I've known Harlan all my life, and he's not going to like this."

I wanted to ask what Mr. Granger had to do with anything, but common sense told me that I would only earn eviction by asking. But then Mr. Jamison went on and explained without any prodding from me.

"Ever since we were boys, Harlan's lived in the past. His grandmother filled him with all kinds of tales about the glory of the South before the war. You know, back then the Grangers had one of the biggest plantations in the state and Spokane County practically belonged to them . . . and they thought it did too. They were consulted about everything concerning this area and they felt it was up to them to see that things worked smoothly, according to the law—a law basically for whites. Well, Harlan feels the same now as his grandmother did back then. He also feels strongly about this land and he resents the fact that you won't sell it back to him. You back the credit with it now and he'll seize this opportunity to take it away from you. You can count on it."

He paused, and when he spoke again his voice had grown so quiet I had to lean forward to hear his next words. "And if you continue to encourage people not to shop at the Wallace store, you could still lose it. Don't forget that Harlan leases that store land to the Wallaces and gets a hefty percentage of its revenue. Before he let the Wallaces set up storekeeping, he was only getting his sharecroppers' money. Now he gets a nice bit of Montier's and Harrison's sharecroppers' money too since both of those plantations are too small to have a store, and he's not hardly going to stand for your interfering with it.

"But even more important than all that, you're pointing a finger right at the Wallaces with this boycott business. You're not only accusing them of murder, which in this case would be only a minor consideration because the man killed was black, but you're saying they should be punished for it. That they should be punished just as if they had killed a white man, and punishment of a white man for a wrong done to a black man would denote equality. Now *that is* what Harlan Granger absolutely will not permit."

Mr. Jamison was silent, waiting; no one else spoke and he went on again.

"What John Henry Berry and his brother were accused of—making advances to a white woman—goes against the grain of Harlan Granger and most other white folks in this community more than anything else, you know that. Harlan may not believe in the methods of the Wallaces, but he'll definitely support them. Believe me on that."

Mr. Jamison picked up his briefcase, ran his fingers through his graying hair, and met Papa's eyes. "The sad thing is, you know in the end you can't beat him or the Wallaces."

Papa looked down at the boys and me awaiting his reply, then nodded slightly, as if he agreed. "Still," he said, "I want these children to know we tried, and what we can't do now, maybe one day they will."

"I do hope that's so, David," murmured Mr. Jamison going to the door. "I truly hope that's so."

In the days that followed Mr. Jamison's visit, Papa, Mama, and Uncle Hammer went to the houses of those families who were considering shopping in Vicksburg. On the fourth day Papa and Uncle Hammer again went to Vicksburg, but this time in the wagon with Mr. Morrison. Their journey took two days and when they returned, the wagon was loaded with store-bought goods.

"What's all that?" I asked Papa as he jumped from the wagon. "That for us?"

"No, Cassie girl. It's things folks ordered from Vicksburg."

I wanted to ask more questions about the trip, but Papa seemed in a hurry to be off again and my questions went unanswered until the following day, when Mr. Granger arrived. Christopher-John and I were drawing water from the well when the silver Packard glided to a smooth stop in the drive and Mr. Granger stepped out. He stared sourfaced at Uncle Hammer's Packard in the barn, then opened the gate to the front yard and stepped briskly across the lawn to the house.

Hastily Christopher-John and I tugged on the well rope, pulled up the water tube, and poured the water into the bucket. Each of us gripping a side of the heavy bucket, we hurried to the back porch where we deposited it, then tiptoed silently through the empty kitchen to the door leading to Mama and Papa's room. Little Man and Stacey, just leaving the room under Mama's orders, allowed the door to remain slightly cracked, and all four of us huddled against it stepladder fashion.

"You sure giving folks something to talk 'bout with that car of yours, Hammer," Mr. Granger said in his folksy dialect as he sat down with a grunt across from Papa. In spite of his college education he always spoke this way. "What they got you doing up North? Bootlegging whiskey?" He laughed dryly, indicating that the question was to be taken lightly, but his eyes tight on Uncle Hammer showed that he intended to have an answer.

Uncle Hammer, leaning against the fireplace mantel, did not laugh. "Don't need to bootleg," he said sullenly. "Up there I got me a man's job and they pay me a man's wages for it."

Mr. Granger studied Uncle Hammer. Uncle Hammer wore, as he had every day since he had arrived, sharply creased pants, a vest over a snow-white shirt, and shoes that shone like midnight. "You right citified, ain't you? Course you always did think you was too good to work in the fields like other folks."

"Naw, that ain't it," said Uncle Hammer. "I just ain't never figured fifty cents a day was worth a child's time, let alone a man's wages." Uncle Hammer said nothing else; he didn't need to. Everyone knew that fifty cents was the top price paid to any day laborer, man, woman, or child, hired to work in the Granger fields.

Mr. Granger ran his tongue around his teeth, making his lips protrude in odd half circles, then he turned from Uncle Hammer to Papa. "Some folks tell me y'all running a regular traveling store up here. Hear tell a fellow can get just 'bout anything he wants from up at Tate's in Vicksburg if he just lets y'all know."

Papa met Mr. Granger's eyes, but did not speak.

Mr. Granger shook his head. "Seems to me you folks are just stirring up something. Y'all got roots in this community. Even got yourselves that loan Paul Edward made from the First National Bank up in Strawberry for that eastern two hundred acres. Course now with times like they are, that mortgage could come due anytime . . . and if it comes due and y'all ain't got the money to pay it, y'all could lose this place."

"Ain't gonna lose it," said Uncle Hammer flatly.

Mr. Granger glanced up at Uncle Hammer, then back to Papa. He took a cigar from his pocket, then a knife to cut off the tip. After he had thrown the tip into the fire, he settled back in his chair and lit the cigar while Papa, Mama, Uncle Hammer, and Big Ma waited for him to get on. Then he said: "This is a fine community. Got fine folks in it—both white and colored. Whatever's bothering you people, y'all just tell me. We'll get it straightened out without all this big to-do."

Uncle Hammer laughed outright. Mr. Granger looked up sharply, but Uncle Hammer eyed him insolently, a smile still on his lips. Mr. Granger, watching him, cautioned sternly, "I don't like trouble here. This is a quiet and peaceful place. . . . I aim to see it stays that way." Turning back to Papa, he continued. "Whatever problems we have, we can work them out. I ain't gonna hide that I think y'all making a big mistake, both for the community and for yourselves, going all the way down to Vicksburg to do your shopping. That don't seem very neighborly—"

"Neither does burning," said Uncle Hammer.

Mr. Granger puffed deeply on his cigar and did not look at Uncle Hammer. When he spoke again it was to Big Ma. His voice was harsh, but he made no comment on what Uncle Hammer had said. "I don't think your Paul Edward would've condoned something like this and risked losing this place. How come you let your boys go do it?"

Big Ma smoothed the lap of her dress with her hands. "They grown and it's they land. I got no more say in it."

Mr. Granger's eyes showed no surprise, but he pursed his lips again and ran his tongue around his teeth. "The price of cotton's mighty low, y'all know that," he said finally. "Could be that I'll have to charge my people more of their crops next summer just to make ends meet. . . . I'd hate to do it, 'cause if I did my people wouldn't hardly have enough to buy winter stores, let alone be able to pay their debts. . . ."

There was a tense, waiting silence before his glance slid to Papa again.

"Mr. Joe Higgins up at First National told me that he couldn't hardly honor a loan to folks who go around stirring up a lot of bad feelings in the community—"

"And especially stirring the colored folks out of their place," interjected Uncle Hammer calmly.

Mr. Granger paled, but did not turn to Uncle Hammer. "Money's too scarce," he continued as if he had not heard, "and folks like that are a poor risk. You ready to lose your land, David, because of this thing?"

Papa was lighting his pipe. He did not look up until the flame had caught in the tobacco and held there. Then he turned to Mr. Granger. "Two hundred acres of this place been Logan land for almost fifty years now, the other two hundred for fifteen. We've been through bad times and good times but we ain't never lost none of it. Ain't gonna start now."

Mr. Granger said quietly, "It was Granger land before it was Logan."

"Slave land," said Papa

Mr. Granger nodded. "Wouldn't have lost this section if it hadn't been stolen by your Yankee carpetbaggers after the war. But y'all keep on playing Santa Claus and I'm gonna get it back—real easy. I want you to know that I plan to do whatever I need to, to keep peace down in here."

Papa took the pipe from his mouth and stared into the fire. When he faced Mr. Granger again his voice was very quiet, very distinct, very sure. "You being white, you can just 'bout plan on anything you want. But I tell you this one thing: You plan on getting this land, you're planning on the wrong thing."

Mama's hand crossed almost unseen to Papa's arm.

Mr. Granger looked up slyly. "There's lots of ways of stopping you, David."

Papa impaled Mr. Granger with an icy stare. "Then you'd better make them good," he said.

Mr. Granger stood to go, a smile creeping smugly over his lips as if he knew a secret but refused to tell. He glanced at Uncle Hammer, then turned and left, leaving the silence behind him.

Chapter

8

"Uh . . . Miz Lillian Jean, wouldja wait up a minute, please?"

"Cassie, you cracked?" cried Stacey. "Cassie, where you . . . get back here! Cassie!"

Stacey's words faded into the gray stillness of the January morning as I turned deaf ears to him and hurried after Lillian Jean. "Thanks for waiting up," I said when I caught up with her.

She stared down at me irritably. "What you want?"

"Well," I said, walking beside her, "I been thinking 'bout what happened in Strawberry back last month."

"Yeah?" commented Lillian Jean suspiciously.

"Well, to tell you the truth, I was real upset for a while there. But my papa told me it don't do no good sitting around being mad. Then I seen how things was. I mean, I should've seen it all along. After all, I'm who I am and you're who you are."

Lillian Jean looked at me with astonishment that I could see the matter so clearly. "Well, I'm glad you finally learned the way of things."

"Oh, I did," I piped readily. "The way I see it— here, let me take them books for you, Miz Lillian Jean—the way I see it, we all gotta do what we gotta do. And that's what I'm gonna do from now on. Just what I gotta."

"Good for you, Cassie," replied Lillian Jean enthusiastically. "God'll bless you for it."

"You think so?"

"Why, of course!" she exclaimed. "God wants all his children to do what's right."

"I'm glad you think so . . . Miz Lillian Jean."

When we reached the crossroads; I waved good-bye to Lillian Jean and waited for the others. Before they reached me, Little Man exclaimed, "Owwww I'm gonna tell Mama! Carrying that ole dumb Lillian Jean's books!"

"Cassie, whatja do that for?" questioned Christopher-John, his round face pained.

"Ah, shoot," laughed T.J. "Ole Cassie jus' learned she better do what's good for her if she don't want no more of Mr. Simms's back hand."

I clinched my fists behind me, and narrowed my eyes in the Logan gaze, but managed to hold my tongue.

Stacey stared at me strangely, then turned and said, "We'd better get on to school."

As I followed, Jeremy touched my arm timidly. "C-Cassie, you didn't have to do that. That—that ole Lillian Jean, she ain't worth it."

I stared at Jeremy, trying to understand him. But he shied away from me and ran down the road after his sister.

"Mama gonna whip you good, too," said prideful Little Man, still fuming as we approached the school. "'Cause I'm gonna sure tell it."

"Naw you ain't," said Stacey. There was a shocked silence as all heads turned to him. "This here thing's between Cassie and Lillian Jean and ain't nobody telling nobody nothin' 'bout this." He stared directly at T.J., caught his eye, and repeated, "Nobody."

"Ah, man!" cried T.J. "It ain't none of my business." Then, after a moment's silence, he added, "I got too many worries of my own to worry 'bout Cassie Uncle Tomming Lillian Jean."

My temper almost flew out of my mouth, but I

pressed my lips tightly together, forcing it to stay inside.

"Them final examinations comin' up in two weeks, man, and ain't no way I can afford to fail them things again," T.J. continued.

"Then you won't," said Stacey.

"Shoot, that's what I thought last year. But your mama makes up the hardest examinations she know how." He paused, sighed, and ventured, "Bet though if you kinda asked her 'bout what kind of questions—"

"T.J., don't you come talking to me 'bout no more cheating!" cried Stacey angrily. "After all that trouble I got in the last time 'count of you. You got questions, you ask Mama yourself, but you say one more word to me 'bout them tests, I'm gonna—"

"All right, all right." T.J. smiled in feigned apology. "It's just that I'm gonna have to figure out somethin'."

"I got a solution," I said, unable to resist just one bit of friendly advice.

"What's that?"

"Try studying."

After Uncle Hammer left on New Year's Day, Papa and I had gone into the forest, down the cow path, and to the misty hollow where the trees lay fallen. For a while we stood looking again at the destruction, then, sitting on one of our fallen friends, we talked in quiet, respectful tones, observing the soft mourning of the forest.

When I had explained the whole Strawberry business to Papa, he said, slowly, "You know the Bible says you're s'pose to forgive these things."

"Yessir," I agreed, waiting.

"S'pose to turn the other cheek."

"Yessir."

Papa rubbed his moustache and looked up at the trees standing like sentinels on the edge of the hollow, listening. "But the way I see it, the Bible didn't mean for you to be no fool. Now one day, maybe I can forgive John Andersen for what he done to these trees, but I ain't gonna forget it. I figure forgiving is not letting something nag at you—rotting you out. Now if I hadn't done what I done, then I couldn't've forgiven myself, and that's the truth of it."

I nodded gravely and he looked down at me. "You're a lot like me, Cassie girl, but you got yourself a bad temper like your Uncle Hammer. That temper can get you in trouble."

"Yessir."

"Now this thing between you and Lillian Jean, most folks would think you should go around doing what she tell you . . . and maybe you should—"

"Papa!"

"Cassie, there'll be a whole lot of things you ain't gonna wanna do but you'll have to do in this life just so you can survive. Now I don't like the idea of what Charlie Simms did to you no more than your Uncle Hammer, but I had to weigh the hurt of what happened to you to what could've happened if I went after him. If I'd've gone after Charlie Simms and given him a good thrashing like I felt like doing, the hurt to all of us would've been a whole lot more than the hurt you received, so I let it be. I don't like letting it be, but I can live with that decision.

"But there are other things, Cassie, that if I'd let be, they'd eat away at me and destroy me in the end. And it's the same with you, baby. There are things you can't back down on, things you gotta take a stand on. But it's up to you to decide what them things are. You have to demand respect in this world, ain't nobody just gonna hand it to you. How you carry yourself, what you stand for—that's how you gain respect. But, little one, ain't nobody's respect worth more than your own. You understand that?"

"Yessir."

"Now, there ain't no sense in going around being mad. You clear your head so you can think sensibly. Then I want you to think real hard on whether or not Lillian Jean's worth taking a stand about, but keep in mind that Lillian Jean probably won't be the last white person to treat you this way." He turned toward me so that he looked me full in the face, and the seriousness of his eyes startled me. He held my chin up with the wide flat of his hard hand. "This here's an important decision, Cassie, very important—I want you to understand that—but I think you can handle it. Now, you listen to me, and you listen good. This thing, if you make the wrong decision and Charlie Simms gets involved, then I get involved and there'll be trouble.

"B-big trouble?" I whispered. "Like the trees?"

"Don't know," said Papa "But it could be bad."

I pondered his words, then I promised, "Mr. Simms ain't never gonna hear 'bout it, Papa."

Papa studied me. "I'll count on that, Cassie girl I'll count real hard on that."

For the month of January I was Lillian Jean's slave and she thoroughly enjoyed it. She even took to waiting for me in the morning with Jeremy so that I could carry her books. When friends of hers walked with us, she bragged about her little colored friend and almost hugged herself with pleasure when I called her "Miz" Lillian Jean. When we were alone, she confided her secrets to me: the boy she had passionately loved for the past year and the things she had done to attract his attention (with no success, I might add); the secrets of the girls she couldn't stand as well as those she could; and even a tidbit or two about her elder brothers' romantic adventures. All I had to do to prime the gossip pump was smile nicely and whisper a "Miz Lillian Jean" every now and then. I *almost* hated to see the source dry up.

At the end of examination day, I shot out of Miss Crocker's class and hurried into the yard. I was eager to get to the crossroads to meet Lillian Jean; I had promised myself to first take care of the examinations and then . . .

"Little Man! Claude! Christopher-John! Come on, y'all!" I cried. "There's Stacey!" The four of us dashed across the yard trailing Stacey and T.J. to the road. When we caught up with them, it was obvious that the jovial mask T.J. always wore had been stripped away.

"She did it on purpose!" T.J. accused, a nasty scowl twisting his face.

"Man, you was cheating!" Stacey pointed out. "What you 'spect for her to do?"

"She could've give me a break. Warn't nothin' but a couple bits of ole paper. Didn't need 'em nohow."

"Well, whatja have them for?"

"Ah, man, leave me be! All y'all Logans think y'all so doggone much with y'all's new coats and books and shiny new Packards!" He swirled around, glaring down at Christopher-John, Little Man, and me. "I'm sick of all y'all. Your mama and your papa, too!" Then he turned and fled angrily up the road.

"T.J.! Hey, man, where you going?" Stacey yelled after him. T.J. did not answer. The road swelled into a small hill and he disappeared on the other side of it. When we reached the crossroads and saw no sign of him on the southern road leading home, Stacey asked Claude, "Where he go?"

Claude looked shame-faced and rubbed one badly worn shoe against the other. "Down to that ole store, I reckon."

Stacey sighed. "Come on then, we'd better get on home. He'll be all right by tomorrow."

"Y'all go on," I said. "I gotta wait for Lillian Jean."

"Cassie—"

"I'll catch up with ya," I said before Stacey could lecture me. "Here, take my books, will ya?" He looked at me as if he should say something else, but deciding not to, he pushed the younger boys on and followed them.

When Lillian Jean appeared, I sighed thankfully that only Jeremy was with her; it could be today for sure. Jeremy, who seemed to be as disappointed in me as Little Man, hurried on to catch Stacey. That was fine, too; I knew he would. I took Lillian Jean's books, and as we sauntered down the road, I only half listened to her; I was sweeping the road, looking for the deep wooded trail I had selected earlier in the week. When I saw it, I interrupted Lillian Jean apologetically. "'Scuse me, Miz Lillian Jean, but I got a real nice surprise for you . . . found it just the other day down in the woods."

"For me?" questioned Lillian Jean. "Ah, you is a sweet thing, Cassie. Where you say it is?"

"Come on. I'll show you."

I stepped into the dry gully and scrambled onto the bank. Lillian Jean hung back. "It's all right," I assured her. "It ain't far. You just gotta see it, Miz Lillian Jean."

That did it. Grinning like a Cheshire cat, she

crossed the gully and hopped onto the bank. Following me up the overgrown trail into the deep forest, she asked, "You sure this is the way, little Cassie?"

"Just a bit further . . . up ahead there. Ah, here it is." We entered a small dark clearing with hanging forest vines, totally hidden from the road.

"Well? Where's the surprise?"

"Right here," I said, smashing Lillian Jean's books on the ground.

"Why, what you do that for?" Lillian Jean asked, more startled than angry.

"I got tired of carrying 'em," I said.

"This what you brought me all the way down here for! Well, you just best get untired and pick 'em up again." Then, expecting that her will would be done with no more than that from her, she turned to leave the glade.

"Make me," I said quietly.

"What?" The shock on her face was almost comical.

"Said make me."

Her face paled. Then, red with anger, she stepped daintily across the clearing and struck me hard across the face. For the record, she had hit me first; I didn't plan on her hitting me again.

I flailed into her, tackling her with such force that we both fell. After the first shock of my actually laying hands on her, she fought as best she could, but she was no match for me. I was calm and knew just where to strike. I punched her in the stomach and buttocks, and twisted her hair, but not once did I touch her face; she, expending her energy in angry, nasty name-calling, clawed at mine, managing to scratch twice. She tried to pull my hair but couldn't, for I had purposely asked Big Ma to braid it into flat braids against my head.

When I had pinned Lillian Jean securely beneath me, I yanked unmercifully on her long, loose hair and demanded an apology for all the names she had called me, and for the incident in Strawberry. At first she tried to be cute—"Ain't gonna 'pologize to no nigger!" she sassed.

"You wanna be bald, girl?"

And she apologized. For herself and for her father. For her brothers and her mother. For Strawberry and Mississippi, and by the time I finished jerking at her head, I think she would have apologized for the world being round had I demanded it. But when I let her go and she had sped safely to the other side of the clearing with the trail in front of her, she threatened to tell her father.

"You do that, Lillian Jean. You just do that and I'm gonna make sure all your fancy friends know how you keeps a secret. Bet you won't be learning no more secrets after that."

"Cassie! You wouldn't do that. Not after I trusted you—"

"You mutter one word of this to anybody, Lillian Jean," I said, attempting to narrow my eyes like Papa's, "just one person and everybody at Jefferson Davis is gonna know who you crazy 'bout and all your other business . . . and you know I know. Besides, if anybody ever did find out 'bout this fight, you'd be laughed clear up to Jackson. You here going on thirteen, getting beat up by a nine-year-old."

I was starting up the trail, feeling good about myself, when Lillian Jean asked, bewildered, "But, Cassie, why? You was such a nice little girl. . . ."

I stared at her astonished. Then I turned and left the forest, not wanting to believe that Lillian Jean didn't even realize it had all been just a game.

"Cassie Logan!"

"Yes'm, Miz Crocker?"

"That's the third time I've caught you day-dreaming this morning. Just because you managed to come in first on the examinations last week doesn't mean a thing this week. We're in a new quarter and everyone's slate is clean. You'll make no A's by daydreaming. You understand that?"

"Yes'm," I said, not bothering to add that she repeated herself so much that all a body had to do was listen to the first few minutes of her lesson to be free to daydream to her heart's content.

"I think you'd just better sit in the back where you're not so comfortable," she said. "Then maybe you'll pay more attention."

"But—"

Miss Crocker raised her hand, indicating that she did not want to hear another word, and banished me to the very last row in front of the window. I slid onto the cold seat after its former occupant had eagerly left it for my warm quarters by the stove. As soon as Miss Crocker turned away, I mumbled a few indignant phrases, then hugged my Christmas sweater to me. I tried to pay attention to Miss Crocker but the cold creeping under the windowsill made it impossible. Unable to bear the draft, I decided to line the sill with paper from my notebook. I ripped out the paper, then turned to the window. As I did, a man passed under it and disappeared.

The man was Kaleb Wallace.

I raised my hand. "Uh, Miz Crocker, may I be excused please, ma'am? I gotta . . . well, you know"

As soon as I had escaped Miss Crocker, I dashed to the front of the building. Kaleb Wallace was standing in frontof the seventh-grade-class building talking to Mr. Wellever and two white men whom I couldn't make out from where I stood. When the men entered the building, I turned and sped to the rear and carefully climbed onto the woodpile stacked behind it. I peeked cautiously through a broken window into Mama's classroom. The men were just entering, Kaleb Wallace first, followed by a man I didn't know and Mr. Harlan Granger.

Mama seemed startled to see the men, but when Mr. Granger said, "Been hearing 'bout your teaching, Mary, so as members of the school board we thought we'd come by and learn something," she merely nodded and went on with her lesson. Mr. Wellever left the room, returning shortly with three folding chairs for the visitors; he himself remained standing.

Mama was in the middle of history and I knew that was bad. I could tell Stacey knew it too; he sat tense near the back of the room, his lips very tight, his eyes on the men. But Mama did not flinch; she always started her history class the first thing in the morning when the students were most alert, and I knew that the hour was not yet up. To make matters worse, her lesson for the day was slavery. She spoke on the cruelty of it; of the rich economic cycle it generated as slaves produced the raw products for the factories of the North and Europe; how the country profited and grew from the free labor of a people still not free.

Before she had finished, Mr. Granger picked up a student's book, flipped it open to the pasted-over front cover, and pursed his lips. "Thought these books belonged to the county," he said, interrupting her. Mama glanced over at him, but did not reply. Mr. Granger turned the pages, stopped, and read something. "I don't see all them things you're teaching in here."

"That's because they're not in there," Mama said.

"Well, if it ain't in here, then you got no right teaching it. This book's approved by the Board of Education and you're expected to teach what's in it."

"I can't do that."

"And why not?"

Mama, her back straight and her eyes fixed on the men, answered, "Because all that's in that book isn't true."

Mr. Granger stood. He laid the book back on the student's desk and headed for the door. The other board member and Kaleb Wallace followed. At the door Mr. Granger stopped and pointed at Mama. "You must be some kind of smart, Mary, to know more than the fellow who wrote that book. Smarter than the school board, too, I reckon."

Mama remained silent, and Mr. Wellever gave her no support.

"In fact," Mr. Granger continued, putting on his hat, "you so smart I expect you'd best just forget about teaching altogether . . . then thataway you'll have plenty of time to write your own book." With that he turned his back on her, glanced at Mr. Wellever to make sure his meaning was clear, and left with the others behind him.

We waited for Mama after school was out. Stacey had sent T.J. and Claude on, and the four of us, silent and patient, were sitting on the steps when Mama emerged. She smiled down at us, seemingly not surprised that we were there.

I looked up at her, but I couldn't speak. I had never really thought much about Mama's teaching before; that was just a part of her being Mama. But now that she could not teach, I felt resentful and angry, and I hated Mr. Granger.

"You all know?" she asked. We nodded as she

slowly descended the stairs. Stacey took one handle of her heavy black satchel and I took the other. Christopher-John and Little Man each took one of her hands, and we started across the lawn.

"M-Mama," said Christopher-John when we reached the road, "can't you ever teach no more?"

Mama did not answer immediately. When she did, her voice was muffled. "Somewhere else maybe, but not here—at least not for a while."

"But how's come, Mama?" demanded Little Man. "How's come?"

Mama bit into her lower up and gazed at the road. "Because, baby" she said finally, "I taught things some folks just didn't want to hear."

When we reached home, Papa and Mr. Morrison were both in the kitchen with Big Ma drinking coffee. As we entered, Papa searched our faces. His eyes settled on Mama; the pain was in her face. "What's wrong?" he asked.

Mama sat down beside him. She pushed back a strand of hair that had worked its way free of the chignon, but it fell back into her face again and she left it there. "I got fired."

Big Ma put down her cup weakly without a word.

Papa reached out and touched Mama. She said, "Harlan Granger came to the school with Kaleb Wallace and one of the school-board members. Somebody had told them about those books I'd pasted over . . . but that was only an excuse. They're just getting at us any way they can because of shopping in Vicksburg." Her voice cracked. "What'll we do, David? We needed that job."

Papa gently pushed the stray hair back over her ear. "We'll get by. . . . Plant more cotton maybe. But we'll get by." There was quiet reassurance in his voice.

Mama nodded and stood.

"Where you goin', child?" Big Ma asked.

"Outside. I want to walk for a bit."

Christopher-John, Little Man, and I turned to follow her, but Papa called us back. "Leave your mama be," he said.

As we watched her slowly cross the backyard to the barren garden and head toward the south pasture, Mr. Morrison said, "You know with you here, Mr. Logan, you got no need of me. Maybe there's work to be had around here. . . . Maybe I could get something . . . help you out."

Papa stared across at Mr. Morrison. "There's no call for you to do that," he said. "I'm not paying you anything as it is."

Mr. Morrison said softly, "I got me a nice house to live in, the best cooking a man could want, and for the first time in a long time I got me a family. That's right good pay, I'd say."

Papa nodded. "You're a good man, Mr. Morrison, and I thank you for the offer, but I'll be leaving in a few weeks and I'd rather you was here." His eyes focused on Mama again, a tiny figure in the distance now.

"Papa," rasped Christopher-John, moving close to him, "M-Mama gonna be all right?"

Papa turned and, putting his arms around Christopher-John, drew him even nearer. "Son, your mama . . . she's born to teaching like the sun is born to shine. And it's gonna be hard on her not teaching anymore. It's gonna be real hard 'cause ever since she was a wee bitty girl down in the Delta she wanted to be a teacher."

"And Grandpa wanted her to be one, too, didn't he, Papa?" said Christopher-John.

Papa nodded. "Your mama was his baby child and

every penny he'd get his hands on he'd put it aside for her schooling . . . and that wasn't easy for him either cause he was a tenant farmer and he didn't see much cash money. But he'd promised your grandmama 'fore she died to see that your mama got an education, and when your mama 'come high school age, he sent her up to Jackson to school, then on to teacher training school. It was just 'cause he died her last year of schooling that she come on up here to teach 'stead of going back to the Delta."

"And y'all got married and she ain't gone back down there no more," interjected Little Man.

Papa smiled faintly at Little Man and stood up. "That's right, son. She was too smart and pretty to let get away." He stooped and looked out the window again, then back at us. "She's a strong, fine woman, your mama, and this thing won't keep her down . . . but it's hurt her bad. So I want y'all to be extra thoughtful for the next few days—and remember what I told you, you hear?"

"Yessir, Papa," we answered.

Papa left us then and went onto the back porch. There he leaned against the porch pillar for several minutes staring out toward the pasture; but after a while he stepped into the yard and crossed the garden to join Mama.

"T.J.? You sure?" Stacey asked Little Willie Wiggins at recess the next day. Little Willie nodded morosely and answered, "Heard it myself. Clarence, too. Was standin' right up 'side him at the store when he told Mr. Kaleb. Come talkin' 'bout how Miz Logan failed him on purpose and then said she wasn't a good teacher and that she the one stopped everybody from comin' up to they store. Said she even was destroyin' school property—talkin' 'bout them books, you know."

"Who's gonna take him?" I cried.

"Hush, Cassie," said Stacey. "How come you just telling this now, Little Willie?"

Little Willie shrugged. "Guess I got fooled by ole T.J. Clarence and me, we told him we was gonna tell it soon as we left the store, but T.J. asked us not to do it. Said he was goin' right back and tell them it wasn't nothin' but a joke, what he said. And he went back too, and I thought nothin' was gonna come of it." He hesitated, then confessed, "Didn't say nothin' 'bout it before 'cause me and Clarence wasn't s'pose to be up there ourselves . . . but then here come Mr. Granger yesterday and fires Miz Logan. I figure that's T.J.'s doin'."

"He probably figured it too," I said. "That's why he ain't in school today."

"Talking 'bout he sick," said Christopher-John.

"If he ain't now, he gonna be," prophesied Little Man, his tiny fists balled for action. " 'Round here telling on Mama."

After school when Claude turned up the forest trail leading to the Avery house, we went with him. As we emerged from the forest into the Avery yard, the house appeared deserted, but then we spied T.J., lazily swinging straddle-legged atop an inner tube hanging from an old oak in the front yard. Stacey immediately charged toward him, and when T.J. saw him coming he tried to swing his long right leg over the tube to escape. He didn't make it. Stacey jumped up on the inner tube, giving them both a jerky ride before they landed hard on Mrs. Avery's azalea bush.

"Man, what's the matter with you?" T.J. cried as he rolled from under Stacey to glance back at the flattened bush. "My mama gonna kill me when she see that bush."

Stacey jumped up and jerked at T.J.'s collar. "Was you the one? Did you do it?"

T.J. looked completely bewildered. "Do what? What you talkin' 'bout?"

"Didja tell it? You tell them Wallaces 'bout Mama?"

"Me?" asked T.J. "Me? Why, man, you oughta know me better'n that."

"He do know you," I said. "How come you think we up here?"

"Hey, now, wait a minute," objected T.J. "I don't know what somebody been tellin' y'all, but I ain't told them Wallaces nothin'."

"You was down there," Stacey accused. "The day Mama caught you cheating, you went down to them Wallaces."

"Well, that don't mean nothin'," said T. J., jerking away from Stacey's grip and hopping to his feet. "My daddy says I can go down there if I wanna. Don't mean I told them ole folks nothin' though."

"Heard you told them all sorts of things . . . like Mama didn't know nothin' and she wasn't even teaching what she s'pose to—"

"Didn't neither!" denied T.J. "Ain't never said that! All I said was that it was her that . . ." His voice trailed off as he realized he had said too much, and he began to laugh uneasily. "Hey, look, y'all, I don't know how come Miz Logan got fired, but I ain't said nothin' to make nobody fire her. All I said was that she failed me again. A fellow got a right to be mad 'bout somethin' like that, ain't he?"

Stacey's eyes narrowed upon T.J. "Maybe," he said. "But he ain't got no right to go running his mouth off 'bout things that ain't s'pose to be told."

T.J. stepped backward and looked nervously over his shoulder to the south, where the fields lay fallow.

The rutted wagon trail which cut through the fields leading from the distant Granger mansion revealed a thin woman stepping briskly toward us. T.J. seemed to take heart from the figure and grew cocky again. "Don't know who's been tellin', but it ain't been me."

A moment's silence passed, and then Stacey, his eyes cold and condemning, said quietly, "It was you all right, T.J. It was you." Then, turning, he motioned us back toward the forest.

"Ain't you gonna beat him up?" cried a disappointed Little Man.

"What he got coming to him is worse than a beating," replied Stacey.

"What could be worse than that?" asked Christopher-John.

"You'll see," said Stacey. "And so will T.J."

T.J.'s first day back at school after almost a week's absence was less than successful. Avoiding us in the morning, he arrived late, only to be shunned by the other students. At first he pretended that the students' attitude didn't matter, but by the afternoon when school was out, he hurried after us, attempting to convince us that he was merely a victim of circumstances.

"Hey, y'all ain't gonna hold what Little Willie said against me, are you?" he asked.

"You still saying what Little Willie said ain't true?" questioned Stacey.

"Why, shoot, yeah!" he exclaimed. "When I catch up with that little rascal, I'm gonna beat him to a pulp, 'round here tellin' everybody I got Miz Logan fired. Ain't nobody even speakin' to me no more. Little Willie probably told them Wallaces that hisself, so he figures to get out of it by tellin' everybody it was—"

"Ah, stop lying, T.J.," I said testily. "Don't nobody believe you."

"Well, I should've known you wouldn't, Cassie. You never liked me noway."

"Well, anyway, that's the truth," I agreed.

"But," said T.J., grinning again and turning toward Little Man and Christopher-John "my little buddy Christopher-John believes me, don't you, fellow? And you still my pal, ain't you, Little Man?'?

An indignant Little Man looked up at T.J., but before he could speak, easygoing Christopher-John said, "You told on Mama, T.J. Now she all unhappy 'cause she can't teach school no more and it's all your fault, and we don't like you no more!"

"Yeah!" added Little Man in agreement.

T.J. stared down at Christopher-John, not believing that he had said that. Then he laughed uneasily. "I don't know what's got into folks. Everybody's gone crazy—"

"Look," Stacey said, stopping, "first you run off with the mouth to them Wallaces and now you blaming Little Willie for what you done. Why don't you just admit it was you?"

"Hey, man!" T.J. exclaimed; grinning his easy grin. But then, finding that the grin and the smooth words no longer worked, his face dropped. "Oh, all right. All right. So maybe what if I did say somethin 'bout Miz Logan? I can't even remember saying nothin' 'bout it, but if both Little Willie and Clarence said I did then maybe I did. Anyways, I'm real sorry 'bout your mama losin' her job and—"

All of us, including Claude, stared distastefully at T.J. and walked away from him.

"Hey, wait. . . . I said I was sorry, didn't I?" he asked, following us. "Look, what's a fellow got to do anyway? Hey, y'all, look, this here is still ole T.J.! I ain't changed. Y'all can't turn on me just 'cause—"

"You the one turned, T.J.," Stacey called over his shoulder. "Now leave us alone. We don't want no more to do with you."

T.J., for the first time comprehending that we were no longer his friends, stopped. Then, standing alone in the middle of the road, he screamed after us, "Who needs y'all anyway? I been tired of y'all always hangin' 'round for a long while now, but I been too nice to tell ya. . . . I should've known better. What I look like, havin' a bunch of little kids 'round all the time and me here fourteen, near grown. . . . "

We walked on, not stopping.

"Got me better friends than y'all! They give me things and treat me like I'm a man and . . . and they white too. . ."

His voice faded into the wind as we left him and we heard no more.

Chapter 9

Spring. It seeped unseen into the waiting red earth in early March, softening the hard ground for the coming plow and awakening life that had lain gently sleeping through the cold winter. But by the end of March it was evident everywhere: in the barn where three new calves bellowed and chicks the color of soft pale sunlight chirped; in the yard where the wisteria and English dogwood bushes readied themselves for their annual Easter bloom, and the fig tree budded producing the forerunners of juicy, brown fruit for which the boys and I would have to do battle with fig-loving Jack; and in the smell of the earth itself. Rain-drenched, fresh, vital, full of life, spring enveloped all of us.

I was eager to be in the fields again, to feel the furrowed rows of damp, soft earth beneath my feet; eager to walk barefooted through the cool forest, hug the trees, and sit under their protective shadow. But although every living thing knew it was spring, Miss Crocker and the other teachers evidently did not, for school lingered on indefinitely. In the last week of March when Papa and Mr. Morrison began to plow the east field, I volunteered to sacrifice school and help them. My offer was refused and I trudged wearily to school for another week.

"I guess I won't be seein' much of y'all after next Friday," said Jeremy one evening as we neared his forest trail.

"Guess not," said Stacey.

"Be nice if our schools ended at the same time."

"You crazy!" I cried, remembering that Jefferson

Davis didn't dismiss until mid-May.

Jeremy stammered an apology. "I—I just meant we could still see each other." He was silent a moment, then brightened. "Maybe I can come over to see y'all sometime."

Stacey shook his head. "Don't think Papa would like that."

"Well . . . I just thought . . ." He shrugged. "It'll sure be lonely without y'all."

"Lonely?" I asked. "With all them brothers and sisters you got?"

Jeremy frowned. "The little ones, they too young to play with, and the older ones . . . Lillian Jean and R.W. and Melvin, I guess I don't like them very much."

"What you saying?" asked Stacey. "You can't not like your own sister and brothers."

"Well, I can understand that," I said soberly. "I sure don't like them."

"But they're his kin. A fellow's gotta like his own kin."

Jeremy thought about that. "Well, Lillian Jean's all right, I guess. She ain't so persnickety since Cassie stopped bein' her friend." He smiled a secret smile to himself. "But that R.W. and Melvin, they ain't very nice. You oughta see how they treat T.J. . . ." He halted, looked up embarrassed, and was quiet.

Stacey stopped. "How they treat him?"

Jeremy stopped too. "I don't know," he said as if he was sorry he had mentioned it. "They just don't do him right."

"How?" asked Stacey.

"Thought you didn't like him no more."

"Well . . . I don't," replied Stacey defensively. "But I heard he was running 'round with R.W. and Melvin. I wondered why. Them brothers of yours must be eighteen or nineteen."

Jeremy looked up at the sun, squinted, then glanced up his forest trail a few feet ahead. "They brung T.J. by the house a couple of times when Pa wasn't home. They treated him almost friendly like, but when he left they laughed and talked 'bout him— called him names." He squinted again at the trail and said hurriedly, "I better go. . . . See y'all tomorrow."

"Mama, how come you suppose R.W. and Melvin putting in time with T.J.?" I asked as I measured out two heaping tablespoons of flour for the cornbread.

Mama frowned down into the flour barrel. "Only one tablespoon, Cassie, and not so heaping."

"But, Mama, we always use two."

"That barrel will have to last us until Papa goes back to the railroad. Now put it back."

As I returned one tablespoon of flour to the barrel, I again asked, "What you think, Mama? How come them Simmses running 'round with T.J.?"

Mama measured out the baking powder and gave it to me. It was a teaspoon less than we had been using, but I didn't ask her about it. It was running low too.

"I don't really know, Cassie," she said, turning to the stove to stir milk into the butter beans. "They may just want him around because it makes them feel good."

"When T.J.'s around me, he don't make me feel good."

"Well, you told me Jeremy said they were laughing at T.J. behind his back. Some folks just like to keep other folks around to laugh at them . . . use them."

"I wonder how come T.J. don't know they laughing at him? You s'pose he's that dumb?"

"T.J.'s not 'dumb,' Cassie. He just wants attention, but he's going after it the wrong way."

I was going to ask what use T.J. could possibly be to anyone, but I was interrupted by Little Man running into the kitchen. "Mama!" he cried. "Mr. Jamison just drove up!" He had been in the barn cleaning the chicken coop with Christopher-John and stubby particles of straw still clung to his head. I grinned at his mussed appearance but didn't have to tease him before he was gone again.

Mama looked at Big Ma, a question in her eyes, then followed Little Man outside. I decided that the cornbread could wait and dashed after them.

"Girl, get back in here and finish mixin' this cornbread!" muttered Big Ma.

"Yes'm," I said. "I'll be right back." Before Big Ma could reach me, I was out the back door running across the yard to the drive.

Mr. Jamison touched his hat as Mama approached. "How doing, Miz Logan?" he asked.

"Just fine, Mr. Jamison," Mama answered. "And yourself?"

"Fine. Fine," he said absently. "Is David here?"

"He's over in the east field." Mama studied Mr. Jamison "Anything wrong?"

"Oh, no . . . no. Just wanted to speak to him."

"Little Man," Mama said, turning, "go get Papa."

"Oh, no—don't do that. I'll just walk on over there if that's all right. I need the exercise." Mama nodded, and after he had spoken to me Mr. Jamison crossed the yard to the field. Little Man and I started to follow after him but Mama called us back and returned us to our jobs.

Mr. Jamison did not stay long. A few minutes later he emerged from the field alone, got into his car, and left.

When supper was ready, I eagerly grabbed the iron bell before Christopher-John or Little Man could claim it, and ran onto the back porch to summon Papa, Mr. Morrison, and Stacey from the fields. As the three of them washed up on the back porch, Mama went to the end of the porch where Papa stood alone. "What did Mr. Jamison want?" she asked, her voice barely audible.

Papa took the towel Mama handed him, but did not reply immediately. I was just inside the kitchen dipping out the butter beans. I moved closer to the window so that I could hear his answer.

"Don't keep anything from me, David. If there's trouble, I want to know."

Papa looked down at her. "Nothing to worry 'bout, honey. . . . Just seems that Thurston Wallace been in town talking 'bout how he's not gonna let a few smart colored folks ruin his business. Says he's gonna put a stop to this shopping in Vicksburg. That's all."

Mama sighed and stared out across the plowed field to the sloping pasture land. "I'm feeling scared, David," she said.

Papa put down the towel. "Not yet, Mary. It's not time to be scared yet. They're just talking."

Mama turned and faced him. "And when they stop talking?"

"Then . . . then maybe it'll be time. But right now, pretty lady," he said, leading her by the hand toward the kitchen door, "right now I've got better things to think about."

Quickly I poured the rest of the butter beans into the bowl and hurried across the kitchen to the table. As Mama and Papa entered, I slid onto the bench beside Little Man and Christopher-John. Papa beamed down at the table.

"Well, look-a-here!" he exclaimed. "Good ole butter beans and cornbread! You better come on,

Mr. Morrison! You too, son!" he called. "These womenfolks done gone and fixed us a feast."

After school was out, spring drooped quickly toward summer; yet Papa had not left for the railroad. He seemed to be waiting for something, and I secretly hoped that whatever that something was, it would never come so that he would not leave. But one evening as he, Mama, Big Ma, Mr. Morrison, and Stacey sat on the front porch while Christopher-John, Little Man, and I dashed around the yard chasing fireflies, I overheard him say, "Sunday I'm gonna have to go. Don't want to though. I got this gut feeling it ain't over yet. It's too easy."

I released the firefly imprisoned in my hand and sat beside Papa and Stacey on the steps. "Papa, please," I said, leaning against his leg, "don't go this year." Stacey looked out into the falling night, his face resigned, and said nothing.

Papa put out his large hand and caressed my face. "Got to, Cassie girl," he said softly. "Baby, there's bills to pay and ain't no money coming in. Your mama's got no job come fall and there's the mortgage and next year's taxes to think of."

"But, Papa, we planted more cotton this year. Won't that pay the taxes?"

Papa shook his head. "With Mr. Morrison here we was able to plant more, but that cotton is for living on; the railroad money is for the taxes and the mortgage."

I looked back at Mama wanting her to speak, to persuade him to stay, but when I saw her face I knew that she would not. She had known he would leave, just as we all had known.

"Papa, just another week or two, couldn't you—"
"I can't, baby. May have lost my job already."

"But Papa—"

"Cassie, that's enough now," Mama said from the deepening shadows.

I grew quiet and Papa put his arms around Stacey and me, his hands falling casually over our shoulders. From the edge of the lawn where Little Man and Christopher-John had ventured after lightning bugs, Little Man called, "Somebody's coming!" A few minutes later Mr. Avery and Mr. Lanier emerged from the dusk and walked up the sloping lawn. Mama sent Stacey and me to get more chairs for the porch, then we settled back beside Papa still sitting on the steps, his back propped against a pillar facing the visitors.

"You goin' up to the store tomorrow, David?" Mr. Avery asked after all the amenities had been said. Since the first trip in January, Mr. Morrison had made one other trip to Vicksburg, but Papa had not gone with him.

Papa motioned to Mr. Morrison. "Mr. Morrison and me going the day after tomorrow. Your wife brought down that list of things you need yesterday."

Mr. Avery cleared his throat nervously. "It's—it's that list I come 'bout, David . . . . I don't want them things no more."

The porch grew silent.

When no one said anything, Mr. Avery glanced at Mr. Lanier, and Mr. Lanier shook his head and continued. "Mr. Granger making it hard on us, David. Said we gonna have to give him sixty percent of the cotton, 'stead of fifty . . . now that the cotton's planted and it's too late to plant more. . . . Don't s'pose though that it makes much difference. The way cotton sells these days, seems the more we plant, the less money we gets anyways—"

Mr. Avery's coughing interrupted him and he

waited patiently until the coughing had stopped before he went on. "I'm gonna be hard put to pay that debt in Vicksburg, David, but I'm gonna. . . . I want you to know that."

Papa nodded, looking toward the road. "I suppose Montier and Harrison raised their percentages too," he said.

"Montier did," replied Mr. Avery, "but far as I know Mr. Harrison ain't. He's a decent man."

"That does it," Mama sighed wearily.

Papa kept looking out into the darkness. "Forty percent. I expect a man used to living on fifty could live on forty . . . if he wanted to hard enough."

Mr. Avery shook his head. "Times too hard."

"Times are hard for everybody," Papa said.

Mr. Avery cleared his throat. "I know. I—I feel real bad 'bout what T.J. done—"

"I wasn't talking 'bout that," said Papa flatly.

Mr. Avery nodded self-consciously, then leaned forward in his chair and looked out into the forest. "But—but that ain't all Mr. Granger said. Said, too, we don't give up this shoppin' in Vicksburg, we can jus' get off his land. Says he tired of us stirrin' up trouble 'gainst decent white folks. Then them Wallaces, they come by my place, Brother Lanier's, and everybody's on this thing that owes them money. Said we can't pay our debts, they gonna have the sheriff out to get us . . . put us on the chain gang to work it off."

"Oh, good Lord!" exclaimed Big Ma.

Mr. Lanier nodded and added, "Gotta go up to that store by tomorrow to show good faith."

Mr. Avery's coughing started again and for a while there was only the coughing and the silence. But when the coughing ceased, Mr. Lanier said, "I pray to God there was a way we could stay in this thing, but we can't go on no chain gang, David."

Papa nodded. "Don't expect you to, Silas."

Mr. Avery laughed softly. "We sure had 'em goin' for a time though, didn't we?"

"Yes," agreed Papa quietly, "we sure did."

When the men had left, Stacey snapped, "They got no right pulling out! Just 'cause them Wallaces threaten them one time they go jumping all over themselves to get out like a bunch of scared jackrabbits—"

Papa stood suddenly and grabbed Stacey upward. "You, boy, don't you get so grown you go to talking 'bout more than you know. Them men, they doing what they've gotta do. You got any idea what a risk they took just to go shopping in Vicksburg in the first place? They go on that chain gang and their families got nothing. They'll get kicked off that plot of land they tend and there'll be no place for them to go. You understand that?"

"Y-yessir," said Stacey. Papa released him and stared moodily into the night. "You were born blessed, boy, with land of your own. If you hadn't been, you'd cry out for it while you try to survive . . . like Mr. Lanier and Mr. Avery. Maybe even do what they doing now. It's hard on a man to give up, but sometimes it seems there just ain't nothing else he can do."

"I . . . I'm sorry, Papa," Stacey muttered.

After a moment, Papa reached out and draped his arm over Stacey's shoulder.

"Papa," I said, standing to join them, "we giving up too?"

Papa looked down at me and brought me closer, then waved his hand toward the drive. "You see that fig tree over yonder, Cassie? Them other trees all around . . . that oak and walnut, they're a lot bigger and they take up more room and give so much shade they almost overshadow that little ole fig. But that fig tree's got roots that run deep, and it belongs in that yard as much as that oak and walnut. It keeps on blooming, bearing good fruit year after year, knowing all the time it'll never get as big as them other trees. Just keeps on growing and doing what it gotta do. It don't give up. It give up, it'll die. There's a lesson to be learned from that little tree, Cassie girl, 'cause we're like it. We keep doing what we gotta, and we don't give up. We can't."

After Mr. Morrison had retired to his own house and Big Ma, the boys, and I had gone to bed, Papa and Mama remained on the porch, talking in hushed whispers. It was comforting listening to them. Mama's voice a warm, lilting murmur, Papa's a quiet, easyflowing hum. After a few minutes they left the porch and their voices grew faint. I climbed from the bed, careful not to awaken Big Ma, and went to the window. They were walking slowly across the moon-soaked grass, their arms around each other.

"First thing tomorrow, I'm gonna go 'round and see how many folks are still in this thing," Papa said, stopping under the oak near the house. "I wanna know before we make that trip to Vicksburg."

Mama was quiet a moment. "I don't think you and Mr. Morrison should go to Vicksburg right now, David. Not with the Wallaces threatening people like they are. Wait awhile."

Papa reached into the tree and broke off a twig. "We can't just stop taking care of business 'cause of them Wallaces, Mary. You know that."

Mama did not reply.

Papa leaned against the tree. "I think I'll take Stacey with me."

"Now, David, no—"

"He'll be thirteen next month, honey, and he needs to be with me more. I can't take him with me on the railroad, but I can take him with me where I go 'round here. And I want him to know business . . . how to take care of it, how to take care of things when I ain't around."

"David, he's just a boy."

"Baby, a boy get as big as Stacey down here and he's near a man. He's gotta know a man's things. He gotta know how to handle himself."

"I know, but—"

"Mary, I want him strong . . . not a fool like T.J."

"He's got more brains and learning than that," Mama snapped.

"I know," Papa said quietly. "Still it worries me, seeing T.J. turning like he is."

"Seems to me it isn't bothering Joe Avery much. He doesn't seem to be doing anything about it."

Papa allowed the silence to seep between them before he said, "It's not like you, honey, to be bitter."

"I'm not bitter," said Mama, folding her arms across her chest. "It's just that the boy's gotten out of hand, and doesn't seem like anybody's doing anything about it."

"The other day Joe told me he couldn't do nothing with T.J. anymore. That's a hard thing for a man to admit."

"He can still put a good strip of leather against his bottom, can't he?" It was clear that Mama was unsympathetic to Mr. Avery's problem.

"Said he tried, but his health's so poor, he ended up with a bad coughing spell. Got so sick from it, he had to go to bed. Said after that Fannie tried to whip the boy, but T.J.'s stronger than her, and it didn't do no good." Papa paused, then added, "He's gotten pretty sassy, too, I understand."

"Well, sassy or not," Mama grumbled, "they'd better figure out some way of getting that boy back on the right track because he's headed for a whole lot of trouble."

Papa sighed heavily and left the tree. "We'd better go in. I've gotta get an early start if I'm gonna get 'round to everybody."

"You're still set on going to Vicksburg?"

"I told you I was."

Mama laughed lightly in, exasperation. "Sometimes, David Logan, I wonder why I didn't marry sweet, quiet Ronald Carter or nice, mild Harold Davis."

"Because, woman," Papa said, putting his arm around her, "you took one look at big, handsome me and no one else would do." Then they both laughed, and together moved slowly to the side of the house.

Seven families, including ours, still refused to shop at the Wallace store even with the threat of the chain gang. Mama said that the number was not significant enough to hurt the Wallaces, only enough to rile them, and she worried, afraid for Papa, Stacey, and Mr. Morrison to make the trip. But nothing she could say could change Papa's mind and they left as planned on Wednesday morning long before dawn.

On Thursday, when they were to return, it began to rain, a hard, swelling summer rain which brought a premature green darkness to the land and forced us to leave our hoeing of the cotton field and return to the house. As the thunder rumbled overhead, Mama peered out the window at the dark road. "Wonder what's keeping them," she said, more to herself than anyone else.

"Probably got held up someplace," said Big Ma "Could've stopped to get out of this storm."

Mama turned from the window. "You're most likely right," she agreed, picking up a pair of Christopher-John's pants to mend.

As the evening fell into total darkness, we grew silent, the boys and I saying very little, Mama and Big Ma concentrating on their sewing, their brows furrowed. My throat grew tight, and without knowing why I was afraid, I was.

"Mama," I said, "they all right, ain't they?"

Mama stared down at me. "Course they're all right. They're just late, that's all."

"But, Mama, you s'pose maybe somebody done—"

"I think you children better go on to bed," Mama said sharply without letting me finish.

"But I wanna wait up for Papa," objected Little Man.

"Me, too," said sleepy Christopher-John.

"You'll see him in the morning. Now get to bed!"

Since there was nothing we could do but obey, we went to bed. But I could not sleep. A cold fear crept up my body, churning my stomach and tightening its grip on my throat. Finally, when I felt that I was going to be sick from it, I rose and padded silently into Mama and Papa's room.

Mama was standing with her back to me, her arms folded, and Big Ma was still patching. Neither one of them heard the door swing open. I started to speak, but Mama was talking and I decided not to interrupt her. ". . . I've got a good mind to saddle Lady and go looking for them," she said.

"Now, Mary, what good would that do?" Big Ma questioned. "You runnin' 'round out there on that mare by yo'self in this darkness and rain?"

"But something's happened to them! I can feel it."

"It's just in yo' mind, child," Big Ma scoffed unconvincingly. "Them menfolks all right."

"No . . . no," said Mama shaking her head "The Wallaces aren't just in my mind, they—" She stopped suddenly and stood very still.

"Mary—"

"Thought I heard something." The dogs started barking and she turned, half running, across the room. Pushing up the lock in a mad haste, she swung the door open and cried into the storm, "David! David!"

Unable to stay put, I dashed across the room. "Cassie, what you doin' up, girl?" asked Big Ma, swatting me as I passed her. But Mama, staring into the wet night, said nothing when I reached her side.

"Is it them?" I asked.

Out of the darkness a round light appeared, moving slowly across the drive, and Mr. Morrison's voice drifted softly to us. "Go on, Stacey," he said, "I got him." Then Stacey, a flashlight in his hand, came into sight, followed by Mr. Morrison carrying Papa.

"David!" Mama gasped, her voice a frightened whisper.

Big Ma standing behind me stepped back, pulling me with her. She stripped the bed to its sheets and ordered, "Put him right here, Mr. Morrison."

As Mr. Morrison climbed the stairs, we could see that Papa's left leg stuck straight out, immobilized by his shotgun strapped to it with a rope. His head was wrapped in a rag through which the dark redness of his blood had seeped. Mr. Morrison eased Papa through the doorway, careful not to hit the strapped leg, and laid him gently on the bed. Mama went immediately to the bed and took Papa's hand.

"Hey, baby . . ." Papa said faintly , "I'm . . . all right. Just got my leg broke, that's all. . . ."

"Wagon rolled over it," said Mr. Morrison, avoiding Mama's eyes. "We better get that leg set.

Didn't have time on the road."

"But his head—" Mama said, her eyes questioning Mr. Morrison. But Mr. Morrison said nothing further and Mama turned to Stacey. "You all right, son?"

"Yes'm," Stacey said, his face strangely ashen, his eyes on Papa.

"Then get out of those wet things. Don't want you catching pneumonia. Cassie, you go to bed."

"I'll get a fire started," said Big Ma disappearing into the kitchen as Mama turned to the closet to find sheets for making a cast. But Stacey and I remained rooted, watching Papa, and did not move until Christopher-John and Little Man made a sleepy entrance.

"What's going on?" asked Little Man, frowning into the light.

"Go back to bed, children," Mama said, rushing to keep them from coming farther into the room, but before she could reach them Christopher-John spied Papa on the bed and shot past her. "Papa, you got back!"

Mr. Morrison swung him upward before he could jar the bed.

"Wh-what's the matter?" asked Christopher-John, wide awake now. "Papa, what's the matter? How come you got that thing on your head?"

"Your Papa's asleep," said Mama as Mr. Morrison set Christopher-John back down. "Stacey, take them back to bed . . . and get out of those clothes." None of us stirred. "Move when I tell you!" Mama hissed impatiently, her face more worried than angry.

Stacey herded us into the boys' room.

As soon as the door dosed behind us, I asked, "Stacey, how bad Papa hurt?" Stacey felt around for the lamp, lit it, then plopped wearily on the side of the bed. We huddled around him. "Well?"

Stacey shook his head. "I dunno. His leg's busted up by the wagon . . . and he's shot."

"Shot!" Christopher-John and Little Man exclaimed fearfully, but I was silent, too afraid now to speak, to think.

"Mr. Morrison says he don't think the bullet hurt him much. Says he thinks it just hit his skin . . . here." Stacey ran his forefinger along his right temple. "And didn't sink in nowhere."

"But who'd shoot Papa?" asked Little Man, greatly agitated. "Can't nobody just shoot Papa!"

Stacey stood then and motioned Christopher-John and Little Man under the covers. "I've said too much already. Cassie, go on to bed."

I continued to sit, my mind unable to move.

"Cassie, go on now like Mama said."

"How the wagon roll over him? How he get shot?" I blurted out angrily, already plotting revenge against whoever had dared hurt my father.

"Cassie . . . you go on to bed!"

"Ain't moving till you tell me!"

"I'll call Mama," he threatened.

"She too busy," I said, folding my arms and feeling confident that he would tell the story.

He went to the door and opened it. Christopher-John, Little Man, and I watched him eagerly. But he soon closed the door and came back to the bed.

"What was they doing?" asked Little Man.

"Big Ma's tending Papa's head."

"Well, what happened out there?" I repeated.

Stacey sighed despairingly and sat down. "We was coming back from Vicksburg when the back wheels come off," he said, his voice a hollow whisper. "It was already dark and it was raining too, and Papa and Mr. Morrison, they thought somebody done messed with them wheels for both of them to come off at the same time like they did. Then when I told them I'd seen two boys near the wagon when we was in Vicksburg, Papa said we didn't have time to unhitch and unload the wagon like we should to put them wheels back on. He thought somebody was coming after us.

"So after we found the wheels and the bolts, Papa told me to hold the reins real tight on Jack to keep him still. . . . Jack, he was real skittish 'cause of the storm. Then Mr. Morrison went and lifted that wagon all by himself. And it was heavy too, but Mr. Morrison lifted it like it wasn't nothing. Then Papa slipped the first wheel on. . . . That's when he got shot—"

"But who—" I started.

"A truck come up the road and stopped behind us while we was trying to get that wheel on, but didn't none of us hear it coming 'cause of the rain and the thunder and all, and they didn't put their lights on till the truck stopped. Anyways, there was three men in that truck and soon as Papa seen 'em, he reached for his shotgun. That's when they shot him and he fell back with his left leg under the wagon. Then . . . then Jack reared up, scared by the shot, and I—I couldn't hold him . . . and . . . and the wagon rolled over Papa's leg." His voice cracked sharply, and he exploded guiltily, "It's m-my fault his leg's busted!"

I thought on what he had said and, laying my hand on his shoulder, I said, "Naw, it ain't. It's them men's."

Stacey did not speak for a while and I did not prod him to go on. Finally, he cleared his throat and continued huskily. "Soon's I could, I . . . I tied Jack to a tree and run back to Papa, but Papa told me not to move him and to get down in the gully. After them men shot Papa, they come down trying to get Mr. Morrison, but he was too fast and strong for 'em. I couldn't see everything that happened 'cause they didn't always stay in front of them headlights, but I did see Mr. Morrison pick up one of them men like he wasn't nothing but a sack of chicken feathers and fling him down on the ground so hard it must've broke his back. Ain't never seen nothin' like it before in my whole life. Then one of them other two that had a gun shot at Mr. Morrison, but he didn't hit him. Mr. Morrison, he ducked away from the headlights into the darkness and they went after him.

"Couldn't see nothin' then," he said, glancing toward the door where Papa lay. "Heard bones cracking. Heard somebody cursing and crying. Then I couldn't hear nothin' but the rain, and I was real scared. 'Fraid they'd killed Mr. Morrison."

"But they didn't," reminded Little Man, his eyes bright with excitement.

Stacey nodded. "Next thing I seen was a man coming real slow-like into the headlights and pick up the man lying in the middle of the road—the one Mr. Morrison thrown down. He got him into the truck, then come back and helped the other one. That one looked like he had a broke arm. It was hanging all crazy-like at his side. Then they turned the truck around and drove away."

"Then what?" Little Man inquired.

Stacey shrugged. "Nothin'. We put on the other wheel and come on home."

"Who was it?" I rasped, holding my breath.

Stacey looked at me and said flatly, "The Wallaces, I think."

There was a fearful moment's silence, then Christopher-John, tears in his dark eyes, asked, "Stacey, is . . . is Papa gonna die?"

"No! Course not!" denied Stacey too quickly.

"But he was so still—"

"I don't want Papa to die!" wailed Little Man.

"He was just sleeping—like Mama said. That's all."

"Well, when he gonna wake up?" cried Christopher-John, the tears escaping down his plump cheeks.

"In—in the morning," said Stacey, putting a comforting arm around both Christopher-John and Little Man. "Jus' you wait and see. He'll be jus' fine come morning."

Stacey, still in his wet, muddy clothes, said nothing else, and neither did the rest of us. All the questions had been answered, yet we feared, and we sat silently listening to the rain, soft now upon the roof, and watching the door behind which Papa lay, and wished for morning.

Chapter 10

"How does it look?" asked Papa as I passed through the sitting room on my way out the side door. Over a week had passed since he had been injured, and this was his first morning up. He was seated by the cold fireplace, his head still bandaged, his broken leg resting on a wooden chair. His eyes were on Mama at her desk.

Mama put down her pencil and frowned at the open ledger before her. She glanced at me absently and waited until I had closed the screen door behind me, then she said, "David, do you think we should go into this now? You're still not well—"

"I'm well enough to know there's not much left. Now tell me."

I hopped down the steps and sat on the bottom one.

Mama was silent a moment before she answered him. "With Hammer's half of the mortgage money, we've got enough to meet the June payment. . . . "

"Nothing more?"

"A couple of dollars, but that's all."

They were both silent.

"You think we should write Hammer and borrow some money?" Mama asked.

Papa did not answer right away. "No . . ." he said finally. "I still don't want him to know 'bout this thing. If he knows I'm not on the railroad, he'll wanna know why not, and I don't wanna risk that temper of his when he finds out what the Wallaces done."

Mama sighed. "I guess you're right."

"I know I am," said Papa. "Things like they are, he come down here wild and angry, he'll get himself hung. Long as things don't get no worse, we can make it without him. We'll meet that June note with the money we got there." He paused a moment. "We'll probably have to sell a couple of the cows and their calves to make them July and August notes . . . maybe even that ole sow. But by the end of August we should have enough cotton to make that September payment. . . . Course we'll probably have to go all the way to Vicksburg to get it ginned. Can't hardly use Harlan Granger's gin this year."

There was silence again, then Mama said, "David, Mama's been talking about going into Strawberry to the market next—"

"No," Papa said, not letting her finish. "Too much bad feeling there."

"I told her that."

"I'll talk to her. . . . Anything we just gotta have before the first cotton come in?"

"Well . . . you picked up batteries and kerosene on that last trip . . . but what we're going to need more than anything is some insecticide to spray the cotton. The bugs are getting pretty bad. . . ."

"What 'bout food?"

"Our flour and sugar and baking powder and such are low, but we'll make out—we don't have to have biscuits and cornbread every day. We're out of pepper and there's not much salt, but we don't just have to have those either. And the coffee's all gone. . . . The garden's coming along nicely, though. There's no worry there."

"No worry," Papa muttered as both of them grew quiet. Then suddenly there was a sharp explosion as if something had been struck with an angry force. "If only this leg wasn't busted!"

"Don't let Stacey hear you saying that, David," Mama cautioned softly. "You know he blames himself about your leg."

"I told the boy it wasn't his fault. He just wasn't strong enough to hold Jack."

"I know that, but still he blames himself."

Papa laughed strangely. "Ain't this something? Them Wallaces aim a gun at my head and I get my leg broke, and my boy's blaming himself for it. Why, I feel like taking a bullwhip to all three of them Wallaces and not stopping till my arm get so tired I can't raise it one more time."

"You're sounding like Hammer."

"Am I? Well, a lot of times I feel like doing things Hammer's way. I think I'd get a powerful lot of satisfaction from whipping Kaleb Wallace and them brothers of his."

"Hammer's way would get you killed and you know it, so stop talking like that. Don't we already have enough to worry about? Besides, both Thurston and Dewberry Wallace are still laid up, so I hear. Some folks even say that Dewberry's back is broken. In any case, Mr. Morrison must have hurt them pretty bad."

"Where is he, by the way? I haven't seen him this morning."

There was an instant of silence before Mama answered. "Out looking for work again since dawn."

"He ain't gonna find nothing 'round here. I told him that."

"I know," agreed Mama. "But he says he's got to try. David . . ." Mama stopped, and when she spoke again her voice had grown faint, as if she hesitated to say what was on her mind. "David, don't you think he ought to go? I don't want him to, but after what he did to the Wallaces, I'm afraid for him."

"He knows what could happen, Mary, but he wants to stay—and, frankly, we need him here. Don't pester him about it."

"But, David, if—"

Before Mama finished, I spied Mr. Morrison coming west from Smellings Creek. I left the step and hurried to meet him.

"Hello, Mr. Morrison!" I shouted as Jack pulled the wagon up the drive.

"Hello, Cassie," Mr. Morrison greeted me. "Your papa awake?"

"Yessir. He's sitting out of bed this morning."

"Didn't I tell you nothin' could keep him down?"

"Yessir, you did."

He stepped from the wagon and walked toward the house.

"Mr. Morrison, you want me to unhitch Jack for ya?"

"No, Cassie, leave him be. I gotta talk to your papa then I'll be back."

"Hey, ole Jack," I said, patting the mule as I watched Mr. Morrison enter the side door. I thought of returning to my seat on the steps, but decided against it. Instead I remained with Jack, thoughtfully digesting all I had heard, until Mr. Morrison came from the house. He went into the barn, then reappeared with the planter, a plowlike tool with a small round container for dropping seeds attached to its middle. He put the planter into the back of the wagon.

"Where you going now, Mr. Morrison?"

"Down to Mr. Wiggins' place. I seen Mr. Wiggins this morning and he asked to use your Papa's planter. He ain't got no wagon so I told him I'd ask your Papa and if it was all right, I'd bring it to him."

"Ain't it kinda late for seeding?"

"Well, not for what he got in mind. He thought he'd plant himself some summer corn. It'll be ready come September."

"Mr. Morrison, can I go with ya?" I asked as he climbed up on the wagon.

"Well, I'd be right pleased for your company, Cassie. But you'll have to ask your mama."

I ran back to the house. The boys were now in Mama and Papa's room, and when I asked if I could go up to Little Willie's with Mr. Morrison, Little Man and Christopher-John, of course, wanted to go too.

"Mr. Morrison said it'd be all right, Mama."

"Well, don't you get in his way. Stacey, you going?"

Stacey sat across from Papa looking despondently at the broken leg. "Go on, son," said Papa gently. "There's nothing to do here. Give you a chance to talk to Little Willie."

"You sure there ain't something I can do for you, Papa?"

"Just go and have yourself a good ride over to Little Willie's."

Since it had been my idea to ask to go, I claimed the seat beside Mr. Morrison, and the boys climbed in back. Little Willie's family lived on their own forty acres about two miles east of Great Faith. It was a fine morning for a ride and the six miles there sped by quickly with Mr. Morrison singing in his bassest of bass voices and ChristopherJohn, Little Man, and me joining in wherever we could as we passed cotton fields abloom in flowers of white and red and pink. Stacey being in one of his moods did not sing and we let him be.

We stayed less than an hour at the Wiggins farm,

then headed home again. We had just passed Great Faith and were approaching the Jefferson Davis School Road when a ragged pickup came into view. Very quietly Mr. Morrison said, "Cassie, get in back."

"But why, Mr. Mor—"

"Do quick, Cassie, like I say." His voice was barely above a friendly whisper, but there was an urgency in it and I obeyed, scrambling over the seat to join the boys. "Y'all stay down now."

The truck braked noisily with a grating shriek of steel. We stopped. The boys and I peeped over the edge of the wagon. The truck had veered across the road, blocking us.

The truck door swung open and Kaleb Wallace stepped out, pointing a long condemning finger at Mr. Morrison.

He swayed unspeaking for a long, terrible moment, then sputtered, "You big black nigger, I oughta cut your heart out for what you done! My brothers laid up like they is and you still runnin' 'round free as a white man. Downright sinful, that's what it is! Why, I oughta gun you down right where you sit—"

"You gonna move your truck?"

Kaleb Wallace gazed up at Mr. Morrison, then at the truck as if trying to comprehend the connection between the two. "That truck in your way, boy?"

"You gonna move it?"

"I'll move it all right . . . when I get good and ready—"

He stopped abruptly, his eyes bulging in a terrified stare as Mr. Morrison climbed down from the wagon. Mr. Morrison's long shadow fell over him and for a breathless second, Mr. Morrison towered dangerously near him. But as the fear grew white on

Kaleb Wallace's face, Mr. Morrison turned without a word and peered into the truck.

"What's he looking for?" I whispered.

"Probably a gun," said Stacey.

Mr. Morrison circled the truck, studying it closely. Then he returned to its front and, bending at the knees with his back against the grill, he positioned his large hands beneath the bumper. Slowly, his muscles flexing tightly against his thin shirt and the sweat popping off his skin like oil on water, he lifted the truck in one fluid, powerful motion until the front was several inches off the ground and slowly walked it to the left of the road, where he set it down as gently as a sleeping child. Then he moved to the rear of the truck and repeated the feat.

Kaleb Wallace was mute. Christopher-John, Little Man, and I stared open-mouthed, and even Stacey, who had witnessed Mr. Morrison's phenomenal strength before, gazed in wonder.

It took Kaleb Wallace several minutes to regain his voice. We were far down the road, almost out of hearing, when his frenzied cry of hate reached us. "One of these nights, you watch, nigger! I'm gonna come get you for what you done! You just watch! One night real soon . . ."

When we reached home and told Mama and Papa and Big Ma what had happened, Mama said to Mr. Morrison, "I told you before I was afraid for you. And today, Kaleb Wallace could've hurt you . . . and the children."

Mr. Morrison looked squarely into Mama's eyes. "Miz Logan, Kaleb Wallace is one of them folks who can't do nothing by himself. He got to have a lot of other folks backing him up plus a loaded gun . . . and I knew there wasn't no gun, leastways not in the truck. I checked."

"But if you stay, he'll get somebody and they'll try to take you, like he said—"

"Miz Logan, don't ask me to go."

Mama reached out, laying a slender hand on Mr. Morrison's. "Mr. Morrison, you're a part of us now. I don't want you hurt because of us."

Mr. Morrison lowered his eyes and looked around the room until his gaze rested on the boys and me. "I ain't never had no children of my own. I think sometimes if I had, I'd've wanted a son and daughter just like you and Mr. Logan . . . and grandbabies like these babies of yours. . . ."

"But, Mr. Morrison, the Wallaces—"

"Mary," said Papa quietly, "let it be."

Mama looked at Papa, her lips still poised to speak. Then she said no more; but the worry lines remained creased upon her brow.

August dawned blue and hot. The heat swooped low over the land clinging like an invisible shroud, and through it people moved slowly, lethargically, as if under water. In the ripening fields the drying cotton and corn stretched tiredly skyward awaiting the coolness of a rain that occasionally threatened but did not come, and the land took on a baked, brown look.

To escape the heat, the boys and I often ambled into the coolness of the forest after the chores were done. There, while the cows and their calves grazed nearby, we sat on the banks of the pond, our backs propped against an old hickory or pine or walnut, our feet dangling lazily in the cool water, and waited for a watermelon brought from the garden to chill. Sometimes Jeremy joined us there, making his way through the deep forest land from his own farm over a mile away, but the meetings were never planned;

none of our parents would have liked that.

"How's your papa?" he asked one day as he plopped down beside us.

"He's all right," said Stacey," 'cepting his leg's bothering him in this heat. Itching a lot. But Mama says that's a sign it's getting well."

"That's good," murmured Jeremy. "Too bad he had to get hurt when he done so's he couldn't go back on the railroad."

Stacey stirred uneasily, looked at Christopher-John, Little Man, and me, reminding us with his eyes that we were not to speak about the Wallaces' part in Papa's injury, and said only, "Uh-huh."

Jeremy was silent a moment, then stuttered, "S-some folks sayin' they glad he got hurt. G-glad he can't go make that railroad money."

"Who said that?" I cried, jumping up from the bank. "Just tell me who said it and I'll ram—"

"Cassie! Sit down and be quiet," Stacey ordered. Reluctantly, I did as I was told, wishing that this business about the Wallaces and Papa's injuries were not so complex. It seemed to me that since the Wallaces had attacked Papa and Mr. Morrison, the simplest thing to do would be to tell the sheriff and have them put in jail, but Mama said things didn't work that way. She explained that as long as the Wallaces, embarrassed by their injuries at the hands of Mr. Morrison, did not make an official complaint about the incident, then we must remain silent also. If we did not, Mr. Morrison could be charged with attacking white men, which could possibly end in his being sentenced to the chain gang, or worse.

"I—I ain't the one said it, Cassie," stammered Jeremy by way of apology.

"Well, whoever saying it ought not be," I said huffily.

Jeremy nodded thoughtfully and changed the

subject. "Y'all seen T.J. lately?"

Stacey frowned, considering whether or not he should answer. There had been much talk concerning T.J. and the Simms brothers, all of it bad. Moe Turner's father had told Papa that T.J. had stopped by with the Simmses once, and after they had left he had discovered his watch missing; the Laniers had had the same experience with a locket. "That T.J. done turned real bad," Mr. Lanier had said, "and I don't want nothin' to do with no thief . . . 'specially no thief runnin' 'round with white boys."

Finally Stacey said, "Don't see him much no more."

Jeremy pulled at his lip. "I see him all the time."

"Too bad," I sympathized.

Stacey glanced reproachfully at me, then lay flat upon the ground, his head resting in the cushion of his hands clasped under his head. "It sure is beautiful up there," he said, pointedly changing the subject again.

The rest of us lay back too. Overhead, the branches of the walnut and hickory trees met like long green fans sheltering us. Several feet away the persistent sun made amber roads of shimmering sunlight upon the pond. A stillness hovered in the high air, soft, quiet, peaceful.

"I think when I grow up I'm gonna build me a house in some trees and jus' live there all the time," said Jeremy.

"How you gonna do that?" asked Little Man.

"Oh, I'll find me some real strong trees and just build. I figure I'll have the trunk of one tree in the bedroom and the other in the kitchen."

"How come you wanna live in a tree for?" Christopher-John inquired.

"It's so peaceful up there . . . and quiet. Cool, too," answered Jeremy. " 'Specially at night."

"How you know how cool it is at night?" I said.

Jeremy's face brightened. " 'Cause I got my bedroom up there."

We looked at him unbelieving.

"I-I do—really. Built it myself and I sleeps up there. Come these hot nights, I just climbs in my tree and it's like going into another world. Why, I can see and hear things up there that I betcha only the squirrels and the birds can see and hear. Sometimes I think I can even see all the way over to y'all's place."

"Ah, shoot, boy, you're a story," I said. "Your place too far away and you know it."

Jeremy's face dropped. "Well . . . maybe I can't see it, but that don't keep me from pretending I do." He was silent a second, then hopped up suddenly, his face bright again. "Hey, why don't y'all come on over and see it? My pa's gonna be gone all day and it'd be lots of fun and I could show y'all—"

"No," said Stacey quietly, his eyes still on the trees overhead.

Jeremy sat back down, deflated. "J-jus' wanted y'all to see it, that's all. . ." For a while he looked hurt by Stacey's cold refusal; then, seeming to accept it as part of the things that were, he again took up his position and volunteered good-naturedly, "If y'all ever get a chance to build y'allselves a tree house, just let me know and I'll help ya. It's just as cool . . ."

Papa sat on a bench in the barn, his broken leg stretched awkwardly before him, mending one of Jack's harnesses. He had been there since early morning, a frown line carved deep into his forehead, quietly mending those things which needed mending. Mama told us not to bother him and we stayed away from the barn as long as we could, but by late afternoon we drifted naturally to it and began our chores. Papa had disappeared within himself and he took no notice of us at first, but shortly afterward he looked up, watching us closely.

When the chores were almost finished, Mr. Morrison arrived from Strawberry, where he had gone to make the August mortgage payment. He entered the barn slowly and handed Papa an envelope. Papa glanced up questioningly, then ripped it open. As he read the letter, his jaw set tightly, and when he finished he smashed his fist so hard against the bench that the boys and I stopped what we were doing, aware that something was terribly wrong.

"They tell you?" he asked of Mr. Morrison, his voice curt, angry.

Mr. Morrison nodded. "I tried to get them to wait till after cotton picking, but they told me it was due and payable immediately. Them's they words."

"Harlan Granger," said Papa quietly. He reached for his cane and stood up. "You feel up to going back to Strawberry . . . tonight?"

"I can make it, but I don't know if this ole mule can."

"Then hitch Lady to it," he said motioning to the mare.

He turned then and went to the house. The boys and I followed, not quite sure of what was happening. Papa entered the kitchen; we stayed on the porch peering through the screen.

"David, something the matter, son?"

"The bank called up the note. I'm going to Strawberry."

"Called up the note?" echoed Big Ma. "Oh, Lord, not that too."

Mama stared at Papa, fear in her eyes. "You going now?"

"Now," he said, leaving the kitchen for their room.

Mama's voice trailed him. "David, it's too late. The bank's closed by now. You can't see anyone until morning. . ."

We could not hear Papa's reply, but Mama's voice rose sharply. "You want to be out on that road again in the middle of the night after what happened? You want us worried to death about you?"

"Mary, don't you understand they're trying to take the land?" Papa said, his voice rising too so that we heard.

"Don't *you* understand I don't want you dead?"

We could hear nothing else. But a few minutes later Papa came out and told Mr. Morrison to unhitch Lady. They would go to Strawberry in the morning.

The next day Papa and Mr. Morrison were gone before I arose. When they returned in the late afternoon, Papa sat wearily down at the kitchen table with Mr. Morrison beside him. Rubbing his hand over his thick hair, he said, "I called Hammer."

"What did you tell him? " Mama asked.

"Just that the note's been called. He said he'd get the money.

"How?"

"He didn't say and I didn't ask. Just said he'd get it."

"And Mr. Higgins at the bank, David," said Big Ma. "What he have to say?"

"Said our credit's no good anymore."

"We aren't even hurting the Wallaces now," Mama said with acid anger. "Harlan Granger's got no need—"

"Baby, you know he's got a need," Papa said, pulling her to him. "He's got a need to show us where we stand in the scheme of things. He's got a powerful need to do that. Besides, he still wants this place."

"But son, that mortgage give us four more years."

Papa laughed dryly. "Mama, you want me to take it to court?"

Big Ma sighed and placed her hand on Papa's. "What if Hammer can't get the money?"

Papa did not look at her, but at Mr. Morrison instead. "Don't worry, Mama. We ain't gonna lose the land. . . . Trust me."

On the third Sunday of August the annual revival began. Revivals were always very serious, yet gay and long planned-for, affairs which brought pots and pans from out-of-the-way shelves, mothball-packed dresses and creased pants from hidden chests, and all the people from the community and the neighboring communities up the winding red school road to Great Faith Church. The revival ran for seven days and it was an occasion everyone looked forward to, for it was more than just church services; it was the year's only planned social event, disrupting the humdrum of everyday country life. Teenagers courted openly, adults met with relatives and friends they had not seen since the previous year's "big meeting," and children ran almost free.

As far as I was concerned, the best part of the revival was the very first day. After the first of three services was dismissed, the mass of humanity which had squished its way into the sweltering interior of the small church poured onto the school grounds, and the women proudly set out their dinners in the backs of wagons and on the long tables circling the church.

Then it was a feast to remember.

Brimming bowls of turnip greens and black-eyed

peas with ham hocks, thick slices of last winter's sugar-cured ham and strips of broiled ribs, crisply fried chicken and morsels of golden squirrel and rabbit, flaky buttermilk biscuits and crusty cornbread, fat slabs of sweet-potato pie and butter pound cakes, and so much more were all for the taking. No matter how low the pantry supplies, each family always managed to contribute something, and as the churchgoers made the rounds from table to table, hard times were forgotten at least for the day.

The boys and I had just loaded our plates for the first time and taken seats under an old walnut when Stacey put down his plate and stood up again. "What's the matter?" I asked, stuffing my mouth with cornbread.

Stacey frowned into the sun. "That man walking up the road. . . ."

I took a moment to look up, then picked up my drumstick. "So?"

"He looks like . . . Uncle Hammer!" he cried and dashed away. I hesitated, watching him, reluctant to leave my plate unless it really was Uncle Hammer. When Stacey reached the man and hugged him, I put the plate down and ran across the lawn to the road. Christopher-John, with his plate still in hand, and Little Man ran after me.

"Uncle Hammer, where's your car?" Little Man asked after we all had hugged him.

"Sold it," he said.

"Sold it!" we cried in unison.

"B-but why?" asked Stacey.

"Needed the money," Uncle Hammer said flatly.

As we neared the church, Papa met us and embraced Uncle Hammer. "I wasn't expecting you to come all the way down here."

"You expecting me to send that much money by mail?"

"Could've wired it."

"Don't trust that either."

"How'd you get it?"

"Borrowed some of it, sold a few things," he said with a shrug. Then he nodded toward Papa's leg. "How'd you do that?"

Papa's eyes met Uncle Hammer's and he smiled faintly. "I was sort of hoping you wouldn't ask that."

"Uh-huh."

"Papa," I said, "Uncle Hammer sold the Packard."

Papa's smile faded. "I didn't mean for that to happen, Hammer."

Uncle Hammer put his arm around Papa. "What good's a car? It can't grow cotton. You can't build a home on it. And you can't raise four fine babies in it."

Papa nodded, understanding.

"Now, you gonna tell me 'bout that leg?"

Papa stared at the milling throng of people around the dinner tables. "Let's get you something to eat first," he said, "then I'll tell you. Maybe it'll set better with some of this good food in your stomach."

Because Uncle Hammer was leaving early Monday morning, the boys and I were allowed to stay up much later than usual to be with him. Long hours after we should have been in bed, we sat on the front porch lit only by the whiteness of the full moon and listened to the comforting sounds of Papa's and Uncle Hammer's voices mingling once again.

"We'll go up to Strawberry and make the payment first thing tomorrow," said Papa. "I don't think I'd better go all the way to Vicksburg with this leg, but Mr. Morrison'll take you there—see you to the train."

"He don't have to do that," replied Uncle

Hammer. "I can make it to Vicksburg all right."

"But I'd rest easier if I knew you was on that train headed due north . . . not off getting yourself ready to do something foolish."

Uncle Hammer grunted. "There ain't a thing foolish to what I'd like to do to them Wallaces. . . Harlan Granger either."

There was nothing to say to how he felt, and no one tried.

"What you plan to do for money?" Uncle Hammer asked after a while.

"The cotton looks good," said Papa. "We do well on it, we'll make out all right."

Uncle Hammer was quiet a moment before he observed, "Just tightening the belt some more, huh?"

When Papa did not answer, Uncle Hammer said, "Maybe I better stay."

"No," said Papa adamantly, "You do better in Chicago."

"May do better but I worry a lot." He paused, pulling at his ear. "Come through Strawberry with a fellow from up in Vicksburg. Things seemed worse than usual up there. It gets hot like this and folks get dissatisfied with life, they start looking 'round for somebody to take it out on. . . . I don't want it to be you."

"I don't think it will be . . ." said Papa, ". . . unless you stay."

In the morning after the men had gone, Big Ma said to Mama, "I sure wish Hammer could've stayed longer."

"It's better he went," said Mama

Big Ma nodded. "I know. Things like they is, it don't take but a little of nothin' to set things off, and Hammer with that temper he got could do it. Still," she murmured wistfully, "I sho' wish he could've stayed. . . ."

On the last night of the revival the sky took on a strange yellowish cast. The air felt close, suffocating, and no wind stirred.

"What do you think, David?" Mama asked as she and Papa stood on the front porch looking at the sky. "You think we should go?"

Papa leaned against his cane. "It's gonna storm all right . . . but it may not come till late on over in the night."

They decided we would go. Most other families had come to the same decision, for the church grounds were crowded with wagons when we arrived. "Brother Logan," one of the deacons called as Papa stepped awkwardly down from the wagon, "Reverend Gabson wants us to get the meeting started soon as we can so we can dismiss early and get on home 'fore this storm hits."

"All right," Papa said, directing us toward the church. But as we neared the building, we were stopped by the Laniers. As the grown-ups talked, Little Willie Wiggins and Moe Turner, standing with several other boys, motioned to Stacey from the road. Stacey wandered away to speak to them and Christopher-John, Little Man, and I went too.

"Guess who we seen?" said Little Willie as Stacey walked up. But before Stacey could venture a guess, Little Willie answered his own question. "T.J. and them Simms brothers."

"Where?" asked Stacey.

"Over there," Little Willie pointed. "They parked by the classrooms. Look, here they come."

All eyes followed the direction of Little Willie's finger. Through the settling dusk three figures ambled with assurance across the wide lawn, the two Simmses on the outside, T.J. in the middle.

"How come he bringin' them here?" asked Moe

Turner angrily.

Stacey shrugged. "Dunno, but I guess we'll find out."

"He looks different," I remarked when I could see T.J. more distinctly. He was dressed in a pair of long, unpatched trousers and, as sticky hot as it was, he wore a suit coat and a tie, and a hat cocked jauntily to one side.

"I s'pose he do look different," murmured Moe bitterly. "I'd look different too, if I'd been busy stealin' other folkses' stuff."

"Well, well, well! What we got here?" exclaimed T.J. loudly as he approached. "Y'all gonna welcome us to y'all's revival services?"

"What you doing here, T.J.?" Stacey asked.

T.J. laughed. "I got a right to come to my own church, ain't I? See all my old friends?" His eyes wandered over the group, but no one showed signs of being glad to see him. His wide grin shrank a little, then spying me he patted my face with his moist hand. "Hey, Cassie girl, how you doin'?"

I slapped his hand away. "Don't you come messing with me, T.J.!" I warned.

Again he laughed, then said soberly, "Well, this is a fine how-do-you-do. I come all the way over here to introduce my friends, R.W. and Melvin, to y'all and y'all actin' like y'all ain't got no manners at all. Yeah, ole R.W. and Melvin," he said, rolling the Simmses' names slowly off his tongue to bring to our attention that he had not bothered to place a "Mister" before either, "they been mighty fine friends to me. Better than any of y'all. Look, see here what they give me." Proudly he tugged at the suit coat. "Pretty nice stuff, eh? Everything I want they give me 'cause they really likes me. I'm they best friend."

He turned to the Simmses. "Ain't that right, R.W. and Melvin?"

Melvin nodded, a condescending smirk on his face which was lost on T.J.

"Anything—just anything at all I want—they'll get it for me, including—" He hesitated as if he were unsure whether or not he was going too far, then plunged on. "Including that pearl-handled pistol in Barnett's Mercantile."

R.W. stepped forward and slapped a reassuring hand on T.J.'s shoulder. "That's right, T.J. You name it and you've got it."

T.J. grinned widely. Stacey turned away in disgust. "Come on," he said, "service is 'bout to start."

"Hey, what's the matter with y'all?" T.J. yelled as the group turned en masse and headed for the church. I glanced back at him. Was he really such a fool?

"All right, T.J.," said Melvin as we walked away, "we come down here like you asked. Now you come on into Strawberry with us like you promised."

"It—it didn't even make no difference," muttered T.J.

"What?" said R.W. "You comin', ain't you? You still want that pearl-handled pistol, don't you?"

"Yeah, but—"

"Then come on," he ordered, turning with Melvin and heading for the pickup.

But T.J. did not follow immediately. He remained standing in the middle of the compound, his face puzzled and undecided. I had never seen him look more desolately alone, and for a fleeting second I felt almost sorry for him.

When I reached the church steps, I looked back again. T.J. was still there, an indistinct blur blending into the gathering dusk, and I began to think that perhaps he would not go with the Simmses. But then the rude squawk of the truck's horn blasted the quiet evening, and T.J. turned his back on us and fled across the field.

Chapter 11

Roll of thunder
hear my cry
Over the water
bye and bye
Ole man comin'
down the line
Whip in hand to
beat me down
But I ain't
gonna let him
Turn me 'round

The night whispered of distant thunder. It was muggy, hot, a miserable night for sleeping. Twice I had awakened hoping that it was time to be up, but each time the night had been total blackness with no hint of a graying dawn. On the front porch Mr. Morrison sat singing soft and low into the long night, chanting to the approaching thunder. He had been there since the house had darkened after church, watching and waiting as he had done every night since Papa had been injured. No one had ever explained why he watched and waited, but I knew. It had to do with the Wallaces.

Mr. Morrison's song faded and I guessed he was on his way to the rear of the house. He would stay there for a while, walking on cat's feet through the quiet yard, then eventually return to the front porch again. Unable to sleep, I resigned myself to await his return by counting states. Miss Crocker had had a big thing about states, and I sometimes found that if

I pretended that she was naming them off I could fall asleep. I decided to count the states geographically rather than alphabetically; that was more of a challenge. I had gotten as far west as the Dakotas when my silent recitation was disturbed by a tapping on the porch. I lay very still. Mr. Morrison never made sounds like that.

There it was again.

Cautiously, I climbed from the bed, careful not to awaken Big Ma, who was still snoring soundly, and crept to the door. I pressed my ear against the door and listened, then slipped the latch furiously and darted outside. "Boy, what you doing here?" I hissed.

"Hey, Cassie, wouldja keep it down?" whispered T.J., invisible in the darkness. Then he tapped lightly on the boys' door again, calling softly, "Hey, Stacey, come on and wake up, will ya? Let me in."

The door swung open and T.J. slipped inside. I pulled my own door closed and followed him. "I-I'm in trouble, Stacey," he said. "I mean I'm r-really in trouble."

"That ain't nothing new," I remarked.

"What you coming here for?" whispered Stacey icily. "Go get R.W. and Melvin to get you out of it."

In the darkness there was a low sob and T.J., hardly sounding like T.J., mumbled, "They the ones got me in it. Where's the bed? I gotta sit down."

In the darkness he groped for the bed, his feet dragging as if he could hardly lift them. "I ain't no bed!" I exclaimed as his hands fell on me.

There was a deep sigh. Stacey clicked on the flashlight and T.J. found the bed, sitting down slowly and holding his stomach as if he were hurt.

"What's the matter?" Stacey asked, his voice wary.

"R.W. and Melvin," whispered T.J., "they hurt me bad." He looked up, expecting sympathy. But our faces, grim behind the light Stacey held, showed no compassion. T.J.'s eyes dimmed, then, undoing the buttons to his shirt, he pulled the shirt open and stared down at his stomach.

I grimaced and shook my head at the sight. "Lord, T.J.!" Stacey exclaimed in a whisper. "What happened?"

T.J. did not answer at first, staring in horror at the deep blue-black swelling of his stomach and chest. "I think something's busted," he gasped finally. "I hurt something awful."

"Why'd they do it?" asked Stacey.

T.J. looked up into the bright light. "Help me, Stacey. Help me get home. . . . I can't make it by myself."

"Tell me how come they did this to you."

" 'Cause . . . 'cause I said I was gonna tell what happened."

Stacey and I looked at each other, then together leaned closer to T.J. "Tell what?" we asked.

T.J. gulped and leaned over, his head between his legs. "I . . . I'm sick, Stacey. I gotta get home 'fore my daddy wake up. . . . He say I stay 'way from that house one more night, he gonna put me out, and he mean it, too. He put me out, I got no place to go. You gotta help me."

"Tell us what happened."

T.J. began to cry. "But they said they'd do worse than this if I ever told!"

"Well, I ain't about to go nowhere unless I know what happened," said Stacey with finality.

T.J. searched Stacey's face in the rim of ghostly light cast by the flashlight. Then he told his story.

After he and the Simmses left Great Faith, they went directly into Strawberry to get the pearl-handled pistol, but when they arrived the mercantile was already closed. The Simmses said that there was no sense in coming back for the pistol; they would simply go in and take it. T.J. was frightened at the thought, but the Simmses assured him that there was no danger. If they were caught, they would simply say that they needed the pistol that night but intended to pay for it on Monday.

In the storage room at the back of the store was a small open window through which a child or a person as thin as T.J. could wiggle. After waiting almost an hour after the lights had gone out in the Barnetts' living quarters on the second floor, T.J. slipped through the window and opened the door, and the Simmses entered, their faces masked with stockings and their hands gloved. T.J., now afraid that they had something else in mind, wanted to leave without the pistol, but R.W. had insisted that he have it. R.W. broke the lock of the gun case with an axe and gave T.J. the much-longed-for gun.

Then R.W. and Melvin went over to a wall cabinet and tried to break off the brass lock. After several unsuccessful minutes, R.W. swung the axe sharply against the lock and it gave. But as Melvin reached for the metal box inside, Mr. Barnett appeared on the stairs, a flashlight in his hand, his wife behind him.

For a long moment no one moved or said a word as Mr. Barnett shone the light directly on T.J., then on R.W. and Melvin their faces darkened by the stockings. But when Mr. Barnett saw the cabinet lock busted, he flew into frenzied action, hopping madly down the stairs and trying to grab the metal box from Melvin. They struggled, with Mr. Barnett getting the better of Melvin, until R.W. whopped Mr. Barnett solidly on the head from behind with the flat of the axe, and Mr. Barnett slumped into a heap upon the floor as if dead.

When Mrs. Barnett saw her husband fall, she dashed across the room and flailed into R.W., crying "You niggers done killed Jim Lee! You done killed him!" R.W., trying to escape her grasp, slapped at her and she fell back, hitting her head against one of the stoves, and did not move.

Once they were outside T.J. wanted to come straight home, but the Simmses said they had business to take care of and told him to wait in the back of the truck. When T.J. objected and said that he was going to tell everybody it was R.W. and Melvin who had hurt the Barnetts unless they took him home, the two of them lit into him, beating him with savage blows until he could not stand, then flung him into the back of the truck and went down the street to the pool hall. T.J. lay there for what he thought must have been an hour before crawling from the truck and starting home. About a mile outside of town, he got a ride with a farmer headed for Smellings Creek by way of Soldiers Road. Not wanting to walk past the Simmses' place for fear R.W. and Melvin had taken the Jackson Road home, he did not get out at the Jefferson Davis School Road intersection, but instead crossed Soldiers Bridge with the farmer and got out at the intersection beyond the bridge and walked around, coming from the west to our house.

"T.J., was . . . was them Barnetts dead?" asked Stacey when T.J. grew quiet.

T.J. shook his head. "I dunno. They sure looked dead. Stacey, anybody find out, you know what they'd do to me?" He stood up, his face grimacing with pain. "Stacey, help me get home," he pleaded. "I'm afraid to go there by myself. . . . R.W. and Melvin might be waitin'. . . . "

"You sure you ain't lying, T.J.?" I asked suspiciously.

"I swear everything I told y'all is the truth. I . . . I admit I lied 'bout tellin' on your mama, but I ain't lyin' now, I ain't!"

Stacey thought a moment. "Why don't you stay here tonight? Papa'll tell your daddy what happened and he won't put—"

"No!" cried T.J., his eyes big with terror. "Can't tell nobody! I gotta go!" He headed for the doors holding his side. But before he could reach it, his legs gave way and Stacey caught him and guided him back to the bed.

I studied T.J. closely under the light, sure that he was pulling another fast one. But then he coughed and blood spurted from his mouth; his eyes glazed, his face paled, and I knew that this time T.J. was not faking.

"You're bad hurt," Stacey said. "Let me get Big Ma— she'll know what to do."

T.J. shook his head weakly "My mama . . . I'll just tell her them white boys beat me for no reason and she'll believe it . . . she'll take care of me. But you go wakin' your grandmama and your daddy'll be in it. Stacey, please! You my only friend . . . ain't never really had no true friend but you. . . . "

"Stacey?" I whispered, afraid of what he might do. As far back as I could remember, Stacey had felt a responsibility for T.J. I had never really understood why. Perhaps he felt that even a person as despicable as T.J. needed someone he could call "friend," or perhaps he sensed T.J.'s vulnerability better than T.J. did himself. "Stacey, you ain't going, are you?"

Stacey wet his lips, thinking. Then he looked at me. "You go on back to bed, Cassie. I'll be all right."

"Yeah, I know you gonna be all right 'cause I'm gonna tell Papa!" I cried, turning to dash for the other room. But Stacey reached into the darkness and caught me. "Look, Cassie, it won't take me but twenty-five or thirty minutes to run down there and back. Really, it's all right."

"You as big a fool as he is then," I accused frantically. "You don't owe him nothin', 'specially after what he done to Mama."

Stacey released me. "He's hurt bad, Cassie. I gotta get him home." He turned away from me and grabbed his pants.

I stared after him; then I said, "Well, you ain't going without me." If Stacey was going to be a fool and go running out into the night to take an even bigger fool home, the least I could do was make sure he got back in one piece.

"Cassie, you can't go—"

"Go where?" piped Little Man, sitting up. Christopher-John sat up too, yawning sleepily. "Is it morning? What y'all doing up?" Little Man questioned. He blinked into the light and rubbed his eyes. "T.J., that you? What you doing here? Where y'all going?"

"Nowhere. I'm just gonna walk T.J. home," Stacey said. "Now go on back to sleep."

Little Man jumped out of bed and pulled his clothes from the hanger where he had neatly hung them. "I'm going too," he squealed.

"Not me," said Christopher-John, lying back down again.

While Stacey attempted to put Little Man back to bed, I checked the porch to make sure that Mr. Morrison wasn't around, then slipped back to my own room to change. When I emerged again, the boys were on the porch and Christopher-John, his pants over his arm, was murmuring a strong protest against this middle-of-the-night stroll. Stacey attempted to persuade both him and Little Man back inside, but Little Man would not budge and Christopher-John, as much as he protested, would not be left behind. Finally Stacey gave up and with T.J. leaning heavily against him hurried across the lawn. The rest of us followed.

Once on the road, Christopher-John struggled into his pants and we became part of the night. Quiet, frightened, and wishing just to dump T.J. on his front porch and get back to the safety of our own beds, we hastened along the invisible road, brightened only by the round of the flashlight.

The thunder was creeping closer now, rolling angrily over the forest depths and bringing the lightning with it, as we emerged from the path into the deserted Avery yard. "W-wait till I get inside, will ya?" requested T.J.

"Ain't nobody here," I said sourly. "What you need us to wait for?"

"Go on, T.J.," said Stacey. "We'll wait."

"Th-thanks, y'all," T.J. said, then he limped to the side of the house and slipped awkwardly into his room through an open window.

"Come on, let's get out of here," said Stacey, herding us back to the path. But as we neared the forest, Little Man turned. "Hey, y'all, look over yonder! What's that?"

Beyond the Avery house bright lights appeared far away on the road near the Granger mansion. For a breathless second they lingered there, then plunged suddenly downward toward the Averys'. The first set of lights was followed by a second, then a third, until there were half a dozen sets of headlights beaming over the trail.

"Wh-what's happening?" cried Christopher-John.

For what seemed an interminable wait, we stood watching those lights drawing nearer and nearer before Stacey clicked off the flashlight and ordered us into the forest. Silently,we slipped into the brush and fell flat to the ground. Two pickups and four cars rattled into the yard, their lights focused like spotlights on the Avery front porch. Noisy, angry men leaped from the cars and surrounded the house. Kaleb Wallace and his brother Thurston, his left arm hanging akimbo at his side, pounded the front door with their rifle butts. "Y'all come on outa there!" called Kaleb. "We want that thieving, murdering nigger of y'all's."

"St-Stacey," I stammered, feeling the same nauseous fear I had felt when the night men had passed and when Papa had come home shot and broken, "wh-what they gonna do?"

"I—I dunno," Stacey whispered as two more men joined the Wallaces at the door.

"Why, ain't . . . ain't that R.W. and Melvin?" I exclaimed. "What the devil they doing—"

Stacey quickly muffled me with the palm of his hand as Melvin thrust himself against the door in an attempt to break it open and R.W. smashed a window with his gun. At the side of the house, several men were climbing through the same window T.J. had entered only a few minutes before. Soon, the frontdoor was flung open from the inside and Mr. and Mrs. Avery were dragged savagely by their feet from the house. The Avery girls were thrown through the open windows. The older girls, attempting to gather the younger children to them, were slapped back and spat upon. Then quiet, gentle Claude was hauled out, knocked to the ground and kicked.

"C-Claude!" whimpered Christopher-John, trying to rise. But Stacey hushed him and held him down.

"W-we gotta get help." Stacey rasped, but none of

us could move. I watched the world from outside myself.

Then T.J. emerged, dragged from the house on his knees. His face was bloody and when he tried to speak he cried with pain, mumbling his words as if his jaw were broken. Mr. Avery tried to rise to get to him, but was knocked back.

"Look what we got here!" one of the men said, holding up a gun. "That pearl-handled pistol from Jim Lee's store."

"Oh, Lord," Stacey groaned. "Why didn't he get rid of that thing?"

T.J. mumbled something we could not hear and Kaleb Wallace thundered, "Stop lyin', boy, 'cause you in a whole lot of trouble. You was in there—Miz Barnett, when she come to and got help, said three black boys robbed their store and knocked out her and her husband. And R.W. and Melvin Simms seen you and them two other boys running from behind that store when they come in town to shoot some pool—"

"But it was R.W. and Melvin—" I started before Stacey clasped his hand over my mouth again.

"—Now who was them other two and where's that money y'all took?"

Whatever T.J.'s reply, it obviously was not what Kaleb Wallace wanted to hear, for he pulled his leg back and kicked T.J.'s swollen stomach with such force that T.J. emitted a cry of awful pain and fell prone upon the ground.

"Lord Jesus! Lord Jesus!" cried Mrs. Avery, wrenching herself free from the men who held her and rushing toward her son. "Don't let 'em hurt my baby no more! Kill me, Lord, but not my child!" But before she could reach T.J., she was caught by the arm and flung so ferociously against the house that she fell, dazed, and Mr. Avery, struggling to reach her, was helpless to save either her or T.J.

Christopher-John was sobbing distinctly now. "Cassie," Stacey whispered, "you take Little Man and Christopher-John and y'all—"

The headlights of two more cars appeared in the distance and Stacey immediately hushed. One of the cars halted on the Granger Road, its lights beaming aimlessly into the blackness of the cotton fields, but the lead car came crazy and fast along the rutted trail toward the Avery house, and before it had rolled to a complete stop Mr. Jamison leaped out. But once out of the car, he stood very still surveying the scene; then he stared at each of the men as if preparing to charge them in the courtroom and said softly, "Y'all decide to hold court out here tonight?"

There was an embarrassed silence. Then Kaleb Wallace spoke up. "Now look here, Mr. Jamison, don't you come messin' in this thing."

"You do," warned Thurston hotly, "we just likely to take care of ourselves a nigger lover too tonight."

An electric tenseness filled the air, but Mr. Jamison's placid face was unchanged by the threat. "Jim Lee Barnett and his wife are still alive. Y'all let the sheriff and me take the boy. Let the law decide whether or not he's guilty."

"Where's Hank?" someone asked. "I don't see no law."

"That's him up at Harlan Granger's," Mr. Jamison said with a wave of his hand over his shoulder. "He'll be down in a minute. Now leave the boy be."

"For my money, I say let's do it now," a voice cried. "Ain't no need to waste good time and money tryin' no thievin' nigger!"

A crescendo of ugly hate rose from the men as the second car approached. They grew momentarily quiet as the sheriff stepped out. The sheriff looked uneasily at the crowd as if he would rather not be here at all, then at Mr. Jamison.

"Where's Harlan?" asked Mr. Jamison.

The sheriff turned from Mr. Jamison to the crowd without answering him. Then he spoke to the men: "Mr. Granger sent word by me that he ain't gonna stand for no hanging on *his* place. He say y'all touch one hair on that boy's head while he on *this* land, he's gonna hold every man here responsible."

The men took the news in grim silence.

Then Kaleb Wallace cried: "Then why don't we go somewhere else? I say what we oughta do is take him on down the road and take care of that big black giant of a nigger at the same time!"

"And why not that boy he working for too?" yelled Thurston.

"Stacey!" I gasped.

"Hush!"

A welling affirmation rose from the men. "I got me three new ropes!" exclaimed Kaleb.

"New? How come you wanna waste a new rope on a nigger?" asked Melvin Simms.

"Big as that one nigger is, an old one might break!"

There was chilling laughter and the men moved toward their cars, dragging T.J. with them.

"No!" cried Mr. Jamison, rushing to shield T.J. with his own body.

"Cassie," Stacey whispered hoarsely, "Cassie, you gotta get Papa now. Tell him what happened. I don't think Mr. Jamison can hold them—"

"You come too."

"No, I'll wait here."

"I ain't going without you!" I declared, afraid that he would do something stupid like trying to rescue T.J. alone.

"Look, Cassie, go on, will ya please? Papa'll know what to do. Somebody's gotta stay here case they take T.J. off into the woods somewhere. I'll be all right."

"Well . . ."

"Please Cassie? Trust me, will ya?"

I hesitated. "Y-you promise you won't go down there by yourself?"

"Yeah, I promise. Just get Papa and Mr. Morrison 'fore they—'fore they hurt them some more." He placed the unlit flashlight in my hand and pushed me up. Clutching Little Man's hand, I told him to grab Christopher-John's, and together the three of us picked our way along the black path, afraid to turn on the flashligh for fear of its light being seen.

Thunder crashed against the corners of the world and lightning split the sky as we reached the road, but we did not stop. We dared not. We had to reach Papa.

Chapter 12

When we neared the house, the dull glow of a kerosene lamp was shining faintly from the boys' room. "Y-you s'pose they already know?" Christopher-John asked breathlessly as we ran up the lawn. "Dunno 'bout that," I said, "but they know we ain't where we s'pose to be."

We ran noisily up onto the porch and flung open the unlatched door. Mama and Big Ma, standing with Mr. Morrison near the foot of the bed, turned as we entered and Big Ma cried, "Lord, there they is!"

"Where have you been?" Mama demanded, her face strangely stricken. "What do you mean running around out there this time of night?"

Before we could answer either question, Papa appeared in the doorway, dressed, his wide leather strap in hand.

"Papa—" I began.

"Where's Stacey?"

"He-he down to T.J.'s. Papa—"

"That boy's gotten mighty grown," Papa said, clearly angry. "I'm gonna teach all of y'all 'bout traipsing off in the middle of the night . . . and especially Stacey. He should know better. If Mr. Morrison hadn't seen this door open, I suppose you would've thought you was getting away with something—like T.J. Well, y'all gonna learn right here and now there ain't gonna be no T.J.s in this house—"

"But, Papa, they h-hurt Claude! " Christopher-John cried, tears streaming down his cheeks for his injured friend.

"And T.J., too," echoed Little Man, trembling.

"What?" Papa asked, his eyes narrowing. "What y'all talking 'bout?"

"Papa, they hurt 'em real bad and . . . and . . ." I could not finish. Papa came to me and took my face in his hands. "What is it, Cassie girl? Tell me."

Everything. I poured out everything. About T.J.'s breaking into the mercantile with the Simmses, about his coming in the night fleeing the Simmses, about the coming of the men and what they had done to the Averys. About Mr. Jamison and the threat of the men to come to the house to get him and Mr. Morrison.

"And Stacey's still down there?" Papa asked when I had finished.

"Yessir. But he hid in the forest. They don't know he's there."

Papa spun around suddenly. "Gotta get him out of there," he said, moving quicker than I had thought possible with his bad leg. Mama followed him into their room, and the boys and I followed her. From over the bed Papa pulled his shotgun.

"David, not with the shotgun. You can't stop them like that."

"Got no other way," he said, stuffing a box of shells into his shirt pocket.

"You fire on them and they'll hang you for sure. They'd like nothing better."

"If I don't, they'll hang T.J. This thing's been coming a long time, baby, and T.J. just happened to be the one foolish enough to trigger it. But, fool or not, I can't just sit by and let them kill the boy. And if they find Stacey—"

"I know, David, I know. But there's got to be another way. Some way they won't kill you too!"

"Seems like they might be planning to do that anyway," Papa said, turning from her. "They come here, no telling what'll happen, and I'll use every bullet I got 'fore I let them hurt anybody in this house."

Mama grabbed his arm. "Get Harlan Granger to stop it. If he says so, they'll go on home."

Papa shook his head. "Them cars had to come right past his house to get to the Averys', and if he'd intended to stop them, he'd stop them without me telling him so."

"Then," said Mama, "force him to stop it."

"How?" asked Papa dryly. "Hold a gun to his head?" He left her then, going back into the boys' room. "You coming, Mr. Morrison?"

Mr. Morrison nodded and followed Papa onto the porch, a rifle in his hand. Like a cat Mama sprang after them and grabbed Papa again. "David, don't . . . don't use the gun."

Papa stared out as a bolt of lightning splintered the night into a dazzling brilliance. The wind was blowing softly, gently toward the east. "Perhaps . . ." he started, then was quiet.

"David?"

Papa touched Mama's face tenderly with the tips of his fingers and said, "I'll do what I have to do, Mary . . . and so will you." Then he turned from her, and with Mr. Morrison disappeared into the night.

Mama pushed us back into her room, where Big Ma fell upon her knees and prayed a powerful prayer. Afterward both Mama and Big Ma changed their clothes, then we sat, very quiet, as the heat crept sticky and wet through our clothing and the thunder banged menacingly overhead. Mama, her knuckles tight against her skin as she gripped the arms of her chair, looked down upon Christopher-John, Little Man, and me, our eyes wide awake with fear. "I don't suppose it would do any good to put you to bed," she said quietly. We looked up at her. She did not mean to have an answer; we gave none, and nothing else was said as the night minutes crept past and the waiting pressed as heavily upon us as the heat.

Then Mama stiffened. She sniffed the air and got up.

"What is it, child?" Big Ma asked.

"You smell smoke?" Mama said, going to the front door and opening it. Little Man, Christopher-John, and I followed, peeping around her in the doorway. From deep in the field where the land sloped upward toward the Granger forest, a fire billowed, carried eastward by the wind.

"Mama, the cotton!" I cried. "It's on fire!"

"Oh, good Lord!" Big Ma exclaimed, hurrying to join us. "That lightning done that!"

"If it reaches those trees, it'll burn everything from here to Strawberry," Mama said. She turned quickly and ran across the room to the side door. "Stay here," she ordered, opening the door and fleeing across the yard to the barn. "Mama, you'd better get some water!" she yelled over her shoulder.

Big Ma hurried into the kitchen with Christopher-John, Little Man, and me at her heels. "What we gonna do, Big Ma?" I asked.

Big Ma stepped onto the back porch and brought in the washtub and began filling it with water. "We gotta fight that fire and try and stop it 'fore it reach them trees. Stand back now out the way so y'all don't get wet."

In a few minutes Mama returned, her arms loaded with sacks of burlap. She quickly threw the sacks into the water and ran back out again. When she returned, she carried two shovels and several more sacks.

"Mama, what you gonna do with all that?" asked

Little Man.

"It's for fighting the fire," she replied hastily.

"Oh," said Little Man, grabbing for one of the shovels as I started to take the other.

"No," Mama said. "You're going to stay here." Big Ma straightened from where she was bent dunking the sacks into the water. "Mary, child, you don't think it'd be better to take them with us?" Mama studied us closely and bit her lower lip. She was silent for several moments, then she shook her head. "Can't anyone get to the house from the Grangers' without our seeing them; I'd rather they stay here than risk them near the fire."

Then she charged each of us, a strange glint in her eyes. "Cassie, Christopher-John, Clayton Chester, hear me good. I don't want you near that fire. You set one foot from this house and I'm going to skin you alive . . . do you hear me now?"

We nodded solemnly. "Yes ma'am, Mama."

"And stay inside. That lightning's dangerous."

"B-but, Mama," cried Christopher-John, "y'all going out here in that lightning!"

"It can't be helped, baby," she said. "The fire's got to be stopped."

Then she and Big Ma laid the shovels across the top of the tub and each took a handle of it. As they stepped out the back door, Mama looked back at us, her eyes uncertain, as if she did not want to leave us. "Y'all be sure to mind now," ordered Big Ma gruffly, and the two of them carrying the heavy tub crossed the yard toward the garden. From the garden they would cut through the south pasture and up to where the cotton blazed. We watched until they were swallowed by the blackness that lay between the house and the fire, then dashed back to the front porch where the view was clearer. There we gazed transfixed as the flames gobbled the cotton and crept dangerously near the forest edge.

"Th-that fire, Cassie," said Christopher-John, "it gonna burn us up?"

"No . . . it's going the other way. Toward the forest."

"Then it's gonna burn up the trees," said Christopher-John sadly.

Little Man tugged at my arm. "Papa and Stacey and Mr. Morrison, Cassie! They in them trees!" Then iron-willed Little Man began to cry. And Christopher-John too. And the three of us huddled together, all alone.

"Hey, y'all all right?"

I gazed out into the night, seeing nothing but the gray smoke and the red rim of the fire in the east "Who's that?"

"It's me," said Jeremy Simms, running up the lawn.

"Jeremy, what you doing out this time of night?" I questioned, taken aback to see him.

"It ain't night no more, Cassie. It's near dawn."

"But what you doing here?" repeated Little Man with a sniffle.

"I was sleepin' up in my tree like I always do—"

"On a night like this?" I exclaimed. "Boy, you *are* crazy!"

Jeremy looked rather shamefaced and shrugged. "Well, anyway, I was and I smelled smoke. I knew it was comin' from thisaway and I was 'fraid it was y'all's place, so I run in and told my pa, and him and me we come on up here over an hour ago."

"You mean you been out there fighting that fire?"

Jeremy nodded. "My pa, and R.W. and Melvin too."

"R.W. and Melvin?" Little Man, Christopher-

John, and I exclaimed together.

"But they was—" I poked Christopher-John into silence.

"Yeah, they got there 'fore us. And there's a whole lot of men from the town out there too." He looked puzzled. "I wonder what they all was doin' out here?"

"How bad is it?" I asked, ignoring his wonderings. "It get much of the cotton?"

Jeremy nodded absently. "Funny thing. That fire come up from that lightning and struck one of them wooden fence posts, I reckon, and sparked that cotton. Must've burned a good quarter of it. . . . Y'all lucky it ain't headed this way."

"But the trees," said Christopher-John. "It gonna get the trees, ain't it?"

Jeremy looked out across the field, shielding his eyes against the brilliance of the fire. "They tryin' like everything to stop it. Your papa and Mr Granger, they got—"

"Papa? You seen Papa? He all right?" cried Christopher-John breathlessly.

Jeremy nodded, looking down at him strangely. "Yeah, he's fine—"

"And Stacey, you seen him?" inquired Little Man.

Again, Jeremy nodded. "Yeah, he out there too."

Little Man, Christopher-John, and I glanced at each other, relieved just a bit, and Jeremy went on, though eyeing us somewhat suspiciously. "Your papa and Mr. Granger, they got them men diggin' a deep trench 'cross that slope and they say they gonna burn that pasture grass from the trench back to the cotton—"

"You think that'll stop it?" I asked.

Jeremy stared blankly at the fire and shook his head. "Dunno," he said finally. "Sure hope so, though." There was a violent clap of thunder, and lightning flooded the field. "One thing would sure help though is if that ole rain would only come on down."

All four of us looked up at the sky and waited a minute for the rain to fall. When nothing happened, Jeremy turned and sighed. "I better be gettin' back now. Miz Logan said she left y'all here so I just come to see 'bout ya." Then he ran down the slope, waving back at us as he went. When he got to the road, he stopped suddenly and stood very still; then he put out his hands, hesitated a moment, and spun around wildly as if he were mad.

"It's rainin', y'all!" he cried. "That ole rain a-comin' down!"

Little Man, Christopher-John, and I jumped from the porch and ran barefooted onto the lawn, feeling the rain fine and cool upon our faces. And we laughed, whooping joyously into the thundering night, forgetting for the moment that we still did not know what had happened to T.J.

When the dawn came peeping yellow-gray and sooted over the horizon, the fire was out and the thunderstorm had shifted eastward after an hour of heavy rain. I stood up stiffly, my eyes tearing from the acrid smoke, and looked out across the cotton to the slope, barely visible in the smoggish dawn. Near the slope where once cotton stalks had stood, their brown bolls popping with tiny puffs of cotton, the land was charred, desolate, black, still steaming from the night.

I wanted to go and take a closer look, but for once Christopher-John would not budge. "No!" he repeated over and over. "I ain't going!"

"But what Mama *meant* was that she didn't want

us near the fire, and it's out now."

Christopher-John set his lips firmly together, folded his plump arms across his chest and was adamant. When I saw that he would not be persuaded, I gazed again at the field and decided that I could not wait any longer. "Okay, you stay here then. We'll be right back." Ignoring his protests, Little Man and I ran down to the wet road.

"He really ain't coming," said Little Man, amazed, looking back over his shoulder.

"I guess not," I said, searching for signs of the fire in the cotton. Farther up the road the stalks were singed, and the fine gray ash of the fire lay thick upon them and the road and the forest trees.

When we reached the burnt-out section of the field, we surveyed the destruction. As far as we could see, the fire line had extended midway up the slope, but had been stopped at the trench. The old oak was untouched. Moving across the field, slowly, mechanically, as if sleepwalking, was a flood of men and women dumping shovels of dirt on fire patches which refused to die. They wore wide handkerchiefs over their faces and many wore hats, making it difficult to identify who was who, but it was obvious that the ranks of the fire fighters had swelled from the two dozen townsmen to include nearby farmers. I recognized Mr. Lanier by his floppy blue hat working side by side with Mr. Simms, each oblivious of the other, and Papa near the slope waving orders to two of the townsmen. Mr. Granger, hammering down smoldering stalks with the flat of his shovel, was near the south pasture where Mr. Morrison and Mama were swatting the burning ground.

Nearer the fence a stocky man, masked like the others, searched the field in robot fashion for hidden fire under the charred skeletons of broken stalks.

When he reached the fence, he leaned tiredly against it, taking off his handkerchief to wipe the sweat and soot from his face. He coughed and looked around blankly. His eyes fell on Little Man and me staring up at him. But Kaleb Wallace seemed not to recognize us, and after a moment he picked up his shovel and started back toward the slope without a word.

Then Little Man nudged me. "Look over there, Cassie. There go Mama and Big Ma!" I followed his pointing finger. Mama and Big Ma were headed home across the field.

"Come on," I said, sprinting back up the road.

When we reached the house, we dragged our feet across the wet lawn to clean them and rejoined Christopher-John on the porch. He looked a bit frightened sitting there all alone and was obviously glad we were back. "Y'all all right?" he asked.

"Course we're all right," I said, plopping on the porch and trying to catch my breath.

"What'd it look like?"

Before either Little Man or I could answer, Mama and Big Ma emerged from the field with Stacey, the sacks now blackened remnants in their hands. We ran to them eagerly.

"Stacey, you all right?" I cried. "What 'bout T.J.?"

"And C-Claude?" stammered Christopher-John.

And Little Man asked, "Papa and Mr. Morrison, ain't they coming?"

Mama held up her hand wearily. "Babies! Babies!" Then she put her arm around Christopher-John. "Claude's fine, honey. And," she said, looking down at Little Man, "Papa and Mr. Morrison, they'll be coming soon."

"But T.J., Mama," I persisted. "What 'bout T.J.?"

Mama sighed and sat down on the steps, laying

the sacks on the ground. The boys and I sat beside her.

"I'm gonna go on in and change, Mary," Big Ma said, climbing the steps and opening our bedroom door. "Miz Fannie gonna need somebody."

Mama nodded. "Tell her I'll be down soon as I get the children to bed and things straightened out here." Then she turned and looked down at Little Man, Christopher-John, and me, eager to know what had happened. She smiled slightly, but there was no happiness in it. "T.J.'s all right. The sheriff and Mr. Jamison took him into Strawberry."

"But why, Mama?" asked Little Man. "He done something bad?"

"They think he did, baby. They think he did."

"Then—then they didn't hurt him no more?" I asked.

Stacey looked across at Mama to see if she intended to answer; then, his voice hollow and strained, he said, "Mr. Granger stopped them and sent them up to fight the fire."

I sensed that there was more, but before I could ask what, Chistopher-John piped, "And—and Papa and Mr. Morrison, they didn't have to fight them ole men? They didn't have to use the guns?"

"Thank the Lord, no," said Mama. "They didn't."

"The fire come up," said Stacey, "and Mr. Morrison come and got me and then them men come down here to fight the fire and didn't nobody have to fight nobody."

"Mr. Morrison come get you alone?" I asked, puzzled. "Where was Papa?"

Stacey again looked at Mama and for a moment they both were silent. Then Stacey said, "Y'all know he couldn't make that slope with that bad leg of his."

I looked at him suspiciously. I had seen Papa move

on that leg. He could have made the slope if he wanted to.

"All right now," Mama said, rising. "It's been a long, tiring night and it's time you all were in bed.

I reached for her arm. "Mama, how bad is it really? I mean, is there enough cotton left to pay the taxes?"

Mama looked at me oddly. "Since when did you start worrying about taxes?" I shrugged, then leaned closer toward her, wanting an answer, yet afraid to hear it. "The taxes will get paid, don't you worry," was all the answer she gave. "Now, let's get to bed."

"But I wanna wait for Papa and Mr. Morrison!" protested Little Man.

"Me too!" yawned Christopher-John.

"Inside!"

All of us went in but Stacey, and Mama did not make him. But as soon as she had disappeared into the boys' room to make sure Little Man and Christopher-John got to bed, I returned to the porch and sat beside him. "I thought you went to bed," he said.

"I wanna know what happened over there."

"I told you, Mr. Granger—"

"I come and got Papa and Mr. Morrison like you asked," I reminded him. "Now I wanna know everything happened after I left."

Stacey sighed and rubbed his left temple absently, as if his head were hurting. "Ain't much happened 'cepting Mr. Jamison tried talking to them men some more, and after a bit they pushed him out the way and stuffed T.J. into one of their cars. But Mr. Jamison, he jumped into his car and lit out ahead of them and drove up to Mr. Granger's and swung his car smack across the road so couldn't nobody get past him. Then he starts laying on his horn.

"You go over there?"

He nodded. "By the time I got 'cross the field to where I could hear what was going on, Mr. Granger was standing on his porch and Mr. Jamison was telling him that the sheriff or nobody else was 'bout to stop a hanging on that flimsy message he'd sent up to the Averys'. But Mr. Granger, he just stood there on his porch looking sleepy and bored, and finally he told the sheriff, 'Hank, you take care of this. That's what folks elected you for.'

"Then Kaleb Wallace, he leaps out of his car and tries to grab Mr. Jamison's keys. But Mr. Jamison threw them keys right into Mrs. Granger's flower bed and couldn't nobody find them, so Melvin and R.W. come up and pushed Mr. Jamison's car off the road. Then them cars was 'bout to take off again when Mr. Granger comes running off the porch hollering like he's lost his mind. 'There's smoke coming from my forest yonder!' he yells. 'Dry as that timber is, a fire catch hold it won't stop burning for a week. Give that boy to Wade like he wants and get on up there!' And folks started running all over the place for shovels and things, then all of them cut back down the road to the Averys' and through them woods over to our place."

"And that's when Mr. Morrison come got you?"

Stacey nodded. "He found me when I followed them men back up to the woods."

I sat very still, listening to the soft sounds of the early morning, my eyes on the field. There was something which I still did not understand.

Stacey nodded toward the road. "Here come Papa and Mr. Morrison." They were walking with slow, exhausted steps toward the drive.

The two of us ran down the lawn, but before we reached the road a car approached and stopped directly behind them. Mr. Jamison was driving.

Stacey and I stood curiously on the lawn, far enough away not to be noticed, but close enough to hear.

"David, I thought you should know . . ." said Mr. Jamison. "I just come from Strawberry to see the Averys—"

"How bad is it?"

Mr. Jamison stared straight out at the road. "Jim Lee Barnett . . . he died at four o'clock this morning."

Papa hit the roof of the car hard with his clenched fist and turned toward the field, his head bowed.

For a long, long minute, none of the men spoke; then Mr. Morrison said softly, "The boy, how is he?"

"Doc Crandon says he's got a couple of broken ribs and his jaw's broken, but he'll be all right . . . for now. I'm going to his folks to tell them and take them to town. Just thought I'd tell you first."

Papa said, "I'll go in with them."

Mr. Jamison pulled off his hat and ran his fingers through his hair, damp against his forehead. Then, squinting, he looked over his shoulder at the field. "Folks thinking," he said slowly, as if he did not want to say what he was about to say, "folks thinking that lightning struck that fence of yours and started the fire. . . . " He pulled at his ear. "It's better, I think, that you stay clear of this whole thing now, David, and don't give anybody cause to think about you at all, except that you got what was coming to you by losing a quarter of your cotton. . . . "

There was a cautious silence as he gazed up at Papa and Mr. Morrison, their faces set in grim, tired lines. ". . . Or somebody might just get to wondering about that fire. . . . "

"Stacey," I whispered, "what's he talking 'bout?"

"Hush, Cassie," Stacey said, his eyes intent on the men.

"But I wanna know—"

Stacey looked around at me sharply, his face drawn, his eyes anxious, and without even a murmur from him I suddenly did know. I knew why Mr. Morrison had come for him alone. Why Mr. Jamison was afraid for Papa to go into town. Papa had found a way, as Mama had asked, to make Mr. Granger stop the hanging: He had started the fire.

And it came to me that this was one of those known and unknown things, something never to be spoken, not even to each other. I glanced at Stacey, and he saw in my eyes that I knew, and understood the meaning of what I knew, and he said simply, "Mr. Jamison's going now."

Mr. Jamison turned around in the driveway and headed back toward the Averys'. Papa and Mr. Morrison watched him leave, then Mr. Morrison walked silently up the drive to do the morning chores and Papa, noticing us for the first time, stared down at us, his eyes bloodshot and unsmiling. "I thought y'all would've been in bed by now," he said.

"Papa," Stacey whispered hoarsely, "what's gonna happen to T.J. now?"

Papa looked out at the climbing sun, a round, red shadow behind the smoggish heat. He didn't answer immediately, and it seemed as if he were debating whether or not he should. Finally, very slowly, he looked down, first at me, then at Stacey. He said quietly, "He's in jail right now."

"And—and what then?" asked Stacey.

Papa studied us. "He could possibly go on the chain gang. . . . "

"Papa, could he . . . could he die?" asked Stacey, hardly breathing.

"Son—"

"Papa, could he?"

Papa put a strong hand on each of us and watched

us closely. "I ain't never lied to y'all, y'all know that."

"Yessir."

He waited, his eyes on us. "Well, I . . . I wish I could lie to y'all now."

"No! Oh, Papa, no!" I cried. "They wouldn't do that to ole T.J.! He can talk his way outa just 'bout anything! Besides, he ain't done nothing *that* bad. It was them Simmses! Tell them that!"

Stacey, shaking his head, backed away, silent, not wanting to believe, but believing still. His eyes filled with heavy tears, then he turned and fled down the lawn and across the road into the shelter of the forest.

Papa stared after him, holding me tightly to him. "Oh, P-Papa, d-does it have to be?"

Papa tilted my chin and gazed softly down at me. "All I can say, Cassie girl . . . is that it shouldn't be." Then, glancing back toward the forest, he took my hand and led me to the house.

Mama was waiting for us as we climbed the steps, her face wan and strained. Little Man and Christopher-John were already in bed, and after Mama had felt my forehead and asked if I was all right she sent me to bed too. Big Ma had already gone to the Averys' and I climbed into bed alone. A few minutes later both Mama and Papa came to tuck me in, talking softly in fragile, gentle words that seemed about to break. Their presence softened the hurt and I did not cry. But after they had left and I saw Papa through the open window disappear into the forest after Stacey, the tears began to run fast and heavy down my cheeks.

In the afternoon when I awakened, or tomorrow or the next day, the boys and I would still be free to run the red road, to wander through the old forest and sprawl lazily on the banks of the pond. Come October, we would trudge to school as always, barefooted and grumbling, fighting the dust and the mud and the Jefferson Davis school bus. But T.J. never would again.

I had never liked T.J., but he had always been there, a part of me, a part of my life, just like the mud and the rain, and I had thought that he always would be. Yet the mud and the rain and the dust would all pass I knew and understood that. What had happened to T.J. in the night I did not understand, but I knew that it would not pass. And I cried for those things which had happened in the night and would not pass.

I cried for T.J. For T.J. and the land.

RELATED READINGS

from Growing Up in the Great Depression

by Richard Wormser

The Logan children were affected by the Depression both at school and at home. The following excerpts explore the changes that took place at that time for African Americans and for school-age children throughout the United States.

Blacks in the Depression

An elderly black man recalls growing up in the depression.

> The Negro was born in depression so the Great American Depression didn't mean much to him. The best he could be was a porter or a shoe shine boy. It only became official when it happened to the white man.

For black people in America during the 1930s, economic depression was a fact of life. Unemployment was always high in the black community; economic opportunities were always limited. The discrimination against black people was profound and widespread throughout the United States. Few stores and factories would hire black workers. Few unions would accept them as members. The few companies that hired blacks usually employed them in the most menial jobs. In the southern states, blacks were segregated from whites. They attended separate schools, sat in separate sections on buses and in movie theaters, used separate drinking fountains and separate rest rooms in public places, and worshipped in separate churches. Black people were not allowed to vote or serve on juries, or to become peace officers, judges, or government officials. Lynchings were so common in the South that newspapers didn't even bother to report many of them. Black people were denied their rights by the courts and by both federal and state legislatures. In the North, although segregation was not official, there were unwritten laws that prevented blacks from entering many private and public places. Still, there was more freedom of movement for black people in the North and they were not subjected to the vicious oppression as in the South. They could vote and attend schools and ride on buses and sit where they wanted. Yet, the prejudice against them was as deep as it was in the South. Race riots, when they occurred, occurred in the North.

As bad as things were before the depression, the crash only made things worse. From the end of the Civil War until 1929, there were many jobs that white Americans considered unsuitable for themselves. This racist attitude resulted in the employment of large numbers of black people as janitors, barbers, elevator operators, street cleaners, garbage collectors, waiters and hotel employees, porters on trains, maids, cooks, laborers, and shoe shine men. On occasion, black workers found jobs as cowboys or railroad firemen, or worked in a few industrial plants such as slaughterhouses and steel mills. A privileged few were able to make a living as entertainers. When the depression came, suddenly these jobs were eagerly sought after by unemployed whites who would grab any job they could get. Not only did they compete with blacks for the same jobs, but many times they completely shut them out. In some places whites would beat or kill any black person who tried to keep his job. The worse the depression became, the more whites demanded those jobs that had traditionally belonged to blacks. In 1930, the year after the crash, unemployment among black workers was 15.7 percent compared to 9 percent for whites. In 1931, 35 percent of blacks were unemployed and 24 percent of whites. The following year 56 percent of the black community was out of work compared to 39 percent of the white.

Anna Arnold Hedgemen describes what Harlem was like when she was growing up in her autobiography, *The Trumpet Sounds:*

> The crashing drop of wages drove Negroes back to the already crowded hovels east of Lenox Avenue. In many blocks, one toilet served a floor of four apartments. Most of the apartments had no private bathrooms or even the luxury of a public bath. All of these tenements were filthy and vermin ridden.
>
> Many families had been reduced to living below street level. Packed in damp, rat-ridden dungeons, they existed in squalor not too different from Arkansas sharecroppers. . . . There were only slits for a window and a tin can for a toilet. . . . Compared to the 20 to 25 percent of their income white families paid for rent, Negro tenants paid 40 to 45 percent. More than half the Negro families were forced to take in lodgers. Frequently all members of a family slept together in one room. Envied was the family who had a night worker as a lodger for he would occupy a bed for the day that would be rented out at night. If a family had a bathtub,

it too would be covered with boards and rented out [as a bed].

. . . a large mass of Negroes were faced with the realities of starvation and turned to public relief . . . (but) the Home Relief Bureau only allowed eight cents a day for food. Meanwhile men, women and children combed the streets and searched garbage cans for food, foraging with dogs and cats. . . .

Richard Wright, in his autobiographical novel, *Black Boy*, writes about what it was like for a black youth growing up in the depression years to have a job a white man felt did not belong to a black man. Wright took a job as a janitor in an optical company in order to learn how to make eyeglasses and earn a decent living. One day, he asked two white employees named Reynolds and Pease, who seemed friendly, to teach him the trade.

"What are you trying to do, get smart, nigger? Reynolds asked me

"No sir," I said.

I was baffled. Perhaps he just did not want to help me. I went to Pease to remind him that the boss said that I was to be given a chance to learn the trade.

"Nigger, you think you're white, don't you?"

"No sir."

"You're acting mighty like it."

"I'm only doing what the boss told me to do," I said.

Pease shook his fist in my face.

"This is a *white* man's work around here," he said.

Eventually Richard Wright was forced to quit. When threats failed to make a black man quit a job, violence was used. As one reporter noted, in the South "dead men not only tell no tales, they create vacancies." Frank Kincaid, a black fireman, was working on a train one night when suddenly a shotgun roared out and a load of buckshot caught him in the head and killed him. A few seconds later, his body was dumped on the side of the tracks and a white man took his place and the train pulled out. By 1933, seven black railroad men had been murdered and seven others wounded.

Lynchings and lynch trials of blacks on phony charges also increased in the South during the depression, and being young was no protection. In 1931, seventeen-year-old Clarence Norris and two friends jumped aboard a freight train in Georgia headed for Birmingham, Alabama, and possible work. They were children of black sharecroppers who lived in poverty and for whom the depression was especially hard. A group of white teenagers was also on the train and tried to force the black youths off. A fight broke out and the black teenagers managed to throw the whites off the train. Angry at being humiliated, the whites, none of whom was seriously injured, notified the local sheriff, who telegraphed ahead to stop the train and arrest the black youths. At a little town called Paint Rock, the sheriff, his deputies, and a number of armed white men stopped the train and arbitrarily arrested nine of the twenty black youths aboard. Most of them did not know one another. There were still several whites on the train as well. To everyone's surprise, two of them turned out to be young white women dressed as boys. Clarence Norris recalled what happened that day:

> When we reached this little old town of Paint
> Rock, Alabama, there was a bunch of white

men with rifles and shotguns waiting for us. They took us off the train and some of them was saying, "Let's lynch these 'niggers.' Let's take them to a tree and hang them." And there was two men with uniforms and buttons. I don't know if they was policemen or firemen or what, but they had these brass buttons and they said, "No. Let's take them to jail." And we never did see no white women. The next day, they brought these two white women to the jail— Victoria Price and Ruby Bates. They lined us up and the sheriff says to Victoria, "Which ones had you?" And she pointed out four of us. "This one and that one, that one and that one." Then they asked Ruby Bates. But she don't say nothing. Then the sheriff says, "No need to ask her. The others must have had her." And that's how a rape charge was framed against us. I never will forget it. That's the way it happened.

The nine youths—collectively known as "the Scottsboro Boys," named for the town in which they were tried—were convicted of rape and sentenced to death. Seven of the nine were teenagers. The death sentence was imposed despite the fact that one of the so-called victims eventually denied she was raped. In addition, there was no physical evidence that the women had been attacked. Even though the Supreme Court overturned the death convictions, Clarence Norris remained in jail almost twenty years before he finally escaped from an Alabama prison. In 1980, he was pardoned by the state of Alabama.

By the middle of the depression it was estimated that over half the black work force in southern cities was unemployed. In the rural areas, where most of the black population worked on farms, black sharecroppers earned $275 a year compared to $417 for white sharecroppers. Laborers earned an average of $175 a year compared to $232 for whites. Black farmers depended upon cotton, and during the depression, prices fell so low that only a very few were able to make enough money to provide for their families. Many went broke or deeper in debt. Even when a young black person was given a job, he was at the mercy of the whites for whom he worked. Henry Winston, who grew up in Mississippi, remembered working as a caddie at a golf course when he was ten years old.

There was this one man who used to play every day and we all hated to caddie for him. He had this cruel habit of taking a golf ball in his hand and cracking it against the head of whoever was caddying for him. Then he would laugh and say, "I want to see which is harder, a golf ball or a nigger's head." To show there was no hard feelings on his part, he would give me a dime—as if money would make the pain go away. I wanted to throw the money in his face, but my family needed the dime—and I needed the job.

The only thing that enabled many black families to survive was public assistance, and even there they faced bigotry. Before the depression, there was very little relief available to anyone. There were no federal programs and the states had limited funds for public assistance. In the South not only did fewer black people than whites receive government help, but the amount of assistance they received was almost one-third less. In Atlanta, Georgia, the average white relief check was $32.66, while blacks received an average of $19.29. The argument given was that "blacks need less than whites. . . ."

Education and Other Dreams

In the 1930s, most Americans believed that to get ahead in life you needed an education. School was the door through which millions of immigrants passed to become Americans. Parents who could neither read nor write themselves insisted that their children get an education so that they could better themselves. Children from comfortable or well-to-do homes were urged to go to college to improve their chances for success.

Just before the depression, almost 10 million children were in school throughout America. After the crash, the number dropped dramatically. By 1930, 3 million children between the ages of six and seventeen had dropped out. Georgia closed 1,318 schools with an enrollment of 170,790 children. In West Virginia 1,000 schools closed their doors. Arkansas's 300 schools averaged only sixty days a year of classes. Throughout the South, schools for black children either closed or cut back. White children went to school five months of the year while black children attended school an average of three months. In parts of Oklahoma, children went to school three days a week or less. At one point, five out of six schools in Alabama were shut down.

Not only were schools shutting down, those that stayed open often had no money to maintain the buildings and pay the teachers. New buildings were out of the question. If a window was broken and a teacher needed new textbooks, the window would stay broken and the students would do without books. One school passed a resolution not to buy new books for ten years, no matter how the world changed. There were no school supplies and few children could afford to buy notebooks and pencils. There was no money for uniforms for sports or for school teams to travel to play each ocher.

For many children, though, school was the only place they could get a decent meal. In Chicago, teachers managed to feed lunch to almost 11,000 hungry children out of their own meager resources despite the fact that they were not being paid. "For God's sake, help us feed these children during the summer," one relief agency cried out in desperation. In New York, an estimated 20 percent of the state's schoolchildren were undernourished. In West Virginia, over 50 percent of the school-age children of miners were underweight. The quality of food was never very good in most schools.

Classes were sometimes doubled up so that one teacher was forced to do the work of two and the other teacher was fired. In some schools, salaries were cut in half. Teachers often went without salaries for long periods of time. In Chicago, a riot broke out when thousands of unpaid teachers demonstrated for the salary they had not received for almost two years between 1931 and 1933. Joined by their students and parents, the teachers marched to the city hall and invaded banks to demand their money. The police were called out and began to beat the striking teachers with clubs. (Political leaders usually found enough money to pay the police to protect them from the angry groups of the unemployed and homeless.) One teacher described her desperate search for a job as follows:

I've been out of normal school for almost two years and have had $4.50 worth of work. Last fall I was promised a job by a school but was disappointed in the last minute by them giving it to a friend. Then I heard about . . . jobs for unemployed teachers and I registered for work right away. . . . I was to be put on a library project at $22.50. The next day I was taken ill with measles which put me out again. Then I started answering advertisements for girls in our paper. I wrote for housework, practical nurse, factory work, anything I could find but nothing came of it.

One Oklahoma woman remembered her parents pushing her to go to school during the dust bowl days.

Mom and Dad were determined we kids were going to school. It didn't matter if there was dust storms, black blizzards, white blizzards, depression or what have you. We was to go and that' s all there was to it. Actually, I didn't mind so much 'cause we had a horse and carriage and Mom would let us hitch her up and ride to school. It was six miles away. We gave as many kids rides as we could so we were very popular.

The depression affected school enrollment in contradictory ways. In many areas, where work was hard to find, teenagers stayed in school because there was no place else for them to go. As a result, many classes were packed full with students who, in normal times, would have entered the work force. However, many children no longer could afford to go to school. Some didn't have carfare; others lacked clothes or books, or lived too far away to walk. A fourteen-year-old Kentucky girl was one of many who wrote of her plight to Mrs. Roosevelt, the president's wife, and asked for help.

I was a freshman at the Painesville High School but had to quit going on account of the depression. The school was about seven miles away. When I was going I had to get up about 5:30 every morning. . . . My parents worked hard to keep me in school but since we lived on a farm and could sell nothing, I had to quit school.

Sometimes the school was too far away to walk and students could not afford the bus fare, even when it was inexpensive. A fourteen-year old Illinois girl wrote:

I want to enter high school but I find it very hard. . . . The school is about six miles away. The bus fare is not free but seventy-five cents a week besides books. If my bus fare were paid I could easily go. . . . You are my only hope. My father is gone for five years and we don't know where.

Many teenagers were ashamed to go to school because they lacked clothes. Farm children sometimes wore clothes that their mothers made out of burlap bags that once contained grain. Two brothers went to school on alternate days because they only had one pair of shoes between them. A sixteen-year-old Michigan girl wrote Mrs. Roosevelt:

I am a high school girl and I must quit school because I am not dressed as other girls are. My clothes are all so shabby from my dress to my shoes. Mrs. Roosevelt, would you kindly look among your things and see if there isn't something you can send me. Please don't let my parents find out that I wrote you asking you for help. I am decent and respectable and you know how some people are. They would laugh at me if they knew I wrote and asked you for old dresses. . . .

Many children's education suffered because they could not afford to buy books or supplies they needed for school. One fourteen-year-old boy pleaded for a donation of books because "I love to learn." A young New Mexican girl asked for a typewriter: "I just love to study and all my wishes are to be a stenographer but my parents are very poor. . . . " A Minnesota farm girl wrote:

I have done a boy's work ever since I was five years old. This week I have been breaking land with a sulky plow and three mules. Is there some way I can hear music and talks and news outside my very small world? I have so little pleasures and pastimes. We are just poor renters on a farm and there is no money for a radio or the books I like to read.

Depression

by Isabel Joshlin Glaser

*Despite the economic troubles caused by
the Depression, some families' riches grew.
Like the Logan family, the speaker of this
poem possessed many things that, to her,
were more valuable than money.*

We heard people were standing
In bread lines in town.
Everywhere people were begging for work
And nothing much to be found,
5   That much we knew.
    But we were fine,
    My sister and I,
There on our grandmother's place.

Living in the tenant's house,
10 Three rooms on a pasture hill,
We had the grass, the trees,
    Fresh air, the sky,
    And all those animals.

We had a father who liked to farm
15 And a mother who built a bookcase,
Then filled it with books and dreams.

People were begging for work . . .
Were standing in lines for food.
It was a terrible time for many,
20 But we had everything, my sister and I.
We were growing up rich.

The Stolen Party

by Liliana Heker,
translated by Alberto Manguel

*Both T.J. Avery and Jeremy Simms thought
that friendships could grow despite
differences in class, race, and ethnicity.
Would the main character in this story
agree with their point of view?*

As soon as she arrived she went straight to the kitchen to see if the monkey was there. It was: what a relief! She wouldn't have liked to admit that her mother had been right. *Monkeys at a birthday?* her mother had sneered. *Get away with you, believing any nonsense you're told!* She was cross, but not because of the monkey, the girl thought; it's just because of the party.

"I don't like you going," she told her. "It's a rich people's party."

"Rich people go to Heaven too," said the girl, who studied religion at school.

"Get away with Heaven," said the mother. . . .

The girl didn't approve of the way her mother spoke. She was barely nine, and one of the best in her class.

"I'm going because I've been invited," she said. "And I've been invited because Luciana is my friend. So there."

"Ah yes, your friend," her mother grumbled. She paused. "Listen, Rosaura," she said at last. "That one's not your friend. You know what you are to them? The maid's daughter, that's what."

Rosaura blinked hard: she wasn't going to cry.

Then she yelled: "Shut up! You know nothing about being friends!"

Every afternoon she used to go to Luciana's house and they would both finish their homework while Rosaura's mother did the cleaning. They had their tea in the kitchen and they told each other secrets. Rosaura loved everything in the big house, and she also loved the people who lived there.

"I'm going because it will be the most lovely party in the whole world, Luciana told me it would. There will be a magician, and he will bring a monkey and everything."

The mother swung around to take a good look at her child, and pompously put her hands on her hips.

"Monkeys at a birthday?" she said. "Get away with you, believing any nonsense you're told!"

Rosaura was deeply offended. She thought it unfair of her mother to accuse other people of being liars simply because they were rich. Rosaura too wanted to be rich, of course. If one day she managed to live in a beautiful palace, would her mother stop loving her? She felt very sad. She wanted to go to that party more than anything else in the world.

"I'll die if I don't go," she whispered, almost without moving her lips.

And she wasn't sure whether she had been heard, but on the morning of the party she discovered that her mother had starched her Christmas dress. And in the afternoon, after washing her hair, her mother rinsed it in apple vinegar so that it would be all nice and shiny. Before going out, Rosaura admired herself in the mirror, with her white dress and glossy hair, and thought she looked terribly pretty.

Señora Ines also seemed to notice. As soon as she saw her, she said:

"How lovely you look today, Rosaura."

Rosaura gave her starched skirt a slight toss with her hands and walked into the party with a firm step. She said hello to Luciana and asked about the monkey. Luciana put on a secretive look and whispered into Rosaura's ear: "He's in the kitchen. But don't tell anyone, because it's a surprise."

Rosaura wanted to make sure. Carefully she entered the kitchen and there she saw it: deep in thought, inside its cage. It looked so funny that the girl stood there for a while, watching it, and later, every so often, she would slip out of the party unseen and go and admire it. Rosaura was the only one allowed into the kitchen. Señora Ines had said: "You yes, but not the others, they're much too boisterous, they might break something." Rosaura had never broken anything. She even managed the jug of orange juice, carrying it from the kitchen into the dining room. She held it carefully and didn't spill a single drop. And Señora Ines had said: "Are you sure you can manage a jug as big as that?" Of course she could manage. She wasn't a butterfingers, like the others. Like that blonde girl with the bow in her hair. As soon as she saw Rosaura, the girl with the bow had said:

"And you? Who are you?"

"I'm a friend of Luciana," said Rosaura.

"No," said the girl with the bow, "you are not a friend of Luciana because I'm her cousin and I know all her friends. And I don't know you."

"So what," said Rosaura. "I come here every afternoon with my mother and we do our homework together."

"You and your mother do your homework together?" asked the girl, laughing.

"I and Luciana do our homework together," said Rosaura, very seriously.

The girl with the bow shrugged her shoulders. "That's not being friends," she said. "Do you go to school together?"

"No."

"So where do you know her from?" said the girl, getting impatient.

Rosaura remembered her mother's words perfectly. She took a deep breath.

"I'm the daughter of the employee," she said.

Her mother had said very clearly: "If someone asks, you say you're the daughter of the employee; that's all." She also told her to add: "And proud of it." But Rosaura thought that never in her life would she dare say something of the sort.

"What employee?" said the girl with the bow. "Employee in a shop?"

"No," said Rosaura angrily. "My mother doesn't sell anything in any shop, so there."

"So how come she's an employee?" said the girl with the bow.

Just then Señora Ines arrived saying *shh shh,* and asked Rosaura if she wouldn't mind helping serve out the hot dogs, as she knew the house so much better than the others.

"See?" said Rosaura to the girl with the bow, and when no one was looking she kicked her in the shin.

Apart from the girl with the bow, all the others were delightful. The one she liked best was Luciana, with her golden birthday crown; and then the boys. Rosaura won the sack race, and nobody managed to catch her when they played tag. When they split into two teams to play charades, all the boys wanted her for their side. Rosaura felt she had never been so happy in all her life.

But the best was still to come. The best came after Luciana blew out the candles. First the cake. Señora

Ines had asked her to help pass the cake around, and Rosaura had enjoyed the task immensely, because everyone called out to her, shouting "Me, me!" Rosaura remembered a story in which there was a queen who had the power of life or death over her subjects. She had always loved that, having the power of life or death. To Luciana and the boys she gave the largest pieces, and to the girl with the bow she gave a slice so thin one could see through it.

After the cake came the magician, tall and bony, with a fine red cape. A true magician: he could untie handkerchiefs by blowing on them and make a chain with links that had no openings. He could guess what cards were pulled out from a pack, and the monkey was his assistant. He called the monkey "partner." "Let's see here, partner," he would say, "Turn over a card." And, "Don't run away, partner: time to work now."

The final trick was wonderful. One of the children had to hold the monkey in his arms and the magician said he would make him disappear.

"What, the boy?" they all shouted.

"No, the monkey!" shouted back the magician.

Rosaura thought that this was truly the most amusing party in the whole world.

The magician asked a small fat boy to come and help, but the small fat boy got frightened almost at once and dropped the monkey on the floor. The magician picked him up carefully, whispered something in his ear, and the monkey nodded almost as if he understood.

"You mustn't be so unmanly my friend," the magician said to the fat boy.

"What's unmanly?" said the fat boy.

The magician turned around as if to look for spies.

"A sissy," said the magician. "Go sit down."

Then he stared at all the faces, one by one. Rosaura felt her heart tremble.

"You, with the Spanish eyes," said the magician. And everyone saw that he was pointing at her.

She wasn't afraid. Neither holding the monkey, nor when the magician made him vanish; not even when, at the end, the magician flung his red cape over Rosaura's head and uttered a few magic words . . . and the monkey reappeared, chattering happily, in her arms. The children clapped furiously. And before Rosaura returned to her seat, the magician said:

"Thank you very much, my little countess."

She was so pleased with the compliment that a while later, when her mother came to fetch her, that was the first thing she told her.

"I helped the magician and he said to me, "Thank you very much, my little countess.' "

It was strange because up to then Rosaura had thought that she was angry with her mother. All along Rosaura had imagined that she would say to her: "See that the monkey wasn't a lie?" But instead she was so thrilled that she told her mother all about the wonderful magician.

Her mother tapped her on the head and said: "So now we're a countess!"

But one could see that she was beaming.

And now they both stood in the entrance, because a moment ago Señora Ines, smiling, had said: "Please wait here a second."

Her mother suddenly seemed worried.

"What is it?" she asked Rosaura.

"What is what?" said Rosaura. "It's nothing; she just wants to get the presents for those who are leaving, see?"

She pointed at the fat boy and at a girl with pigtails who were also waiting there, next to their mothers. And she explained about the presents. She knew, because she had been watching those who left before her. When one of the girls was about to leave, Señora Ines would give her a bracelet. When a boy left, Señora Ines gave him a yo-yo. Rosaura preferred the yo-yo because it sparkled, but she didn't mention that to her mother. Her mother might have said: "So why don't you ask for one, you blockhead?" That's what her mother was like. Rosaura didn't feel like explaining that she'd be horribly ashamed to be the odd one out. Instead she said:

"I was the best-behaved at the party."

And she said no more because Señora Ines came out into the hall with two bags, one pink and one blue.

First she went up to the fat boy, gave him a yo-yo out of the blue bag, and the fat boy left with his mother. Then she went up to the girl and gave her a bracelet out of the pink bag, and the girl with the pigtails left as well.

Finally she came up to Rosaura and her mother. She had a big smile on her face and Rosaura liked that. Señora Ines looked down at her, then looked up at her mother, and then said something that made Rosaura proud:

"What a marvelous daughter you have, Herminia."

For an instant, Rosaura thought that she'd give her two presents: the bracelet and the yo-yo. Señora Ines bent down as if about to look for something. Rosaura also leaned forward, stretching out her arm. But she never completed the movement.

Señora Ines didn't look in the pink bag. Nor did she look in the blue bag. Instead she rummaged in her purse. In her hand appeared two bills.

"You really and truly earned this," she said

handing them over. "Thank you for all your help, my pet."

Rosaura felt her arms stiffen, stick close to her body, and then she noticed her mother's hand on her shoulder. Instinctively she pressed herself against her mother's body. That was all. Except her eyes. Rosaura's eyes had a cold, clear look that fixed itself on Señora Ines's face.

Señora Ines, motionless, stood there with her hand outstretched. As if she didn't dare draw it back. As if the slightest change might shatter an infinitely delicate balance.

from Black Women in White America: A Documentary History

edited by Gerda Lerner

I Was a Negro Come of Age

by Ellen Tarry

Ellen Tarry was born in Birmingham, Alabama, in 1906. Her parents were mulattos, that is, persons of mixed race. Legally, therefore, Ellen was considered to be black, even though she had blond hair, blue eyes, fair skin, and could easily pass for white. This account from her autobiography, The Third Door: The Autobiography of an American Negro Woman, *describes her first experience with the realities of black life in the 1920s.*

I felt like a real grown-up lady when I finally won consent to go to a party without a chaperon. I was more than a little excited when one of the boys who took me out borrowed an automobile and called for me. Mama was giving my escort her final instructions on what time I should come home when a car drove up. A light was flashed on our porch, then on the house next door before the driver stopped alongside a parked car that belonged to a man I had heard our new neighbors call "Shorty." Anxious to be on our way, we promised to be home "early" and started down the steps.

"Wait!" my mother screamed as two white policemen jumped out of the automobile with drawn guns and moved toward Shorty's car.

"Get out of there!" we heard one of them call to the two Negro men sitting in the parked automobile.

"And get out with your hands in the air" yelled the other. "You boys got corn in this car and we gonna find it tonight!"

"Well, what you standing there like dummies for?" the first officer continued. "You *have* got whisky, haven't you?"

"No, sir!" the Negroes cried, their arms high in the air.

"We'll see," the officer said as he and his partner started searching the car.

Watching from our vine-covered porch, it looked as if the policemen were trying to turn the automobile into something for a junk dealer's yard. Cushions were thrown in the street, tools were scattered about and we could hear boards being ripped from the floor, all although it was already evident that the zealous enforcers of Birmingham's dry law were laboring in vain.

"We didn't get you tonight," one of them said, wiping the sweat from his face. "But we've had a tip on you boys and we'll catch you yet!"

The rare sight of two white men working so hard—and in vain—must have amused Shorty, the smaller of the two Negroes, and he giggled.

"So it tickles you, eh?" shouted one of the officers. "Well, laugh this off!"

There was a succession of thuds as the butt of the

officer's revolver cracked against the little Negro's skull again and again. He raised his arms to ward off the blows, but they came too fast and with too much force. He fell and his body lay crumpled and still on the pavement as his friend stood helpless, his black hands high above his head.

"Guess that'll teach him not to be so smart the next time," laughed the other policeman as he walked over to the prostrate form and gave it a kick. The Negro groaned and the white men laughed louder.

I suddenly realized this was not a bad dream. Shorty was real and so were the two men standing over him, especially the one who had raised his foot again.

"You dirty dog!" I screamed, "you're kicking a man who's flat on his back!"

A hand was clasped over my mouth. "Shut up, you little simpleton!" Mama muttered. "Don't you know they could do the same thing to you and I couldn't do a thing about it?"

Shorty groaned again before I could grasp the full meaning of what my mother had said to me. She tried to block me but I ran around her, down the steps, and into the street where Shorty lay with his attackers towering over him. I could hear words coming out of my mouth but I was past fear. The officers peered at me for a second, then ordered Shorty's friend to "get" and he ran up the street.

The men were still laughing when they drove away. Suddenly, I saw that the street was in darkness except for the corner light. The porches were empty, front shades were drawn. Mama was behind the vines and my escort was leaning over the fence retching as he vomited out his fear. There was nobody in the street but Shorty and me.

At that moment words and phrases which had lurked in the nether regions of my consciousness took on meaning. I knew that Shorty and I were alone; nobody wanted anything to do with us at the moment. They would say we were "hotheaded," that we didn't "know our place." Shorty was only half-conscious, but for the first time in my life I knew who and what I was. . . . I was a Negro come of age! All my life I must have looked at things which I had refused to see. Now I both saw and understood.

My legs felt weak and I sat on the curb. I remembered the boy whom I had first heard whisper "race riot." Soon after, I remembered, I saw Papa put a gun in the drawer of a table in the parlor. Then came the parade in the middle of the night. A Ku Klux Klan parade, they said.

I remembered how Mama took me out of bed and carried me to the parlor where I saw Papa, in his old-fashioned night shirt, standing by the front window. He was as still as a statue and his fists were clenched. There had been the clatter of horses' hooves as the light from a fiery cross held high by white-robed men on horseback flashed a warning of destruction to all Jews, Catholics, and Negroes. Papa had opened the table drawer. As the reflection from the burning cross lighted up our room, it glistened against the steel of the revolver in his hand. Mama tightened her grip on my arm but I broke away and pressed my nose against the windowpane, the better to see the men who rode white horses and carried fiery crosses. After the last clop-clop died away there was a long stillness.

As I sat there . . . I closed my eyes and saw again the frightened faces of Negro mothers when white men stalked through our neighborhood, jingling money in their pockets. Now I knew why schoolchildren shouted, "Yaller is roguish, but black is honest." . . .

Shorty stirred, then dragged himself to the curb where he sat with his head between his knees. We had never spoken in our lives. Tonight there was no need for words.

"Why," I asked myself, "did I ever think I was needed in Africa? Alabama was my Africa. Catholic or Protestant, white, black, or yellow, whatever I was, was wrong. I wanted to hide. But there was no hiding place and nobody to tell me why. The world— it could not be God's world. It was the white man's world and I was not white. . . ."

I Did Not Really Understand What it Meant To Be a Negro

by Daisy Lee Bates

Daisy Lee Bates was born in 1920 in Huttig, Arkansas and educated in Little Rock, Arkansas. In her autobiography, The Long Shadow of Little Rock: A Memoir, *Bates tell about a turning point in her life.*

I was born Daisy Lee Gatson in the little sawmill town of Huttig, in southern Arkansas. . . . As I grew up in this town, I knew I was a Negro, but I did not really understand what that meant until I was seven years old. My parents, as do most Negro parents, protected me as long as possible from the inevitable insult and humiliation that is, in the South, part of being "colored." . . .

One afternoon, shortly after my seventh birthday, my mother called me in from play.

"I'm not feeling well," she said. "You'll have to go to the market to get the meat for dinner."

I was thrilled with such an important errand. I put on one of my prettiest dresses and my mother brushed my hair. She gave me a dollar and instructions to get a pound of center-cut pork chops. I skipped happily all the way to the market.

When I entered the market, there were several white adults waiting to be served. When the butcher had finished with them, I gave him my order. More white adults entered. The butcher turned from me and took their orders. I was a little annoyed but felt since they were grownups it was all right. While he was waiting on the adults, a little white girl came in and we talked while we waited.

The butcher finished with the adults, looked down at us and asked, "What do you want, little girl?" I smiled and said, "I told you before, a pound of center-cut pork shops." He snarled, "I'm not talking to you," and again asked the white girl what she wanted. She also wanted a pound of center-cut pork chops.

"Please may I have my meat?" I said, as the little girl left. The butcher took my dollar from the counter, reached into the showcase, got a handful of fat chops and wrapped them up. Thrusting the package at me, he said, "Niggers have to wait 'til I wait on the white people. Now take your meat and get out of here!" I ran all the way home crying.

When I reached the house, my mother asked what had happened. I started pulling her toward the door, telling her what the butcher had said. I opened the meat and showed it to her. "It's fat, Mother. Let's take it back."

"Oh, Lord, I knew I shouldn't have sent her. Stop crying now, the meat isn't so bad."

"But it is. Why can't we take it back?"

"Go on out on the porch and wait for Daddy." As she turned from me, her eyes were filling with tears.

When I saw Daddy approaching, I ran to him, crying. He lifted me in his arms and smiled. "Now, what's wrong?" When I told him, his smile faded.

"And if we don't hurry, the market will be closed," I finished.

"We'll talk about it after dinner, sweetheart." I could feel his muscles tighten as he carried me into the house.

Dinner was distressingly silent. Afterwards my parents went into the bedroom and talked. My mother came out and told me my father wanted to see me. I ran into the bedroom. Daddy sat there, looking at me for a long time. Several times he tried to speak, but the words just wouldn't come. I stood there, looking at him and wondering why he was acting so strangely. Finally he stood up and the words began tumbling from him. Much of what he said I did not understand. To my seven-year-old mind he explained as best he could that a Negro had no rights that a white man respected.

He dropped to his knees in front of me, placed his hands on my shoulders, and began shaking me and shouting.

"Can't you understand what I've been saying?" he demanded. "There's nothing I can do! If I went down to the market I would only cause trouble for my family."

As I looked at my daddy sitting by me with tears in his eyes, I blurted out innocently, "Daddy, are you afraid?"

He sprang to his feet in an anger I had never seen before. "Hell, no! I'm not afraid for myself, I'm not afraid to die. I could go down to that market and tear him limb from limb with my bare hands, but I am afraid for you and your mother."

That night when I knelt to pray, instead of my usual prayers, I found myself praying that the butcher would die. After that night we never mentioned him again. . . .

Incident

(For Eric Walrond)

by Countee Cullen

*Sometimes a single word or action can
have a powerful affect on a person's life.*

Once riding in old Baltimore,
    Heart-filled, head-filled with glee,
I saw a Baltimorean
    Keep looking straight at me.

5 Now I was eight and very small,
    And he was no whit bigger,
And so I smiled, but he poked out
    His tongue, and called me, "Nigger."

I saw the whole of Baltimore
10   From May until December;
Of all the things that happened there
    That's all that I remember.

Equal Opportunity

by Jim Wong-Chu

*At one time, Chinese immigrants to both
Canada and the United States were
discriminated against. However, the
struggle for equality can take curious
turns.*

in early canada
when railways were highways

each stop brought new opportunities

there was a rule

5   the chinese could only ride
the last two cars
of the trains

that is

until a train derailed
10   killing all those
in front

(the chinese erected an altar and thanked
   buddha)

a new rule was made

the chinese must ride
15   the front two cars
of the trains

that is

until another accident
claimed everyone
20   in the back

(the chinese erected an altar and thanked
     buddha)

after much debate
common sense prevailed

the chinese are now allowed
25   to sit anywhere
on any train

The Clearing

by Jesse Stuart

How does fear and hatred of strangers begin? How might a fire affect the relationship between neighbors who are being less than neighborly towards each other?

Finn and I were pruning the plum trees around our garden when a rock came cracking among the branches of the tree I was pruning.

"Where did that come from?" I asked Finn, who was on the ground below piling the branches.

"I don't know," he said.

Then we heard the Hinton boys laughing on the other side of the valley. I went back to pruning. In less than a minute, a rock hit the limb above my head, and another rock hit at Finn's feet. Then I came down from the tree. Finn and I started throwing rocks. In a few minutes, rocks were falling like hailstones around them and around us. The land was rocky on both sides of the valley, and there were plenty of rocks to throw.

One of the rocks hit Finn on the foot, and one of our rocks hit the largest Hinton boy's head.

"Think of it," Finn said. "We fight before we know each other's names! What will it be as time goes on?"

We fought all afternoon with rocks. At sunset the Hinton boys took off up the path and over the hill. We went home. When Pa asked why we hadn't finished pruning the trees, we told him.

"I told you," he said to Mom. "You'll see whether

we can live apart!"

"Wait until we get to know each other," Mom said.

"But how are we ever going to know people like them?" Pa asked.

"Oh, something will happen," she replied calmly. "You'll see."

The next day, Mort Hinton was with his boys. They climbed higher on the hill, cutting the briers and brush and tree branches and stacking them neatly into piles. Finn and I pruned our trees.

"I'll say one thing for the Hintons," Mom said. "They're good workers."

"When they don't throw rocks," Finn said.

On the fourth day, my guinea hens flew across the valley where the Hintons were clearing land.

"Get these hens back on your side of the valley," Mort Hinton yelled. "Get 'em back where they belong."

I didn't want to put my hens in the hen house. But I had to. I knew Mort Hinton would kill them. I wanted to tell him that they would help his land. They'd get rid of insects that might destroy his crop. But I was afraid to tell him anything.

A week had passed before my guinea hens got out and flew across the valley.

"If you don't keep your hens on your side of the valley," Mort Hinton hollered to me, "I'll wring their necks."

That night I put my guinea hens in again. I fixed the hen house so they couldn't get out and roam the hills as they had always done. While Finn, Pa, and I cleared land on one side of the valley, the Hintons cleared on the other side.

Though we'd never been close enough to the Hintons to talk with them, and we didn't want to get that close, we found ourselves trying to do more work than the four of them. Every day, that early March, rain or sunshine, four Hintons worked on their side of the valley, and Pa, Finn, and I worked on our side. One day a Hinton boy hollered at us, "You can't clear as much land as we can."

"Don't answer him," Pa said.

When April came and the Hintons had finished clearing the hill and had burned the brush, Mort Hinton brought a skinny mule hitched to a plow and started plowing the new ground. He plowed slowly the first day. The second day my hens got out again and flew across the valley to the plowed ground. Mort Hinton caught two of them. The others flew back home when he tried to catch them. Then he yelled across to where we were plowing our new ground and told us what he had done.

"I feel like taking a shotgun and sprinkling him," I said.

"Your hens were on his land," Mom said. "He told you to keep them off his land."

Mort Hinton plowed his new ground by working from daylight until dusk, while the boys carried armloads of roots from the field and stacked them in great heaps. By the first of May, they had made this ground soil like a garden. Then came a rainy season in early May, and they carried baskets of tobacco plants and set them in the newly plowed rows.

"They're workers, all right," Pa said.

On a dark night about a week later, I watched a moving light from my upstairs window. It came from the direction of the Hintons', over the hill and down into the valley below our house. In a few minutes, I heard footsteps on the porch. Then there was a loud knock on our door. I heard Pa get out of bed and open the door.

"I'm Mort Hinton," a voice said. "My wife sent for your wife."

I heard Mom getting out of bed.

"I'll be ready in a minute," she called out.

Neither Pa nor Mort said another word.

"I'll be back when everything is all right," Mom said as she hurried off.

I watched the lantern fade from sight as Mort Hinton and Mom went down the path into the deep valley below the house. In two minutes or more, it flashed into sight again when they reached Hintons' tobacco field. The light moved swiftly up and over the hill.

The next morning, Pa cooked breakfast for us. He muttered about the Hintons as he stood near the hot stove frying eggs.

"They are friendly enough when they need something over there," Pa said.

We were ready to sit down to breakfast when Mom came home.

"Dollie Hinton's got a healthy girl baby," were Mom's first words as she sat down for a cup of coffee.

"What did they name the baby?" Glenna asked.

"They've not named her yet," Mom said. "I think they plan to call her Ethel. They're tickled to death. Three boys and now a girl!"

"What kind of people are they, anyway?" Pa asked.

"Like other people," Mom said. "They don't have much furniture in their house. They're working hard to pay for their farm."

"Will they be any better neighbors?" Pa asked.

"I think so," Mom said. "That hill over there is not a fence between us any longer."

"There's more than a hill between us," I said. "What about my hens Mort Hinton caught? Did he say anything about 'em last night?"

"And what about the Hinton boy that hit me on the foot with a rock?" Finn said. "I'd like to meet up with him sometime."

By the time we had finished our breakfast, Mort Hinton was plowing the young tobacco. His three sons were hoeing the tender plants with long-handled hoes.

"You'd think Mr. Hinton would be sleepy," Mom said. "He didn't go to bed last night. And the boys slept on the hay in the barn loft."

Pa, Finn, and I didn't have too much sympathy for the Hintons. Through the dining-room window, we could look across the valley and watch Mort keep the plow moving steadily. We watched his boys dig with their hoes, never looking up from the ground.

"This will be a dry, sunny day," Pa said. "We'll burn the brush piles on the rest of our clearing."

We gathered our pitchforks, hoes, and rakes and went to the hill where we had cleared ground all spring. There were hundreds of brush piles on our twenty acres of cleared ground. The wind was still. The sun had dried the dew from the leaves that carpeted the ground between the brush piles.

"It's the right time to burn," Pa said. "I can't feel any wind. The brush has aged in these piles until it is as dry as powder."

Pa struck a match to the brush pile at the bottom of the clearing. The fire started with little leaps over the leaf-carpeted ground. Finn, Pa, and I set fire to the bottom of the clearing until we had a continuous line of fire going up the slope. Then a wind sprang up from nowhere. And when flames leaped from brush pile to brush pile, Pa looked at me.

"This is out of control," Pa said. "Grab a hoe and start raking a ring."

"I'm afraid we can't stop it," Finn said. "We'll have to work fast to save the orchards."

"Run to the house and get Sal and Glenna," Pa yelled.

"Look, Pa," Finn said, pointing down the hill.

Mort Hinton was in front. He was running up the hill. His three sons were running behind him, each with a hoe across his shoulder.

"It's out of control," Pa shouted to Mort before he reached us.

"We've come to help," Mort said.

"Can we keep it from the orchards?" Pa asked.

"Let's run to the top of the hill and fire against it," Mort said. "I've burnt hundreds of acres of clearings on hillsides, and I always fire the top first and let it burn down! I fire the bottom last. Maybe we'll not be too late to save the orchards!"

Mort ran up the hill and we followed. Finn and I didn't speak to his boys, and they didn't speak to us. But when we started raking a ring side by side, we started talking to the Hintons. We forgot about the rock fight. Now wasn't the time to remember it, when flames down under the hill were shooting twenty to thirty feet high. In no time, we raked the ring across the top of the clearing. And the fire Mort Hinton set along the ring burned fiercely down the hill and made the ring wider and wider. Only once did fire blow across the ring, and Pa stopped it then.

As soon as we had this spot under control, we raked a ring down the west side near the peach orchard. Mort set a line of fire along this ring and let it burn toward the middle of the clearing. Then we raked a ring on the east side and fired against the fire that was approaching our plum trees and our house.

Soon the leaping flames met in the clearing. We had the fire under control. Our clearing was burned clean as a whistle.

"How much do I owe you?" Pa asked Mort Hinton.

"You don't owe me anything," Mort said. "We're just paying you back for the help your wife gave us."

"Then let's go to the house for dinner," Pa said.

"Some other time," Mort said. "We must go home and see about Dollie and the baby."

As we went down the hill, Finn and I talked with the Hinton boys about fishing and wild-bee trees, while Pa and Mort laughed and talked about weather and crops.

The Five-Dollar Dive

by Yvonne Nelson Perry

*Bullies like T.J. and Lillian Jean build up
their own egos by taking advantage of
their victims. Consequently, the victims
usually feel powerless and weak. What
effects does Jojo's bullying have on the
narrator of this story?*

They brought the guy out at four Saturday
afternoon.

They had him on a stretcher, wrapped in a gray
blanket. It must have been a job, bringing him down
that rough trail from the falls. The men carrying him
were dripping In sweat.

As I stood by the ambulance, watching them load
up, Jojo appeared at my side.

"A tourist," he snickered. "Shoulda stayed in
Waikiki."

Pock-faced Jojo, only fourteen, but already bigger
than my father, a stevedore on the Honolulu docks.

Everyone says Jojo is slow, you know, in the head,
but he manages to get money and school lunches
away from the rest of us kids.

That's why I'm here. Jojo bet me I couldn't dive off
the top of the falls.

Diving at the falls is dangerous. If you don't know
what you're doing, you get hurt. Like that tourist. You
see, there's this big rock that juts up from the pool's
bottom. It's right where you land when you dive off
the different ledges. If you go off the lower ones, no
problem. You don't go under that deep. You dive off
the higher ones, you better know exactly where that

underwater rock is or you'll hit it head-on.

Checking out the rock's position is tricky. The water in the pool is dark unless the sun's shining on it. Even then, you can barely see the shadow of that monster under there. Sometimes when I dive, I have to shift back and forth, back and forth, squinting, until I see it.

Anyway, today is the day. Dive off the top of the falls or give Jojo five bucks. You don't tell Jojo what the bet is, he tells you. Remember, he's bigger than the rest of us, and you never know what he's going to do. One day, Benny Sato wouldn't give Jojo his sushi, so Jojo picked him up and threw him over the schoolyard fence. Benny broke his arm when he landed on it wrong; he told the school nurse he was goofing around and fell.

Now, Jojo grabbed my shoulder and pushed me toward the trail that led to the falls.

"Come on, Packy. Dive time," he said.

"Maybe the falls are closed, Jojo. You know, because of that guy." I jerked my thumb toward the ambulance easing out of the dirt parking lot, no siren necessary.

"What's the matta', kid? You afraid?"

To show him I wasn't, I raced for the trail. At that moment I wasn't afraid of diving, I was afraid of Jojo.

The trail rises gradually as it winds through the narrow valley, thick with ginger and ti. Breadfruit trees crowd out the sky, making the trail dark. It always smells like rotten guavas and something else. The guys pee in the bamboo clumps along the way; I guess the girls do it in the pool.

We pounded up the half-mile trail; I could hear Jojo behind me, grunting as he ran flat-footed over the muddy footpath.

As we rounded the last bend, I heard the roar of

the waterfall. When I broke out into the open area near the pool, some of the kids from school were in the water. Others were sitting around, strumming ukes, kicking back.

"Hey, Packy! You see the guy?"

"Man, you shoulda been here."

They crowded around, all giving details of the diving accident at once.

Jojo appeared a few moments later. Everyone fell silent; they must have remembered the bet. Only Jojo's sister, Kalei, sunning with the older girls, called to him.

"Show 'em how, Jojo!" she said. She stood on the far bank, wet white tee shirt clinging to her nut-brown body.

Older than her brother, Kalei couldn't wait for Jojo to play football so she could fool around with the team. The football coach wanted Jojo this year, but Mr. Price, our principal, said eighth-grade boys couldn't play. The other teams were glad; bad enough he was going to start next year.

As Jojo strutted over to me, I looked up at the falls. Water tumbled down fifty-five feet, making a foamy circle where it hit the pool. The white water calmed down quickly, however, as the circle widened. When it reached the edges of the pool, it lapped softly against smooth mossy rocks.

"Let's go, Pack Rat."

Jojo elbowed me and pointed to the top ledge.

Nodding, I took off my shirt, tossed it aside, and dove in. I swam across the pool to the rocks beside the falls, pulled myself out of the water, and started to scale the lava cliff.

Jojo was right behind me.

Looking for handholds and crevices for my feet took all my attention. The falls cascaded a few feet away, spraying me with a fine cool mist. Stopping to rest, I glanced down and saw everyone looking up at us. I couldn't hear them, I only saw their mouths open and shut, open and shut.

Jojo grabbed one of my ankles.

"Chickenin' out?" he shouted up at me.

I jerked my foot away in answer and started climbing again.

A few more feet and I scrambled onto the topmost ledge. I had never been this high before. I didn't stand up until Jojo was beside me; we stood up together.

Without a word, we squared off and jung-keena-po'ed to see who would dive first. I threw paper: hand open, fingers spread wide. On the same downstroke, Jojo held out two fingers: scissors to cut my paper.

I had to dive first.

I turned and faced the pool.

Stepping forward, I gripped my toes over the slippery edge. With knees slightly flexed and arms raised, I got ready to dive.

Peering down, I tried to locate the underwater rock. I couldn't see its shadow anywhere.

I stepped back from the edge and turned to Jojo.

"I can't find the rock," I told him.

"You're just chicken, man," he said, sticking his neck out like one.

"We're diving too late, Jojo."

"You're chicken, man."

"That guy's accident made us get up here too late."

"Like I said, Pack, you're chicken."

"There's no sun on the water, Jojo."

"Chicken!"

"Jojo, I can't see the rock!"

"You lose, buddy! You owe me!"

He punched a fist into my chest.

I went down on one knee, lost my balance, and tumbled head-first off the ledge.

As I fell, a gust of wind blew through the kukui trees surrounding the pool. Silver-green leaves fluttered, the last rays of afternoon sun hit the water.

I saw the shadow of the rock.

As I plunged through the dark surface of the water, I twisted my body to one side.

It was ice-cold, blind-black underwater.

I kept my arms extended, trying to protect myself from the rock.

Then I brushed against it, my hands sliding down its slimy side.

I pushed away. I was safe, home free.

Heart pounding, I clawed my way back up to the surface.

Bursting upward into the light, I grinned with relief and waved my arms wildly at the cheering crowd around the pool.

"Way to go, Pack! Way to go!" they said.

Even Kalei stood and clapped.

Treading water, I gulped a mouthful and blew a stream skyward. Now Jojo would owe me five bucks if he didn't follow me down.

"You did it, Packy! You did it!" someone shouted.

Swimming to the side of the pool, I suddenly realized I didn't want Jojo's money. I just wanted to do something better than him.

I climbed out of the water and turned to look up at the ledge.

"No!" I shouted.

Jojo was already in motion, doing a perfect swan dive through the still air.

They brought him out at six that evening.

Acknowledgements

(continued from page ii)

Jesse Stuart Foundation: "The Clearing" by Jesse Stuart from *Ladies Home Journal*, August 1954; Copyright 1954 by Jesse Stuart, renewed by the Jesse Stuart Foundation. By permission of Jesse Stuart Foundation, P. O. Box 391, Ashland, KY 41114.

John Daniel and Company, Publishers: "The Five Dollar Dive" from *The Other Side of the Island: A Collection of Short Stories* by Yvonne Nelson Perry. Copyright © 1994 by Yvonne Nelson Perry. Reprinted by permission of John Daniel and Company.

Arsenal Pulp Press, Ltd: "Equal Opportunity" from *Chinatown Ghosts* by Jim Wong-Chu; Copyright © 1986 by Jim Wong-Chu. Reprinted by permission of Arsenal Pulp Press.

GRM Associates, Inc.: "Incident" from *Color* by Countee Cullen; Copyright 1925 by Harper & Brothers; Copyright 1953 by Ida M. Cullen. Reprinted by permission of GRM Associates, Inc., Agents for the Estate of Ida M. Cullen.